ONE WE

CHALLENGES FOR
INTERNATIONAL BROADCASTING
IDENTITY, ECONOMICS, INTEGRATION

LA RADIODIFFUSION
INTERNATIONALE
FACE À SES DÉFIS
IDENTITÉ, ASPECTS ÉCONOMIQUES, INTÉGRATION

CHALLENGES FOR INTERNATIONAL BROADCASTING

IDENTITY, ECONOMICS, INTEGRATION

LA RADIODIFFUSION INTERNATIONALE FACE À SES DÉFIS

IDENTITÉ, ASPECTS ÉCONOMIQUES, INTÉGRATION

Edited by
Elzbieta Olechowska and Howard Aster

Mosaic Press
Oakville, Ont. - Buffalo, N.Y.

Canadian Cataloguing in Publication Data

Challenges for international broadcasting: identity, economics, integration

Papers presented at the third conference of a series, held in Vancouver, B.C.,
Mar. 20-23, 1994.
ISBN 0-88962-591-3

1. International broadcasting - Congresses.
2. Radio broadcasting - Congresses. I. Olechowska, Elzbieta.
II. Aster, Howard.

HE8697.4.C53 1994   384.54C95-930992-6

Published by MOSAIC PRESS, P.O. Box 1032, Oakville, Ontario, L6J 5E9,
Canada. Offices and warehouse at 1252 Speers Road, Units #1&2, Oakville,
Ontario, L6L 5N9, Canada and Mosaic Press, 85 River Rock Drive, Suite 202,
Buffalo, N.Y., 14207, USA.

Mosaic Press acknowledges the assistance of the Canada Council, the Ontario
Arts Council, the Ontario Ministry of Culture, Tourism and Recreation and the
Dept. of Canadian Heritage, Government of Canada, for their support of our
publishing programme.

Cover and book design by Susan Parker
Printed and bound in Canada
ISBN 0-88962-591-3

In Canada:
MOSAIC PRESS, 1252 Speers Road, Units #1&2, Oakville, Ontario, L6L 5N9,
Canada. P.O. Box 1032, Oakville, Ontario, L6J 5E9
In the United States:
MOSAIC PRESS, 85 River Rock Drive, Suite 202, Buffalo, N.Y., 14207
Distributed in UK and Western Europe by:
DRAKE INTERNATIONAL SERVICES, Market House, Market Place,
Deddington, Oxford OX15 OSF

ACKNOWLEDGEMENTS

We would like to express our deep appreciation to the large number of people and institutions who have supported the **CHALLENGES FOR INTERNATIONAL BROADCASTING** series of conferences in the past and who have supported the **CHALLENGES III** conference which took place in Vancouver, B.C., from March 20th - March 23rd, 1994.

The Executive Director and the Program Director of Radio Canada International, Terry Hargreaves and Allan Familiant, both of whom have lent their unending encouragement and support for the conferences; the entire staff of Radio Canada International which has worked tirelessly to make the conferences a continuing success; The Niagara Institute which became involved this year and offered their support; The Canadian Broadcasting Corporation which has always found ways and means to support the conferences in all parts of Canada; Lorn Curry of Radio Canada International, Vancouver office who worked diligently to ensure that every organizational detail was in place; the Department of Foreign Affairs, Bureau for Assistance for Central and Eastern Europe which provided funding to bring to Canada a significant number of broadcasters from Central & Eastern Europe and the former Soviet Union; the Department of Canadian Heritage and the Minister who provided support for simultaneous translation; the Department of Communications at Simon Fraser University and its Chair, Prof. Robert Anderson; Dean of Arts at Laval University, Francois Demers who hosted Challenges II in Quebec City and has continued to support the series; the Interdisciplinary Committee on Communist and East European Affairs at McMaster University which hosted Challenges I and continues to offer its support; all the new friends and attendees at Challenges III, all the "veterans" and supporters of previous Challenges conferences; the staff at Hotel Vancouver; the staff at the CBC Broadcast Centre in Toronto who welcomed visitors from Central & Eastern Europe and from the former Soviet Union; to the staff at Radio Canada in Montreal who prepared a similar program in Montreal; the staff of the Europe Service of RCI in Montreal who assisted in the preparation of this manuscript.

Elzbieta Olechowska & Howard Aster
December, 1994

TABLE OF CONTENTS

INTRODUCTION

This volume brings together the papers and proceedings of the third conference of Challenges for International Broadcasting which was held in Vancouver, B.C., Canada on March 20th-March 24th, 1994. The previous conferences were held in Hamilton, Ontario in March 1990 and in Quebec City, Quebec in March 1992. The papers and proceedings of those conferences have been published as *Challenges for International Broadcasting* edited by Howard Aster, (Mosaic Press, Oakville, ON., 1992), and *Challenges for international Broadcasting: The New Democracies: The Means and the Message* edited by Francois Demers, Howard Aster and Elzbieta Olechowska, (Les Presses Inter-Universitaires, Ste. Foy, Que., 1993).

The overall theme of the 1994 conference was "Identity, Economics and Integration". To a large extent, the continuing challenge facing international broadcasters, especially international radio broadcasters, remains "who are we, what do we do, how do we fit into the evolution of broadcasting and communications in the 21st century?" To address these issues, it was thought that the themes of identity, economics and integration could serve as useful intellectual tools. We believe that the contents of this volume justify our expectations. The issues are substantial, the perspectives of the participants reflect both similarities and wide differences, the solutions appear to be complex and perplexing.

There are a number of extremely powerful issues which emerge from this volume which are worth noting. First, international radio broadcasters are fully aware of the impact of television and telecommunications on their medium. Radio will not disappear. The questions remain how and in what manner do international radio broadcasters fit into the evolution of national and global broadcasting and telecommunications systems? Some of the answers to those questions are contained in this volume.

Second, while there are numerous challenges facing international broadcasters, national broadcasters, especially in those states of the former Soviet Union, are becoming increasingly cognizant of their own difficulties, dilemmas and problems. And, they are looking to international broadcasters for understanding and assistance. In effect, new relationships are being formed, new arrangements are being forged and new partnerships are evolving.

Third, the issue of public broadcasting as opposed to state broadcasting is an enormously vital and important issue. Many of the problems explored in this volume relate to the endless search for a viable basis for non-state, non-private broadcasting. Clearly, the future of public broadcasting in international and national broadcasting is of endless concern.

This volume also reflects to a large extent the dialogue between and among the broadcasters themselves. As editors, we have purposely chosen to include edited versions of the discussions which took place at the end of each session of the conference. To us, these encounters reflect "the profession in evolution" and also are the fundamental documentary materials which future historians, scholars, broadcasters and policy makers will be able to utilize.

One of the intentions which propelled us to seek publication of the volume emerging from these conferences was the belief that there was a genuine gap in the academic literature relating to international broadcasting. The Challenges volumes begin to fill that gap. In addition, one of our other intentions in the Challenges conferences was to bring together practitioners, academics and policy-makers in the field of international broadcasting. With hindsight, I can say that we have only succeeded to a certain degree in that objective. There is still a relative paucity of interest in the academic community in the myriad issues relating to international broadcasting. A further objective we set for ourselves was to enhance the national and international profile of international broadcasters.

To some degree, we believe that the Challenges conferences have, indeed, provoked some government concerns and interest in international broadcasting, in Canada, at least. With some satisfaction, the constituency for international broadcasting in Canada participated in a special set of hearings of the Standing Committee on Transport and

Communications of the Canadian Senate. Whether the report of the Committee will affect government policy is still an open question.

Following the report of the Senate Committee, the Special Joint Committee of the Senate and of the House of Commons on Reviewing Canadian Foreign Policy recommended that "every effort should be made to exploit more fully the potential of RCI in particular to project Canada abroad."

There is no doubt that through efforts like the Challenges conferences, at least some national governments are recognizing the significance of international broadcasting.

As long as there is a willingness on the part of the international broadcasting community and a valid intellectual and professional reason to meet in conference, there will be a commitment on the part of the present conference organizers to plan and to execute these biennial conferences. The next conference whose intellectual agenda will rotate around the issue of "repositioning" international broadcasting in terms of national and international agenda provisionally scheduled for May, 1996 in St. John's, Newfoundland.

One final note. It has been a great pleasure and a genuine delight to work these past four years with Elzbieta Olechowska, Manager, Europe Service of Radio Canada International on the Challenges conferences and volumes. I look forward to many future projects of "co-operation and friendship".

Howard Aster
December, 1994

In the last volume of CHALLENGES, I promised to make sure that at the next conference all participants are well aware of our intention to publish the proceedings and would present their organizations not only with the other participants in mind but also for the much larger and diverse r e a d i n g public to whom this volume is addressed in the first place.

That's the reason for Chapter 1 where you'll find a unique, "live" WHO IS WHO in international broadcasting perhaps, not complete but certainly fully authentic.

We decided to keep the presentations in the form they were made to highlight their distinctive character. The same editorial policy was applied to the whole volume. We thought it was important to give the reader a sense and a true reflection of the sound of the conference. After all we were listening and talking to dozens of people from over thirty different countries and for us radio broadcasters, s o u n d is essential.

Our intention and hope is that when you read the book, you'll hear at least some of that sound.

From the point of view of the broadcasting community the reason for participating in the Challenges series is to meet other broadcasters and share with them ideas and experience.

For the foreign guests an important element is getting to know Canada as a country - that's why the conference travels almost literally from "Bonavista to Vancouver Island" - and getting to know Canada as a strong broadcasting presence.

We feel that Canadian experience in the area of public radio born and growing within well established democratic traditions has a lot to offer to media people from countries in political and ideological transition and turmoil.

To illustrate, we have already an example of a direct outcome of the conference: two of the recently democratic countries incorporated in their structures of public broadcasting the office of ombudsman which impressed the executives who visited CBC in Toronto and Radio-Canada in Montreal.

We hope that this volume will also serve as an aide-mémoire to our guests from the young democracies, to be consulted when they face their specific situations and problems at home, ceteris paribus very similar to what the other broadcasters face all across the world. What struck us at the conference was how much we can learn from their experience of dynamic transition and how futile it would be to try to implant our established western model in a vastly different context. Still the ideas are there and it is less painful to learn from the mistakes of others. Whether you really c a n is of course another question.

In the acknowledgements, Howard and I spoke about people who in various ways made this conference possible. I would like to add my own personal deeply felt thanks to those who since the beginning were part of the Challenges series and to those who joined us along the way. Many people at RCI work for the success of the series but it is only fair to start with those who really decide, Allan Familiant and Terry Hargreaves: without their support, advice and ideas we would have never got beyond Challenges I; the other colleagues I have to name because of the importance of their contribution are Misha Brodsky who helps with the logistics and takes special care of guests from Central & Eastern Europe and Ginette Bourely who with Roger Tetrault's help deals with the French language part of Challenges books. And many others most of whom are listed among the participants.

We all share a cycle of concerns and joys which returns every two years: the development of the intellectual focus of each event, the prospectus, several drafts of the program, funding nightmares, logistics and finally the conference itself and as a kind of anti-climax the publication of proceedings. All of us working on Challenges know the particular brand of satisfaction mixed with relief you experience once the cycle ends. It does so now and I would like to put on record how much I enjoyed going through it again.

My special thanks go to someone who officially is not part of RCI but through Challenges became our honorary colleague, Howard Aster of McMaster University, a former member of the CBC Board of Directors, who is the academic arm of this complex matrix of the conference sponsorship and whose idea the whole thing was in the first place.

If I may have another wish, this time already for CHALLENGES IV, I would like to hear in St. John's Newfoundland even more distinctly different voices, especially from areas less represented at the previous three Challenges: Africa, Middle East and Latin America. We are developing a strategy to make this wish come true.

Elzbieta Olechowska
December, 1994

CHAPTER ONE
WHO IS WHO

Editors' Note:

The community of international broadcasters is large and disparate. Over the past four years, the CHALLENGES FOR INTERNATIONAL BROADCASTING conferences have been fortunate in attracting a large and ever-growing group of broadcasters to this biennial event.

One of the paradoxes of international broadcasting is that the broadcasters themselves rarely have the opportunity to meet each other in conference and to provide each other with summary statements of who they, what they do, what their goals and objectives may be.

In the pages that follow, you will get an overview from the international broadcasters themselves. Of particular interest is the representation of some twenty one broadcasters from the former Soviet Union.

WALTER SCRAGG
PRESIDENT
ADVENTIST WORLD RADIO
SILVER SPRINGS - MARYLAND - USA

Adventist World Radio, like many other organizations, is going through a period of change and readjustment in radio broadcasting. It is owned and operated by the Seventh-Day Adventist Church. In its programming, it reflects the holistic world view of the Church. Programs are prepared in one hour blocks and include health, family life, social concerns, music and development programming as well as Gospel broadcasts, and on occasion, agriculture programs as well. It's not your ordinary run-of-the-mill, back-to-back, religion station; we try to do things a little differently than that.

The Adventist World Radio operates two major broadcasting facilities which it owns. AWR-Asia, on the island of Guam, has two 100 kW transmitters and we we are now in the process of installing a third one. Four 4x4 antennas direct signals to East, South East, and South Asia.

AWR-Latin America, in Costa Rica, operates 3x50 kW, 2x20 kW and 1x5 kW shortwave transmitters with log periodic and quad antennas directed to the Americas. In addition, AWR operates a 5 kW transmitter in Guatemala and a 10 kW transmitter in Italy.

In addition to that, we lease time. Transmitters are leased in Russia (Moscow, Novosibirsk, Samara, and, until recently, Ekaterinburg), Slovakia (Rimskaya Sobota) and Africa (Gabon). Our most recent acquisition has been the leasing of two 250 kW transmitters in Slovakia, which are beamed towards Africa, the Middle East and India. We are finding that it is a very effective way of carrying out our purpose. Programming for these stations is assembled at the AWR-Europe headquarters in Darmstadt, Germany, and then released in DAT format at the broadcast sites.

AWR broadcasts about 1000 hours a week in 34 languages. Before the end of 1994, a further 4 languages will be added. It is quite an extensive and busy operation.

We program a little differently from most broadcasters. Wherever possible, programs are produced in the country to which the broadcasts are directed so that programs are accessed from that country and then rebroadcast back to it. The effect of this is to keep us always in touch with the needs of the local community and the way in which they want to express things rather than using expatriate people who very quickly, in our experience, drift away from being really in touch with what's happening in their country. While this does not allow for timely programs, the content is always related to the actual situation in the country and language usage keeps pace with changes. The programming philosophy of AWR has resulted in about 50 studios producing programs for broadcast release.

AWR plans to commence the use of satellite distribution of programming before the end of 1996. As a result of that we also expect to get into downlinking, and rebroadcast from AM and FM facilities will become a reality. Plans are also being developed to begin news broadcasts in 1997.

DEREK WHITE
GENERAL MANAGER, INTERNATIONAL
BROADCASTING
AUSTRALIAN BROADCASTING CORPORATION, RADIO
AUSTRALIA
SYDNEY - AUSTRALIA

The ABC has recently bestowed on me a new title, not necessarily a welcome one, General Manager, International Broadcasting. I mention that not for reasons of ego but because it combines the old and the new of international broadcasting, the familiar and perhaps the feared. On the one hand Radio Australia is the traditional public service, publicly funded, that is by the taxpayer, through the government, and we are an international shortwave station now feeling its way into rebroadcasting and satellite delivery through new and adventurous systems like the cable system in Japan and WRN World Radio Network in Europe, and now North America.

Radio Australia is a regional broadcaster to Asia and the Pacific in eight regional languages, plus English. Its target audience is not Australian expatriates but people in those countries. People who value and sometimes need independent, reliable news and information. We are all comfortable with that philosophy and with those functions even if they are too little known within Australia.

Contrast the new! Australia Television, the ABC's year old television satellite service to South East Asia, is a commercially funded, English language service, operated by a public broadcaster and until now, free of advertisements. It is an international broadcast which offers entertainment as well as news, pictures as well as sound, satellite quality and not shortwave static. In Indonesia as in India, the village has a dish. Is it surprising that already within the ABC, there is pressure to divert resources away from Radio Australia to Australia Television, cries that shortwave is dead and survival for Radio Australia is greater involvement through television? We are involved, with T.V. news in three languages coming from the Radio Australia newsroom through a little television studio. Also, Radio Australia is cooperating in a coproduction with Australian Television in a current affairs program. You will excuse my feeling a little schizophrenic. I might add that in one year, Australia Television has had more publicity than Radio Australia in ten.

Finally, a third dimension. As Assistant Director of the ABC's domestic radio system, I represent the link between our domestic and overseas radio services, soon to share a new studio complex and increasingly sharing programs and resources. Yet I believe Radio Australia's separate identity as an international broadcaster is crucial to its existence. I question whether, given the likely development of a direct satellite to receive radio, there is point for any government to continue to fund an international broadcaster whose services are directed primarily at expatriates. Why not simply broadcast the domestic service?

I am pleased that this conference, while still largely viewing international broadcasting as radio, acknowledges television. Not to do so would be to ignore reality. I am pleased that we will be considering, albeit briefly, direct satellite radio. In my view, that is the future, indeed the life raft, for transnational radio, even if my enthusiasm has been somewhat dampened by recent discussions in London.

Radio Australia is fortunate in having shortwave still widely used for domestic services in its target countries: Papua New Guinea, Indonesia, Vietnam and China. Given the choice however, of a good picture or poor sound, will they listen or watch in the future?

I look forward to having my faith restored over the next few days.

GRAHAM MYTTON
HEAD, AUDIENCE RESEARCH & CORRESPONDENCE
BRITISH BROADCASTING CORPORATION
WORLD SERVICE
LONDON - UNITED KINGDOM

As you may have heard, the BBC World Service is subject to a major reorganization. Some three or four years ago, a number of us were involved in planning for the future in a series of groups called World Service 2000, or WS 2000. Our mandate was to plan for the future of the World Service and we decided, at that time, that a regional structure should replace the rather antiquated structure that we had, and, in fact, still have, of three separate divisions: one for Europe, one for the overseas (curiously named), and one for English. (Really a structure which goes back to World War II.) Nothing was done however. The Managing Director at that time, John Tusa, retired at the end of 1992. The new Managing Director, Bob Phillis, was appointed a year ago and set in train immediate work on a World Service review. The results of that review are now being implemented.

The BBC's international activities are being reorganized along six regions. Each of those regions has a Head. The Heads have all been appointed except for one. They will be responsible for all output by the BBC to those areas. That has not been the case until now. There's been conflicting and sometimes rather muddled planning. The point now is that each region will be headed by one Director or Head, who is responsible for all output to those areas, both in English and in other languages.

There is still a global English service but it will be regionalized by the timing of programs so that you won't get plays in the morning, for instance... so that the programs you get in the morning will be more suitable for morning listening. We hope there will also be a greater degree of regional output, rather like the African output at the moment, which is designed especially for Africa.

The result of all this has been much delayering, that is to say much reduction in senior posts. I don't know how many redundances there will be but at least 12 of my senior colleagues will be loosing their job. So, it's not a very happy time from that point of view in Bush House.

Meantime we have negotiated a new Triennium. You remember we have a three year agreement with the government for broadcasting. We've lost some funding. The new Triennium starts in two weeks time, in the beginning of April. We've lost about 5 million pounds. However we've had very strong political support from parliament with the third largest number of backbenchers signing what is called an "early day motion" in support of the BBC. The loss of 5 million pounds has been offset by that and also by the fact that the BBC is now in much more control of its own strategic planning: the hours it broadcasts, the languages it broadcasts in, and we are developing a new relationship with the Foreign Office.

One last point. There are many things to resolve and much more to tell you. One important area is to define the BBC's wider international role as not only a public service broadcaster but as a successful commercial media organization with television and enterprises and program sales, much has yet to be announced about that. What is clear is that the future importance of the BBC World Service as an international public service radio is underlined and guaranteed.

Incidentally, whatever you may hear to the contrary, I don't believe shortwave is dead, it's not even dying, it is facing a mature and vital old age. In my research, audiences are growing, not falling.

ANGUEL NEDIALKOV
DIRECTOR
RADIO BULGARIA
SOFIA - BULGARIA

As an international broadcaster, Radio Bulgaria is an integral part of the Bulgarian National Radio which runs two 24-hour domestic programs and five regional radio stations, which operate in the competitive media of five international broadcasters on FM (Deutsche Welle, RFI, Radio Free Europe, the BBC and VOA) and 19 private commercial radio stations.

The external service of the Bulgarian National Radio has been in existence since 1936 and now it runs programs in 12 languages beamed to North and South America, Western Europe, the Balkans, the Middle East and Australia. With program output of nearly 350 hours weekly, Radio Bulgaria is seventh in Europe and among the top 20 public international broadcasters in the world.

The reforms in the Bulgarian National Radio (and Radio Bulgaria correspondingly) had to be carried out over the past year and a half in an extremely hostile political and economic environment with the war in former Yugoslavia raging less than 100 miles from the Bulgarian border and economic pressures which had a negative impact on international broadcasting.

Nevertheless, we learned the bitter lessons in a hard battle of survival and succeeded in sustaining its program output and high editorial standards. Moreover, we resumed broadcasts to Asia and North Africa, we will be opening Russian broadcasts this fall, and we are planning to go ahead with Romanian broadcasts in the near future. Last year we started FM broadcasts for ethnic Turks who comprise about 8% of Bulgaria's population.

Radio Bulgaria is putting great effort into expanding its transcription service and is planning to open a monitoring service which will also transcribe news from the domestic and international broadcasters of neighbouring states.

For the time being, we rely on shortwave and AM transmitters but our efforts are also concentrated on satellite relay of our broadcasts and on exploring new channels for reaching our audiences around the world.

ALEXANDER PICHA
DIRECTOR, RADIOZURNAL
CESKY ROZHLAS
PRAGUE - THE CZECH REPUBLIC

The Czech Radio, established under public law, has enjoyed a long 71-year tradition. Currently it consists of three nation-wide radio stations and eight regional studios. The first channel, called "Radiozurnal", is a news and pop music oriented station. The second channel, called "Praha", is a family station for all generations. The third channel, called "Vltava", which stands for culture, presents radio plays, artistic programmes and classical music. The Czech Radio also provides international broadcasting as a state order.

Our public radio is financed 90% from licence fees and 10% from revenues arising from advertising and sponsoring. International broadcasting is financed by the Czech government. Its separate annual budget is about 2 million US dollars (in 1993 its was 3.5 million US dollars).

The Director General of the Czech Radio is elected by a nine member Czech Radio council, the members of which are elected by parliament. Following a staff reduction, the Czech Radio currently employs about 1800 people, 65 of which work in the foreign broadcasting department. They broadcast in Czech, in English, in German, Russian and Spanish.

Today, the Czech Radio finds itself in the most critical situation of its history. During the last three years, new competition has emerged. Today there are 56 private radio stations. A number of regional private radios have done better as far as rate of listeners is concerned. Two out of three nation-wide programmes have, however, retained their highest rate of listeners although, in the light of the competition of nation-wide private radios, our rate of listeners has dropped to its lowest level so far. The news and music oriented programme "Radiozurnal" has achieved a rate of listeners of about 30% and the family oriented station "Praha", of about 25%. Our news coverage is generally considered to be the most reputable one. Not even one private radio has made any attempt to compete with our radio in the most serious radio production, such as fairy-tale programmes for children, radio plays or classical music transmissions.

Another serious problem of the Czech Radio is the transmission network. By law, the Czech Radio is entitled to own, for its three nation-wide stations, only two FM networks and one AM network. The first new program "Radiozurnal", by law, transmits on the FM network. The second temporarily leased AM network will have to be returned within six months to a private radio. The longwave transmitter is very expensive for us so we can only use it a part of each day. The family oriented programme "Praha" transmits, by law, on a very expensive AM network. Only in the evenings and in the mornings can it run simultaneously, even on the regional transmitters' FM network. The third cultural programme may, by law, transmit on its own FM network. Our foreign broadcasting is transmitted only on shortwave because our government refuses to pay the longwave transmitter.

A further problem the Czech Radio has to face currently is the problem of financing. As I mentioned before, 90% of our budget comes from licence fees. Twenty Crowns a month represents the radio licence fee, which is less than US $1, about 70 cents. The licence fee has remained the same for the last three years, even though inflation has risen by several percentage points. Payment of the transmission network only takes up just over a third of the entire Czech Radio budget. The radio licence fee, however, is determined by the Czech Ministry of Finance. Parliament has as yet failed to adopt a law on the collection of radio fees which means that the number of non-payers is rising.

The biggest problem for the Czech Radio, however, may be the completion of the new radio building which was designed and built according to monstrous plans by the former communist regime. The Czech Radio owns this building under a law and its completion will cost about US $80 million, which is three times the annual budget of the Czech radio.

Our young "top management" must solve all these problems without subsidies or any other help from the state. Despite these problems, the Czech Radio remains the most listened to and most prestigious radio in the Czech Republic. We also met all the requirements resulting from our membership in the EBU.

ARNO SELDERS
HEAD, TECHNICAL DIRECTOR'S OFFICE
DEUTSCHE WELLE - GERMANY

Deutsche Welle is a journalistic international broadcasting service that started more than 40 years ago on May 3rd, 1953, with the first transmission with a 20 kW shortwave transmitter. Today we transmit daily, with 90-hour programs in 40 different languages, with 55 transmitters placed all over the world, with a total power of 15,300 kW.

Apart from these facilities, we use 17 audio subcarriers on the satellite Eutelsat II F1 for Europe, Middle-East, North Africa, on Intersat -K for North, Central and South America, on SATCOM C-4 for North America and the Caribbean, and on ASTRA 1-B for Central Europe, to distribute our German program in stereo quality, since January 1st this year, and our foreign language programs currently mono quality.

In April 1992 we started regular transmissions of current affairs T.V. programs in German, English and Spanish, and currently we transmit 40 hours daily. This is via worldwide satellites Eutelsat II F1, Intersat-K and Satcom-C4. In exchange for time segment on our Eutelsat II F1 transponder with Worldnet, we use Worldnet satellite, Spacenet 2, for North America and the Caribbean, INTERSAT 505 AND 601 for Africa and Asia, and INTERSAT 508 for East Asia, Australia and New Zealand. The agreement will run out in 1995. That is exactly when we start new transmission via ASIA 2 transponder which we have leased from January 1st, 1996.

Apart from that, several hundred T.V. stations and cable networks in West and East Europe, South and North America, and Asia, are rebroadcasting our programs. A transcription service for television produces programs in German, English, French and Russian. These programs are transmitted by several hundred T.V. and cable network stations in North America, Asia and East Europe.

Now some figures concerning our organization. Currently we have 2,100 employees working in the editorial, engineering and other sections. In the next few years we will have to reduce the number of staff by approximately 300.

Deutsche Welle is financed through funds from the federal government. Our budget was originally DM 650 million but due to budget pressures, we had to reduce it by 10%.

JUHANI NIINISTÖ
HEAD, EXTERNAL BROADCASTING
YLE RADIO FINLAND
HELSINKI - FINLAND

In Finland, external broadcasting is run by the National Broadcasting Company. The external operations are fairly closely tied with the domestic operations. Over the past few years in particular, this relationship has turned out to be quite successful as the domestic national broadcasting organization realized that the existence of a good external broadcasting service is an asset for the company in its competition against local commercial operators. As we have about 50 commercial operators in Finland and while you can advertise, whatever you listen to domestically, when you go to the Canary Islands or to North America, the only Finnish station you can listen to is YLE.

The financing of external broadcasting is based solely on the licence fee. There are no governmental subsidies at all.

Our primary task is to serve the expatriates abroad which we are doing with more than 40 hours a day. The second task is to provide news about Finland and Northern Europe - that's basically Finland and the rest of the Scandinavian countries, and to some extent the Baltic republics - news in English, German, French and Russian. At this time, we are the only broadcaster which broadcasts in French from Northern Europe, after the decision by Radio Sweden to stop their broadcasts in French.

The scope of our external broadcasting is, however, enlarged by the local presence. We are available in Finland as an all-news network, all news AM station in Helsinki, in Finnish and Swedish. Then we run an FM outlet which also relays some leading international broadcasters such as the BBC, Voice of America, Radio Australia, Deutsche Welle, Radio France and NPR, Washington.

The domestic availability has greatly enhanced our profile in Finland. A recent survey about our image indicated that over 75% of the over-25 population in Finland was aware of the existence of external broadcasting.

DONG YU-CHING
DEPUTY DIRECTOR
THE VOICE OF FREE CHINA
TAIPEI - TAIWAN

The international service of the Broadcasting Corporation of China operates with two stations, the Voice of Free China and the Voice of Asia. The Voice of Free China was established in 1949, so this will be the 44th year of the Voice of Free China. The Voice of Asia was established in 1979, so this will be its 13th year.

Currently the Voice of Free China broadcasts in 15 languages including five Chinese dialects and ten foreign languages. The five Chinese dialects are Mandarin, Hakka, Amoy, Cantonese and Chaochau. The ten foreign languages are English, French, German, Arabic, Thai, Vietnamese, Japanese, Korean, Indonesian and Spanish. Beginning the 28th of this month, we will start the Russian service, adding one more foreign language.

The Voice of Asia broadcasts in four languages and is targeted to China and the South-East Asian nations. We use Mandarin, which is Chinese, and three other foreign languages: Thai, Indonesian and English.

Both of the stations are set up to introduce Taiwan to the world.

We currently have a staff of about 250 operating under a budget of 10 million US dollars. Each year we receive about 70,000 letters from all over the world. We have a large audience in China, especially for the Voice of Asia.

ARNOLD KLOTINS
DIRECTEUR GÉNÉRAL
LATVIJAS RADIO
RIGA - LETTONIE

J'ai aujourd'hui à parler de la radio d'un petit pays de quelques 2.5 millions d'habitants, un pays situé à l'est de la Mer Baltique, et faisant de la Suède son vis-à-vis obligé et estimé; ce pays est la Lettonie avec sa capitale Riga.

Créée en 1925, la Radio lettone fut le 19e diffuseur européen. Hélas, en 1940, la vie pour elle a eu une parenthèse douloureuse: l'occupation soviétique en fit, durant cinq décennies, la grande muette, la soumettant aux propagandes idéologiques que vous connaissez bien. Muette mais non soumise, comme devait le prouver l'activité, y compris l'activité clandestine, qui pendant les années de la Perestroïka lui permit de se restructurer et d'être aussi efficace que, par exemple, dans la semaine tragique de l'hiver 1991, le temps de liberté et d'indépendance, scellé par le sang de trois journalistes.

Le patrimoine de nos archives sonores, riche aujourd'hui de quelques 200,000 unités, maintient aussi de l'emploi pour 500 collaborateurs dont un choeur, un théâtre radiophonique, un orchestre de jazz, un groupe musical d'enfants, un groupe dramatique d'enfants, et plusieurs solistes.

Nous faisons 88 heures de diffusion quotidienne, réparties entre trois chaînes: Une première chaîne dite intégrale, polyvalente, sans spécificité de programme. Une seconde, également multifonctionnelle mais déjà plus sélective quant aux programmes, donnant priorité aux émissions éducatives ou culturelles à l'intention des jeunes qui ont leur heure musicale. A cela s'ajoutent des émissions pour les minorités résidant sur notre territoire, et des retransmissions de programmes étrangers.

Une troisième chaîne s'est donnée une vocation plus littéraire et musicale plus classique. C'est une chaîne de musique sérieuse et de la littérature du théâtre radiophonique.

A côté de ces trois chaînes majeures il faut signaler quelques émissions en ondes courtes, destinées à l'étranger, en suédois, en anglais et en allemand.

Il existe chez nous un double financement. Le budget d'État nous subventionne à hauteur de 80% des dépenses engagées. Le 20%

restant nous vient de la publicité et demain, sans doute, du produit d'une redevance généralisée actuellement à l'étude.

D'autre part, nos statuts ont été redéfinis par la loi sur l'audiovisuel en mars 1992 ainsi que par le Cahier des charges dont le contrôle relève d'un Conseil de l'audiovisuel mis en place par la même loi.

Pour conclure, hier nous n'étions qu'une radio d'État soumise impérativement au bon vouloir du pouvoir. Aujourd'hui, déjà une radio presque de service public, notre autonomie est grande, d'autant plus grande que depuis cette loi, la radiodiffusion n'est plus un monopole d'État. C'est-à-dire que la radio lettone est entourée depuis peu par quelques dizaines de diffuseurs privés commerciaux. La lutte pour les auditeurs est commencée mais ce serait une autre histoire à raconter...

KAZIMIERA MAZGELIENE
PROGRAM DIRECTOR
LITHUANIAN RADIO
VILNIUS - LITHUANIA

Lithuanian Radio and TV is the largest mass-media organization in Lithuania. It is administered by a council appointed by the Sejm. The council consists of writers, philosophers, politicians, representatives of the clergy. It focuses its attention on formulating the cultural strategy for radio and television. At the council's recommendations licences are issued to commercial radio and TV companies. The are currently over 200 such companies. Lithuanian Radio and TV is financed by the government as well as from its own revenue. The revenue is generated through advertizing and services to the public and other organizations, including foreign TV and radio companies.

A bill has been recently drafted which proposes to change the status of the radio from government radio to public radio. We hope that the bill will be passed by the Sejm in the nearest future. Lithuanian Radio joined the EBU in 1992.

Radio broadcasts were started in Lithuania in 1926. At that time, there were 300 radio sets in Lithuania. Today 3,700,000 potential listeners have access to approximately 1,500,000 radio sets. Lithuanian Radio broadcasts for a total of 41 hours a day. The first channel broadcasts round the clock on AM, FM and on shortwave. In terms of content, this channel carries information, news, popular music and advertizing. It also has a phone-in facility. The second channel is on the air for 17 hours a day and broadcasts on AM and FM. Most of the programs on this channel are of a cultural or religious nature. They target both Lithuanians and ethnic minorities.

Prior to the declaration of independence, Lithuanian Radio was broadcasting mostly in Lithuanian, which it continues to do. It also had programs in Russian, Polish and English. In 1990 Byelorussian, Ukrainian, Tatar and Yiddish programs were added. We also plan to start broadcasts in German. Today Lithuanian Radio is more international than it used to be at the time when internationalism was one of the slogans of communism. The international service of Lithuanian Radio broadcasts in Lithuanian and English, half an hour a day in each language.

ROMAN CZEJAREK
VICE-PRESIDENT
POLSKIE RADIO
WARSAW - POLAND

At Polish Radio, I am responsible for finance, personnel and operational issues such as programming changes and cooperation with regional public radio stations (which is very important in Poland at the moment.)

As you can see, I am a rather young person. By Polish standards, this is unusual but it is a sign of the fundamental changes which took place in Polish radio broadcasting at the end of last year.

Briefly, Polish Radio offers four national programs:

The first is the main radio program of Polish Radio. It broadcasts news, talk shows, golden oldies and classic rock. It has about 15 million listeners, which is about 68% of the adults in Poland. The average age of our listeners is over 35.

The second program broadcasts mainly classical music, programs about literature and the arts. It has about one million listeners, mostly upper class.

The third program is more for young people, students. It offers frequent news headlines, pop music, talk shows, and targets listeners between the ages of 15 to 40 about three million listeners.

The fourth program is educational, for special groups of listeners such as children, teachers, pensioners, blind people, young mothers, etc.

We also have a special fifth program transmitting in nine languages: English, German, Russian and other languages used in countries bordering Poland.

Polish Radio is 69 years old. Since January 1st, we have a new status as a form of joint stock company. All stocks belong to the state, represented by the Ministry of Finance, but the state cannot influence the programming policy of our broadcasting companies.

National Polish Radio is a public system: one nationwide station in Warsaw and 17 regional companies. All regional stations of Polish radio received independent status on January 1st.

Since January 1st, we also have a special Program Council which consists of 15 people; ten from different political parties of the Polish parliament and five nominated by the National Council for Radio and Television.

At the present, they are working on a special code which will solve the question of how various political parties can present their points of view on air, on public radio stations, a privilege allowed under the law by parliament.

My colleagues and I from the Executive Board of Polish Radio have much work to do. We must change the Polish public broadcasting system, which is a bit outdated, into a newer and stronger public radio organization, while fighting competition from commercial radio stations. This is not an easy task in a country such as Poland.

LEVON ANANIKIAN
DIRECTOR GENERAL
RADIO ARAKS
YEREVAN - ARMENIA

It is a well-known fact that also in radio the beginning was the Word.

It was in 1943, at the time of the fiercest battles of World War II, that Radio Armenia addressed its first words to listeners outside the country. Armenia was calling home its sons and daughters who had left their native land during World War I to take refuge in hospitable Arab countries. The native land of Armenians was Soviet Armenia. Such was Radio Armenia's first ideology. Streams of expatriates started returning home. Many of them came to discover that their native land was not only Soviet Armenia but Soviet Siberia as well.

After World War II came the Cold War which was as fierce and relentless as the real one. Both on land and in the air, the infamous "phantom of communism" set up a powerful propaganda machine to disseminate its ideology throughout the world. Radio Armenia started broadcasts in Arabic, then followed up with programs in Kurdish, Persian and Turkish. Sometimes my older colleagues tried to tell the truth not only to Armenians living in Arab countries but to Arabs as well, or both to Armenians living in Iran and to Iranians. However, these attempts were immediately censured by higher authorities. To counterbalance official Radio Armenia and probably all other government-controlled radios, an alternative "Radio Yerevan" was born. You know quite well that this "Radio" used to provide witty answers to intelligent and sometimes silly questions. Radio Yerevan infused us with the energy which sustained us and helped us survive and function.

Radio Armenia was reborn in 1990, after democratic forces had won the parliamentary elections, still under the Soviet regime. When we got rid of censorship, truth finally could be told in our broadcasts. Changes have also occurred in the tasks and responsibilities assigned to Radio Armenia, two major ones being the strengthening of the independence of the Republic of Armenia and the promotion of friendship with neighbouring countries. The program of dissemination of the communist ideology has been replaced by programs aiming to restore for Armenians scattered all over the world the faith in a rebirth an independent and free homeland.

This is one of the reasons why Radio Armenia broadcasts today in 12 languages 10 hours a day. Our broadcasts target Armenians who live far from their native land and who have forgotten their mother tongue, as well as Europeans, Americans, Asians, Australians who want to know the truth about what is happening in Armenia and Nagorno-Karabakh.

The Republic of Armenia which suffered a devastating earthquake in 1988 and had to bear its terrible aftermath, both physical and moral, has been subjected by the neighboring countries to a blockade for over five years now. The conflict between Georgia and Abkhazia has aggravated our situation as the only railway connecting Armenia to the outside world has been cut.

It is the warmth and the light which the Armenian people have been sharing with the mankind since time immemorial that has sustained us and helped us survive three hard winters in cold, darkness and half-starvation. Can you see yourself writing up your programs with a pencil and a dim candle as your only source of light? Can you visualize yourself in your studio with your coat and gloves on? Or getting meagre two dollars for a report, roundup, commentary or even a small piece of information? This is exactly the amount our journalists get per month. This money can buy them nothing but bread. Very often, when gas pipelines and railway tracks explode one after another, it is the sky that remains our only hope. No, it is not God, it is airplanes that bring to Armenia humanitarian aid from various countries. Our people have proven more than once that man can hold out against any physical and moral hardships. They continue proving this with their lives every hour of every day. However, it cannot go on forever.

For us, radio journalists, our best encouragement is the response that we get to our programs. Last winter alone, under conditions of an inefficient international mail service, we received letters from more than eighty countries. Every letter, mind you, letter, not a report to get a QSL card, was warming our hearts as we felt that our voice, our words had been reaching our listeners. To prove my statement I would like to show you this pretty picture. It is a view of a beautiful city. The picture has been punctured with a needle to mark the building in which our listener Mr. Eric Walton listens to programs broadcast by Radio Armenia. The city on this picture is Vancouver.

BABEK HUSEYN OGLU-MAMEDOV
PRESIDENT
RADIO AZERBAIIAN
BAKU - AZERBAIJAN

Since as president of this company I represent both Azerbaijan TV and radio, I would like to apologize in advance if in my short speech I also talk of television.

Radio Azerbaijan has been broadcasting for almost seventy years now. The broadcasts were inaugurated in 1926 both in Azeri and, since it was during Soviet times, in Russian. Today Radio Azerbaijan broadcasts a total of 53 hours a day, including 10 hours of foreign-language broadcasts. We broadcast in Turkish for 2 hours a day, in Arabic, Persian, English, German and French, one hour each. We also have daily broadcasts for the Azeri diaspora, approximately 3 hours a day, since, as you may know, over 30 million Azeris live outside Azerbaijan.

In Azerbaijan, radio currently plays a more important role than TV since we have a war on our territory. Approximately 20 % of the Azerbaijan territory is under Armenian military occupation. There are 1,200,000 refugees in the country who have been deprived of, among other things, the possibility to watch TV. That is why people in Azerbaijan now listen more to the radio than watch TV. Consequently, we are paying great attention to radio in order to spread the truth about Azerbaijan and, what is most important, to break the information blockade around our country.

For the above reason we have lately introduced broadcasts in English, French and German. Our English broadcasts reach Canada, therefore, we receive letters from our Canadian listeners. Our radio station has been named after a hero of our national legend, Dedek Kurgut. This station has been receiving letters from Canada which is so far and, yet, so close.

We have many nationalities in our country. Aside from the indigenous population, Armenians continue to live in Nagorno-Karabakh. Therefore we also have daily broadcasts in Armenian. Furthermore, we have ethnic minorities in Azerbaijan who receive broadcasts in Kurdish, Lezghin and Talyzh. And, of course, about 500,000 Russian-speaking people live in Azerbaijan. So, both our channels have daily broadcasts in Russian. These are music, literary and information programs.

Aside from regional and foreign-language broadcasting services, our radio company has two channels. They are called the first and the second programs. The second program is also called Aras. Each of them broadcasts for eighteen hours a day. The first program targets audiences exclusively in our republic, whereas the second one, Aras, has a wider range since for its broadcasts we rent transmitters from Russia. In the past, these transmitters were used to jam broadcasts of the Voice of America, Deutsche Welle, Radio Liberty/Free Europe. After jamming had been halted under Gorbachev during Perestroika, idle transmitters were offered for rent to republics of the former Soviet Union. We have been renting these transmitters from Russia. These transmitters are very powerful, therefore radio signals reach even Canada. This second channel, Aras, broadcasts information, music, literary programs. It also carries some programs, as I have already mentioned, in languages of the ethnic minorities living in Azerbaijan, again music, literary and information programs. I repeat once again, both channels broadcast programs in Russian. They target Russian-speaking audiences, inside and outside Azerbaijan, and bring them the truth about Azerbaijan.

ALEKSEY S. VLASENKO
PROGRAM DIRECTOR
RADIO BELARUS
MIENSK - BELARUS

Belorussian broadcasting celebrates this year the 70th anniversary of its activities. It began in 1924 with the foundation of the joint stock company "Radio Program".

Radio Belarus today broadcasts 35 hours a day, on AM, FM and shortwave. A network of broadcasting stations has been developed that provides broadcasting all over the country. Different programs of Radio Belarus can be heard in neighbouring countries, in Western Europe, North America, in fact, on all the continents.

A distinctive feature of Belorussian programming is cable broadcasting which guarantees very high quality of program transmission. The number of cable receivers gives evidence of the high popularity of cable broadcasting among our listeners. There are about 3.5 million cable radio receivers in the country with a population of 10 million. One can find such a receiver in every Belorussian home. After a sociological survey, we found that more than 80% of our audience gets information solely from cable radio. There are also other radio receivers of widely varying standards, although they don't provide such quality of transmission as cable radio receivers do.

Belorussian journalists make programs for the broadest range of listeners including children. The scope of our work is reflected in the makeup of our creative journalistic units. We have the following departments: programs for children and teen-agers, programs for youth, musical programs, literary and drama programs, social and economic programs, public and political programs, information, sports, sociological research and mail.

Regular study of the most favourable conditions for radio listening for our audiences and broadcasting at a suitable time in accordance with listeners' interests, has given Byelorussian Radio the largest audience in comparison with television, newspapers and magazines.

Belorussian Radio intends to begin FM-range broadcasting this year. Also, we are negotiating with the partners concerned about additional information which would meet the broadcasting needs of our radio listeners.

TERRY HARGREAVES
EXECUTIVE DIRECTOR
RADIO CANADA INTERNATIONAL
MONTREAL - CANADA

At Radio Canada International, we classify ourselves as a small to medium size international broadcaster. I think it's a little closer to small when it comes to staff and budget at least. We have a staff of about 115. The budget is approximately $16 million a year.

We broadcast in seven languages, a minimum of 230 hours a week. We have nine transmitters in Sackville, New Brunswick, two overseas. Then we have relay agreements with Austria, Germany,

Portugal, Cyprus, China, Korea and Japan, which simultaneously broadcast our programs to other areas.

The languages we broadcast in are English, French, Arabic, Ukrainian, Russian, Spanish and standard Chinese. In this way, we cover most parts of the globe.

Our primary role is to reflect Canada honestly to the rest of the world. Our secondary role is to keep in touch with Canadians overseas. As part of keeping in touch with Canadians overseas, we also run a shortwave service with daily shortwave programs for Canadian peacekeepers in Yugoslavia, the Golan Heights and in Somalia. This week, we are in the process of installing four satellite downlinks in Yugoslavia - so they will have 24-hour a day of Canadian radio - and one in the Golan.

On the budget scene, we had a major cut in 1991 where we dropped seven languages and lost half of our staff. Since then we have suffered a few other cuts, not as severe, and we hope this situation will stabilize soon.

We also do a lot of rebroadcasting across the world, English language lessons, business programs, self-help programs, classical music programs, pop music programs and a service of news. For instance, we have rebroadcasting in 26 cities in Russia, 15 cities in China, in Ukraine, Estonia, Latvia, Lithuania, Moldova, Kazakhstan, Namibia, and in Latin America we have just started - we have ten stations that are carrying our material on a regular basis and 42 which will be starting shortly.

SERGEY KORZOUN
RÉDACTEUR-EN-CHEF
RADIO ÉCHO DE MOSCOU
MOSCOU - RUSSIE

Il y a deux ans, en présentant ma radio à la conférence précédente, j'ai dit que nous n'avions pas d'ambitions internationales. Nous n'avons toujours pas ces ambitions internationales mais en ces deux ans, nous avons quand même commencé quelques émissions en arménien, en yiddish, en tatar et en ukrainien, donc quatre autres langues par rapport au russe figurent dans nos émissions. Évidemment ce sont des émissions spéciales destinées aux communautés qui parlent ces langues et qui habitent à Moscou. Ce sont des émissions bilingues, c'est-à-dire qu'il y a une annotation ou bien traduction directe en russe puisque notre rayon d'action c'est Moscou et ses environs.

La radio *È* a été entendue pour la première fois sur les ondes le 22 août 1990. Elle a vécu avec les Moscovites toutes les péripéties et tous les développements politiques et économiques en Russie et à Moscou de ces derniers temps.

Notre auditoire potentiel est d'environ 15 millions de personnes. C'est justement la population de la région que nous couvrons par nos émetteurs, en ondes moyennes et en FM, version est-orientale pour le moment.

Nous employons environ 80 personnes. Nous émettons 24 heures sur 24, ce qui n'était pas encore le cas il y a deux ans.

Notre plus grande ambition est de donner une information objective, non politisée. Évidemment, nous nous branchons sur les développements politiques mais nous ne prenons pas parti pour qui que ce soit dans toutes les batailles politiques, économiques ou autres. La seule cause que nous défendons est celle de la liberté de parole et j'aurai l'occasion d'en parler davantage durant le séminaire qui suivra.

JAMES LATHAM
STATION MANAGER
RADIO FOR PEACE INTERNATIONAL
SAN JOSE - COSTA RICA

I bring warm, sunny greetings from all of the staff at Radio for Peace International to all of you today. I believe RPI is possibly the smallest of the radio stations represented here in respect to staff size and transmitting capacity. The station is a joint project of the University for Peace which was created at the 1992 UN General Assembly and the US based, not for profit corporation Earth Communications.

The station went on the air in September of 1987 with a single transmitter, a single studio and a single office. Today we've just completed a new office/studio facility that houses several studios and offices, as well as a new antenna system and transmitting system. We are currently operating with five transmitters from Costa Rica.

The station is located in the rolling hills of the central valley of Costa Rica. It provides a voice for the geographically and culturally diverse community. This is the reason we call ourselves "global community radio". Radio for Peace International, a few years ago, joined an organization called AMARC which is the international association of community broadcasters. I must admit it was difficult to get them to understand that you could be a shortwave broadcaster and serve a global community. Now there are several shortwave broadcasters who belong to that organization.

The programming content of Radio for Peace International relates to issues of peace education, environmental and social justice issues, the improvement of cross-cultural understanding, conflict resolution issues, issues affecting the lives of women.

Languages currently broadcast from RPI are Spanish, English, and for the people of Haiti, French Creole.

On May 1, 1991, RPI inaugurated a new department, a feminist department, which explores issues such as poverty, womens' rights as human rights, the environment, violence against women, discrimination, racism, militarism, sexuality, education, art, culture, all from a gender perspective.

RPI is funded by listeners. We also receive funding from non profit foundations in the United States and abroad. I must say we are very positive about the future of shortwave. We realize, as all of you here, that there are great challenges ahead for us, but we have been growing in a very tough market and we're looking forward to the future.

KEVIN KLOSE
DIRECTOR
RADIO LIBERTY
read by
EUGENE PARTA
DIRECTOR, MEDIA AND OPINION RESEARCH
RADIO FREE EUROPE/RADIO LIBERTY
MÜNICH - GERMANY (USA)

The post-Cold War era poses extraordinary challenges for our unique radio stations. The Clinton Administration and the U.S. Congress, faced with giant federal deficits, last year agreed to consolidate U.S. international broadcasting to save money and better coordinate broadcast activities. That legislation, by the way, is right now in its final stages.

Radio Free Europe and Radio Liberty, beacons of news and information for millions of listeners in East Europe and Eurasia for more than 40 years, have borne much of the cuts. Our budget will be reduced nearly two-thirds, from $210 million today to not more than $75 million in 1995-96.

Our total staff of some 1,600 will go to about 600. The toll is grim, the news difficult to bear. Our Hungarian Service and Radio Free Afghanistan have already been silenced. Broadcast hours for a number of other services will be cut too.

Yet, with congressional support and administration commitment, we are pressing on with our unfinished mission: to help strengthen democracy in newly sovereign, post-Soviet states. We are going to make do with less, but we are going to do it.

Since the fall of the Berlin Wall in 1989, RFE/RL has created, across the former region, the largest coordinated surrogate radio network of any international broadcaster to this region. With news bureaus in virtually every eastern capital, from Warsaw to Almaty, Tallinn to Sophia, our local freelancers, stringers and specialists provide remarkable contact with populations struggling to get accurate, useful news and information about themselves and the new world around them.

RFE/RL's regional round-tables, cross-reporting, and capital-to-capital links foster trans-national, civil dialogue. Anchored in Munich but lively and inter-active from country to country, our news

25

and current affairs programming helps the region stay plugged in and talking - a democratic bulwark against isolation, regional fear and xenophobia.

Earlier this year, RFE/RL's "South Slavic Service" went on the air, broadcasting in Serbian and Croatian to the war-scarred Balkans. We are proud to join the international broadcast community in such vital work. Amid budget reductions, this attests to the vitality of our mission.

In all, we broadcast in 22 languages a total average daily airtime of 112.4 plus hours.

Our shortwave and medium wave transmitter sites in Germany, Portugal and Spain, are increasingly supplemented by retransmission agreements with local and national, private or state-affiliated AM-FM stations and networks, and I believe many of you here are now carrying RFE/RL broadcasts on your own networks. Local affiliates can sell advertising around RFE/RL current affairs programs. The idea is straightforward: free enterprise and free speech, working together to build sturdy, independent radio media.

Comments by Eugene Parta.

I would like to add a few points because you may have read about a few items in the press which Kevin didn't address in his general message. One concerns the possible move of Radio Free Europe/ Radio Liberty to Prague. This subject is under study at the moment. In a move that has been much appreciated both by the Board for International Broadcasting and RFE/RL, the Czech government very generously made available the former Czechoslovak parliament building in Prague, which could be a broadcast centre for the entire organization. The idea behind a move to Prague is that in time of downsizing and budget cuts, Prague would offer a considerably less expensive milieu to function in than Munich which has one of the highest operating costs in all of Europe. This project is presently under study and the second report from the consulting firm Arthur Andersen is due in about two weeks. The Board will take a final decision on this in three weeks. As I understand it, the Board will be making a decision purely on the basis of the cost merits, the potential cost savings involved.

Another item has to do with relocation of some of the broadcast services into the countries to which they have been broadcasting. This summer the Polish service and the Czech service will respectively go to Warsaw and Prague, in reduced form. They will receive some central support from Munich but essentially the idea is that these will be become indigenous broadcasting entities in the countries to which they have moved.

I would see this as being a model for a number of the other broadcasting units as well, although no final decisions have been made on that.

The third has to do with the issue of staff cuts. 1600 to 600 sounds very drastic. However, under the perceived legislation, many of the support functions that are now within the radios themselves would be consolidated under the USIA with the Voice of America, such as engineering and various other personnel aspects. The research institute of which I am part, will have an independent status. So when we talk of a downsizing to 600, that is drastic but there are a number of other support functions that traditionally have been part of that 1600 and will not be included in that 600.

MASAOMI SATO
DIRECTOR GENERAL
RADIO JAPAN NHK
TOKYO - JAPAN

I am delighted to be able to participate in the sessions of Challenges for International Broadcasting III, organized by RCI and others.

We, at Radio Japan, broadcast 420 hours a week in 22 languages. Starting next month, we plan to increase it to 445 hours a week. However, we do not intend to increase our shortwave broadcasting any further in the future. Instead, we plan to provide visual services to the world.

Radio Japan has already been re-broadcasting its programs through a communications satellite to North America and Europe.

In the near future, NHK plans to introduce visual services to Asia to begin with. We believe that broadcasting in Asia will be competitive and listeners will have many programs to choose from.

We believe these sessions will be quite meaningful to the future of international broadcasting.

VIKTOR IVANOVICH NABRUSKO
DIRECTOR & DEPUTY CHAIRMAN
WORLD SERVICE RADIO UKRAINA
UKRAINIAN STATE RADIO & TV COMPANY
KIEV - UKRAINE

The State Broadcasting Company of Ukraine is the basis for national radio and TV in Ukraine. It is financed by the state. Its programs cover the whole territory of the country and certain regions abroad.

About Ukrainian television: The first national channel has 15 hours of broadcasting on socio-political issues, culture, entertainment, sports and other programs. The second channel, having 14 hours of broadcasting, is a combined one which includes programs of national, local and Russian TV companies. The third national channel broadcasts programs of the Russian TV company "Ostankino".

According to the Law on Radio and Television recently adopted by the Ukrainian parliament, Ukrainian television will undergo deep restructuring. The Law states that one broadcasting company cannot broadcast on more than two TV and three radio channels over the territory of the country (this doesn't include cable networks and World Service). Thus, in the near future, Ukrainian TV will have the following structure: Channel 1 will be national. Programs will be made and broadcast from Kiev. Channel 2 will be combined. It will broadcast national and local programs as well as programs made jointly with foreign companies. Channel 3 will be the technical state channel. It will broadcast programs of non-state companies and of the Russian company "Ostankino", from Kiev.

About Ukrainian radio: The Law doesn't envisage radical changes for Ukrainian radio. Presently, it has the following structure. There are three channels. Concerning channel 1: Since the last reorganization of Ukrainian radio, the situation in the world information system has changed radically. What are the main features of this new system? Firstly Ukrainian radio is now national, ideologically, organizationally and technologically independent of any structures located beyond the territory of Ukraine. Secondly, increased broadcasting and the formation of four channels has permitted Ukraine to be well represented in the world and the CIS.

Thirdly, Ukrainian radio has experienced qualitative changes with the following objective: To meet the spiritual and pragmatic demands of the audience. This is done by offering different programming of channels which gives listeners a wider choice, and by democratization of the programs live to air. Many programs have become a factor of the socio-political process in the country.

Channel 2 ("Promin") offers round the clock information, music and entertainment geared to the young listeners. Channel 3 is a round the clock music, art and drama channel.

Now a word about Radio Ukraine's World Service: Over the past several years, it has increased its broadcasting from 7.5 to 31 hours per day. This includes the Ukrainian, English, German and Romanian sections. Radio Ukraine's World Service broadcasts to more than 60 countries of the world and receives about 20,000 letters a year.

Being a station of independent Ukraine, RU World Service has radically changed its ideological programming. A propagandist station of the former Soviet Union, it is now a state factor of foreign political activities of Ukraine, objectively informing its listeners about all socio-political processes in Ukraine and abroad. The main principles are impartiality, fairness and plurality of views.

The methodology of programming has also changed. Instead of propagandist activities, it now makes informational and analytical programs. The informational policy of Radio Ukraine's World Service has also changed. Before, 70% of the information came from TASS and Moscow Radio. Now only 10% of the news comes from abroad, the rest is provided by the State Broadcasting Company of Ukraine and adapted to World Service specifications.

VALENTINA ZLOBINA
HEAD OF RESEARCH
RADIO MOSCOW INTERNATIONAL
MOSCOW - RUSSIA

Radio Moscow International today is Russia's State Broadcasting Company. Until recently, it was an integral part of Russia's State TV and Broadcasting Company "Ostankino".

On December 22, 1993, President Yeltsin signed executive orders aimed at revamping Russia's media. It was decided, among other things, that a government-managed radio company to be known as "The Voice of Russia" should be created on the basis of radio Moscow International, with a view to upgrading Russia's international radio programs. This is a history-making decision for us because, for the first time in its long history, the network emerges as an independently-acting company.

Addressing listeners abroad on New Year's Eve and Christmas, Armen Oganessyan, Chairman of Russia's network for international broadcasts, said that radical changes that might send Radio Moscow's listeners into a state of shock could hardly be expected. Now that it has attained a better standing, and that its technical and financial needs will get more attention, the network must simply upgrade its performance.

We believe that Radio Moscow International, as never before, can serve Russia's interests, remaining a unique public diplomacy instrument. A major task for radio Moscow International is to help the world community comprehend the new Russia, its new foreign policy and domestic democratic reforms.

Some facts about RMI's history:

In 1929, RMI began regular broadcasts in German, English and French. In the 1940's, the Voice of Moscow could already be heard in most countries of Europe, the Middle East, Southeast Asia, Japan, North and Latin America.

At present, Radio Moscow International broadcasts in 46 foreign languages for 156 hours a day. The number of languages and air time remained the same as in the previous year. Yet, in 1989, Radio Moscow broadcasted in 66 languages for 235 hours a day. Changes were prompted by financial difficulties and search for the best format of broadcasts.

Key problems for Radio Moscow International are its status and funding. Staff of Radio Moscow International, its senior officials, the President of Russia, the government and the parliament, have been discussing the future of the station. Numerous listeners joined in the discussion and organized a kind of forum in support of Radio Moscow International by mail, fax and phone. Much effort is required to fully inform the Russian public of what Radio Moscow has been doing so that Russia's nationals understand that Radio Moscow International today can promote Russia's interests better than ever.

Today RMI has launched a project to open English language television broadcasts. There are plans for daily English language TV broadcasts to North America, Western Europe, and Asia.

The Teleino Productions Association has already used the "Moscow Global" satellite channel to air several experimental programmes for audiences in the United States through the "Conus Communications" national network. Teleino Productions can also be seen on Russia's Ostankino TV channels. Their list includes the popular monthly show "Paradise Cocktail", documentaries, and programmes devoted to Russia's cultural and spiritual revival.

A few words about our commercial activities:

RMI is prepared to develop and conduct a comprehensive advertising campaign, produce radio commercials and place them in its most popular programmes broadcast in 46 foreign languages. A number of firms in Europe, the United States, and Asia have already used this opportunity successfully.

RMI offers other services as well. For instance, it helps to secure contracts for using certain radio frequencies and segments of air time to broadcast programmes to the whole world or the territory of the CIS, or for leasing transmitters of the studio complex and communication satellites.

The audience research service:

The Audience Research Service was set up at Radio Moscow in 1970. Annually, 15 studies on countries and regions are conducted at the broadcasting studios' request. The results of listening polls figure in various analytical accounts and in a special publication: "Audience". The service supplies broadcasting studios with different monthly publications such as "Statistics and Commentaries", "RMI Foreign Post" (comments and remarks), "Questions from RMI Listeners Abroad", "Analysis of Letters in Figures, Structure and Content".

RMI has extensive archives of audience surveys in various countries, covering the past 25 years. We are prepared to share the data with other radio stations in open working relationships. We could exchange the results of our studies, include in our polls questions of interest for other radio stations, cooperate in drafting questionnaires and perfecting the technology of studies, arrange the exchange of employees from services for audience study for professional training, exchange articles on the work of services for audience study for publication in professional journals.

BERT STEINKAMP
DIRECTOR, PLANNING & DEVELOPMENT
RADIO NEDERLAND WERELDOMROEP
HILVERSUM - THE NETHERLANDS

It won't be difficult to keep my presentation within three minutes because I do not propose to give you a lot of statistics about Radio Nederland today. The information would be out of date within a month. Why? External Broadcasting from the Nederlands started in 1927. When we turned 65 two years ago, the Managing Director at that time, Minne Dijkstra, prepared a report of introspection entitled "Culture and Structure". It was a fairly negative report. For some of the activities, the only reason was that we had been doing it for 20 years. Our Board picked it up from there and decided we should restructure. At the moment, we are in the hands of an interim Manager whose duty is to "turn the house around" to a new phase. On June 1st, a new and hopefully permanent Managing Director will take over. The name of the new person was released only this morning, it is Lodewijk Bouwens.

We shall be dropping a number of languages because we believe they no longer provide value for money. We shall increase our output to Europe. We will develop cooperative ventures with the countries of Eastern Europe and the former Soviet Union.

We are not facing a budget cut which is rather exceptional these days. But we must reinvest in new activities at the cost of existing activities. We shall have to reinvest in quality because we are not satisfied with our present level of quality. We shall study privatization of some of the logistic facilities, which I believe is a new concept in broadcasting. We will also study the sale and lease back of a relay station. I'm sure that in two years, we shall be able to report to you what our accumulated wisdom has provided us with.

MARIAN BISTRICEANU
DEPUTY EDITOR-IN-CHIEF
RADIO ROMANIA
BUCHAREST - ROMANIA

First, some figures relating to the audience of Radio Romania which broadcasts from Bucharest, the capital city of our country. According to Audience Research, of all the radio stations broadcasting in Romania, or broadcasting in various countries to Romania, in Romanian, the Romanian News' first channel is the most listened to, with 65% of all people listening in to a radio station.

The Romanian National Public Radio Company, which is Radio Romania, broadcasts on five programs. The first channel which is news and current affairs and does feature reports. The second channel, cultural and artistic programs. The third channel, youth and children programs. Then two local channels called "The Bucharest Antenna". Incidentally, when we started broadcasting about six years ago, the first program on Radio Romania was called "The Bucharest Antenna". The program was started again about four years ago. We also have a local channel for the villages and the farmers in the area around the capital city.

The first channel is on a 24-hour basis. The second channel broadcasts for 16 hours a day. Third for 17 hours a day. The local channel, "The Bucharest Antenna", for 7 hours a day. The village channel for 5 hours a day.

We also have programs in Hungarian and German, from Bucharest, for Romania, in German for one hour and in Hungarian for one hour.

Radio Romania International started broadcasting 55 years ago. It broadcasts daily on four programs, simultaneously on medium and shortwave, for 35 hours a day in 14 languages: English 7 hours, Romanian 5 hours, Aromanian 1 hour, Spanish 4.5 hours, French 3 hours, German 2 hours, Arabic 2 hours, Portuguese 2 hours, Italian 2 hours, Russian 1.5 hours, Turkish 1 hour, Greek 1 hour, Iranian 1 hour, Serbian 1 hour and Hungarian 1/2 hour.

TATYANA N. ANDREYEVA
DEPUTY DIRECTOR
RADIO ROSSII SANKT-PETERBURG KANAL 5
ST-PETERSBURG - RUSSIA

Our broadcasts are delivered via the first cable channel and cover the entire territory of Russia. These are morning programs which feature our analysis of everything that happens in Russia as well as information programs. We also broadcast every Wednesday for 6 hours via Radio Rossii. It is very important for Russia to listen to and to understand how the situation is analyzed and evaluated in St. Petersburg.

The second company, the one for which I work is called St.Petersburg-Channel 5. In this company I am the manager of Radio St. Petersburg which will be 70 years old this year. We have 500 employees. Our cable broadcasts via the first channel reach the same audiences as those of Radio Rossii. Our AM broadcasts can be received by approximately 10 million listeners all over the Northwest Russia. Programs are broadcast for 18 hours a day. Radio St. Petersburg also has a second channel which is called Radio Classics. It plays classical music from our archives that has been recorded throughout the history of Radio St. Petersburg. This channel stays on the air for 20 hours a day.

Radio St. Petersburg provides its listeners with a great variety of programs. About 50 % of broadcast time is given to information programs which deal with political, economic and social issues. The balance are literary and music programs, drama, including shows for children and young people. This variety of genres and programs explains why we have such a big staff.

Radio St. Petersburg has two orchestras, a symphony orchestra and a folk-music orchestra. We also have three choirs, a children's choir, an adult choir, and a theater company. This structure has developed traditionally since financing has always been provided by the state. Our operations continue to be financed by the state but, at the same time, we are embarked on the course of self-financing. Our financing also comes from advertising revenue. Of course, the financial situation of our radio company is as difficult as that of the Ostankino Radio Company and Radio Rossii since the government budget funds are limited. Our company may have to become a shareholding company and look for other means of financing its operations.

ALEXANDRU DOROGAN
DIRECTEUR
RADIOTELEVIZIUNEA NATIONALA A REPUBLICII MOLDOVA
CHISINAU - MOLDOVA

L'histoire de Radio Moldova est vieille de 64 ans. Nous émettons sur deux champs: le premier poste de radio avec des programmes axés sur les actualités et le deuxième poste avec des programmes culturels et cognitifs, de littérature et musique.

Nous avons encore un réseau local de radio. Nous avons aussi un département de programmes qui sont émis dans les langues des communautés de la capitale de Moldova: en russe, ukrainien, bulgare, gagaouze qui est une langue turque et en yiddish. En 1992 nous avons créé un service international, Radio Moldova International. Nous émettons chaque jour 4.5 heures en français, en espagnol et en roumain.

PÈRE PASQUALE BORGOMEO
DIRECTEUR GÉNÉRAL
RADIO VATICANA
VATICAN

J'aimerais vous rappeler le caractère atypique de Radio Vatican. Malgré son ancienneté (inauguré en 1931), sa restructuration pour être à la page et la réduction du personnel de 11% en cinq ans, notre budget ne baisse pas. Au contraire, le budget monte. Nous sommes en train de démontrer que pour faire des économies, il faut faire des investissements. La solution présente, nous disons "provisoire", est la suivante: nous continuons à transmettre en ondes courtes mais en même temps nous avons commencé à diffuser par satellite, pour une phase que nous appelons "retransmission", donc nous avons des coûts doubles. Heureusement, les stations surtout catholiques, mais pas exclusivement, qui reprennent les programmes d'information de Radio Vatican contribuent au coût du satellite. Donc c'est un peu un soulagement pour les finances.

Radio Vatican est une station de taille moyenne. 300 heures de programmes par semaine, 34 langues. Le personnel représente 54 nationalités. Les 430 personnes que nous avions doivent devenir 385. Il paraît que le seuil de 400 est tabou. Il faut être en-dessous de ce chiffre.

Je crois que nous avons réussi prouver à nos autorités que jamais Radio Vatican n'a été aussi économique, si on compte le coût de chaque auditeur. C'est-à-dire qu'à travers la retransmission, nous avons, en Europe au moins, et non seulement en Europe occidentale, une multiplication de l'auditoire.

J'aimerais féliciter les organisateurs, Radio Canada International et les institutions universitaires qui l'appuient, d'avoir réussi à réunir ici autant de collègues de l'Europe orientale et de l'Europe centrale. Ils se disent reconnaissants d'être là, et c'est noble de leur part de le dire, mais il ne faudrait pas oublier que ce n'est pas seulement à leur avantage de participer à ces réunions, c'est aussi à notre avantage. Dieu sait combien il nous manque le rapport, le contact, le dialogue et la connaissance de nos collègues.

RICHARD MCCLEAR
GENERAL MANAGER
RAVEN RADIO KCAW
SITKA, ALASKA - USA

Raven Radio (KCAW) is a small community radio station located about 1,000 km north of here. We serve Sitka, Alaska, a town of 8,600, via FM, and the surrounding villages using satellite fed translators. Radio Raven serves a total of around 11,000 listeners. The station has a full-time staff of six and over 60 community volunteers providing programming. Our part of Alaska sells very little to the south 48 states; we sell our fish to the European Union and the Pacific rim, our pulp to Taiwan, Japan, China and Egypt, so our listeners are very interested in world affairs. That is why we rebroadcast BBC, CBC, Deutsche Welle, Radio Nederland and other international broadcasters.

Raven Radio is one of 27 small community stations in the Alaska Public Radio Network (APRN). I served as Chair of the network for several years. APRN produces a daily satellite feed service that includes newscasts, a news magazine, economic news, specials, call-in programs, and especially programs for indigenous people in Alaska. APRN maintains bureaus in Anchorage, Juneau, Fairbanks and Washington DC to cover Alaskan and Native American news.

A major part of APRN's effort is dedicated to working with and training indigenous people in Alaska. All our stations are controlled by local community Boards and 12 of those Boards are controlled by native Alaskans. APRN runs the Indigenous Broadcast Center in Anchorage. The center provides training to native Alaskan broadcasters in Anchorage and sends people out to provide training at the stations. The center coordinates events with south 48 indigenous broadcasters and cooperates with other northern broadcasters, including the CBC Northern Service and Greenlands Radio, in covering activities like the Inuit Circumpolar Conference and the Arctic Northern Games.

APRN also produces National Native News, the only daily national news program produced by and for native Americans, for American Public Radio. The program is on over 100 stations in the south 48 states and consists of a daily newscast and native arts features. National Native News also produces special programs on topics of interest to native Americans.

Finally APRN is seeking better relations with our neighbours across the Bering Straits as Alaska renews its traditional and historic ties with the Russian Far East. Because of this, I am particularly interested in meeting with the delegates from the Russian Far East who will speak following me.

After this presentation, you may wonder why I am at a meeting of international broadcasters. Aside from wanting to meet with broadcasters from across the straits from Alaska, I am interested in meeting with broadcasters from Eastern Europe because I just finished working for several months with Radio Tirana, in Albania, on a grant from the German Marshall Fund. There I worked as a management advisor and I trained journalists. I am very interested to hear experiences of other people who have worked in Eastern Europe so that when I return to Tirana, I can bring some of that to bear in what I do there.

BORIS V. MAXIMENKO
DIRECTOR GENERAL
TIKHYI OKEAN
PRIMORSKAYA TELERADIOKOMPANIA
VLADIVOSTOK - RUSSIA

The Vladivostok State TV and Radio Company is one of 89 regional broadcasting companies in Russia. It is one of the largest TV and radio companies in Siberia and the Far East.

Our company is 63 years old. Within our broadcasting area there is a radio station which is called Tikhiy Okean (Pacific Ocean). Our broadcasts target regions of the Arctic, Indian and Pacific Oceans. They are received in Canada and in the United States. We also get letters from European countries and even from ships working in the Atlantic Ocean.

We broadcast on AM and on shortwave. The main objective of this radio station is to inform crews of Russian fishing, freight, navy and research ships about life in Russia and abroad.

I would like to thank the organizers of this meeting, this conference. We have discovered you and I hope that you will discover us.

FOAUD A. TAHER
ASSISTANT DEPUTY MINISTER
MINISTRY OF INFORMATION
BROADCASTING SERVICE OF THE KINGDOM
OF SAUDI ARABIA
RIYADH - SAUDI ARABIA

As we are the custodians of the Islamic holy places, we have a duty to send our message to all Islamic people all over the globe.

We have four local stations broadcasting on FM and AM in Arabic and one in English and French. We also have an external service on shortwave in 14 languages, which broadcasts 70 hours each day.

CHEN WEB-BING
PRESIDENT
SHANGHAI PEOPLE'S BROADCASTING STATION
SHANGHAI - PEOPLE'S REPUBLIC OF CHINA

I would like to convey my thanks to Radio Canada International and the other sponsors for this invitation. We hope this conference will broaden and deepen our friendships, facilitate mutual understanding and promote cooperation to strive for the development of broadcasting.

Concerning the prospect of radio, broadcasters often discuss the challenges from newspapers and television and the competition among radio stations both internal and external. We think that while competition and challenge pose a threat to radio, they also bring about real opportunities. As means of mass media, newspapers and television have their own characteristics and glamour but radio has its irreplaceable superiorities, its rapid transmission of information, its great capacity, its wide coverage and its convenient reception. In the face of competition and challenge, our response is to incorporate the strong points of others and take full advantage of our own, to establish a radio station with characteristics typical of Shanghai and typical of China. An important part of our policy is to promote international exchange and cooperation and to explore the great potential of radio together.

Since October 1992, the Shanghai People's Broadcasting Station has faced a new competitive situation. This competition has changed our old broadcasting model and has stimulated the initiative and creativity of our reporters, editors, and all our staff. With eight frequencies, we have been able to establish eight sub-stations: news, economics, art, music, English, traffic news, language teaching and the Voice of Pu Jiang. With a staff of only 200, we have been able to make 8 sets, 145 programmes, including 49 live ones, which total 128 hours a day.

In November 1993, we succeeded in holding the Fourth Shanghai International Music Festival whose scale and programme quality are far above those of the previous three festivals. During that period, 59 broadcasting stations and corporations of 44 countries and regions supplied us with 139 sets of music programmes for contest.

Several hundred friends from 27 countries and regions attended this Music Festival. The eight international judges invited for the first time by the Music Festival decided on the 16 awards named after gold, silver and brass chimes of ancient Chinese musical instruments. The national special music programme "The Tune of Old China" submitted by Radio Shanghai had the honour of winning the Gold Chime Award. The scale of activities and the number of programmes of this festival far surpassed those of the previous three festivals. The sound of radio echoed in Shanghai so that the year 1993 was called "the year of radio". The practical experience of recent years tells us that if only we seize the opportunity, take up the challenge, and turn pressure into motivation, we can bring radio out of this difficult position.

As for the prospects for radio, we should not be over-optimistic. Instead, we should have a sense of crisis and a sense of responsibility. As the Chinese saying goes: "Be prepared for danger in times of peace". We are expecting to explore this theme with our counterparts from other countries in this conference.

This year is the 45th anniversary of the Shanghai People's Broadcasting Station. In October 1994, we are going to hold an international symposium on the theme of "Challenges of the 21st Century". I would like to take this opportunity to extend our cordial invitation to everybody attending today's conference.

VLADIMIR STEFKO
DIRECTOR GENERAL
SLOVENSKY ROZHLAS
BRATISLAVA - SLOVAKIA

Slovak Radio was the first in the former Eastern block to reach the status of public service broadcasting institution under the law. This happened July 1st, 1991, when Parliament passed an Act on Slovak Radio. Slovak Radio is a member of the EBU. Its beginnings go back to the year 1926.

After November 1989, new management started to work based on principles of democracy and pluralism. According to the aforementioned Act, Slovak Radio is now separate from the former unitarian Czecho-Slovak Radio.

Until last year, Slovak Radio operated four programme networks. Due to lack of finances, one of them had to be cancelled this year. At present, Slovensko 1 is the universal channel, broadcasting most of Slovak Radio's news and current affairs output. It offers artistic programmes as well. Slovensko 2 is a combined channel: morning air time brings regional broadcasting whereas programmes of literature and music can be heard afternoons. Slovensko 2 - Rock FM is a non political music station for leisure, intended mostly for young people.

We also have traditional broadcasts for national minorities: 39 hours weekly for about half a million Hungarian fellow-citizens; 13 hours weekly for 31,000 Ruthenians and Ukrainians; two half-hour programes a month are prepared for 5.5 thousand Carpathian Germans; and two half-hour programes for the 85,000 Romanian minority. Slovak Radio has three regional studios and a modest network of foreign correspondents in Washington, Bonn, Budapest, Moscow and Prague.

Until last year, Slovak Radio was financed from three sources: 68% from licence fees, 14% from a state subsidy, and 18% from its own commercial activities including advertising. Due to the severe state restrictions in 1993, the commercial activities of Slovak Radio were reduced.

The state subsidy was withdrawn as well and it has not been allocated for 1994 either. Slovak Radio is facing serious subsistence difficulties. The State only covers external broadcasting realized in English, German, French and Russian, and in the Slovak language for communities of Slovaks living abroad. External broadcasting covers Western and Eastern Europe, Southern and Northern America, Australia and parts of Asia. External broadcasting operates in accordance with the principles of public service radio.

Lately, forceful support of private commercial stations is being noticed on the part of the State, while public service radio is being suppressed in many respects. That is why the existence of the Slovak Radio Symphony Orchestra and Folk Instruments Orchestra is challenged. The Big Band radio, Bratislava, was dismissed last year.

Slovak Radio is headed by a Director General who is appointed by parliament on the basis of the Radio Council's proposal. The Radio Council is appointed by parliament and has nine members - independent personalities (writers, publicists, public authorities) without political membership.

Slovak Radio is housed in a modern building with up-to-date technology but at the present, it is suffering from an acute lack of finances.

HELENE ROBILLARD-FRAYNE
DIRECTRICE, PROGRAMMATION ET
DIFFUSION DE LA RADIO FRANCAISE
SOCIÉTÉ RADIO-CANADA
MONTRÉAL - CANADA

Je représente ici la radio domestique. La radio à Radio-Canada existe depuis 1936. Il y a deux réseaux de langue française en radio et deux en langue anglaise. Je parlerai aujourd'hui des réseaux de langue française.

La tête des réseaux de langue française est à Montréal. La tête des réseaux de langue anglaise est à Toronto. Le siège social qui chapeaute radio française et anglaise et télévision, est à Ottawa.

Nous avons donc deux réseaux de langue française: un AM et un FM. Le réseau AM comprend 15 stations. Nous diffusons de l'Atlantique au Pacifique. Nous couvrons donc six fuseaux-horaires. C'est quand même un réseau assez complexe. Le réseau AM peut rejoindre potentiellement 99% des francophones canadiens. C'est une programmation de type généraliste composée d'informations, de magazines sur la vie quotidienne et de chansons de langue française de divers pays de même que d'ici. On a très peu de chansons de langue anglaise à notre antenne. Ce réseau diffuse 19.5 heures par jour.

Chacune des 15 stations du réseau AM produit environ 35 heures de production régionale par semaine, le reste étant de la programmation réseau. Une priorité, plus particulièrement depuis deux ans, a été de donner une plus grande place aux productions faites dans une région et diffusée sur l'ensemble du réseau, en plus de cette production strictement régionale pour diffusion régionale.

Notre réseau FM est spécialisé en musique classique et en émissions culturelles parlées: théâtre radiophonique, documentaires, etc. Le réseau FM ne couvre pas tout le Canada. Il ne va que de Moncton au Nouveau-Brunswick jusqu'à Toronto. Par exemple, ici on ne peut recevoir le réseau FM de Radio-Canada, sauf une sélection d'émissions en soirée. Par contre, ici on peut capter notre station AM de langue française.

La radio de Radio-Canada est aussi active dans le domaine international. Nous collaborons avec des radios de vos pays dans le cadre de la CRPLF, la Communauté des radio publics de langue française, qui comprend la France, la Suisse et la Belgique. Nous faisons des co-productions sur une base hebdomadaire. Nous faisons aussi des échanges d'émissions.

Nous sommes présents à l'UER, l'Union européenne de radiodiffusion, surtout dans le domaine des concerts. Nous diffusons des concerts des pays membres de l'UER et faisons aussi des offres de concerts à ces pays.

Pour ce qui est de notre auditoire... Au Canada il y a peut-être 700 stations de radio. Sur une base hebdomadaire, nous avons environ 800,000 auditeurs pour nos deux réseaux. C'est une compétition qui s'est accrue, que ce soit strictement dans le domaine radiophonique, ou dans toute la concurrence médiatique en général, mais depuis 10 ans, notre auditoire s'est maintenu.

Pour ce qui est de l'avenir, deux points sont à souligner. Le CRTC qui est l'organisme de réglementation, a renouvelé nos licences pour sept ans, jusqu'en l'an 2000. Le développement qui suscite beaucoup d'espoir à la radio de Radio-Canada mais aussi chez tous les radiodiffuseurs privés au Canada, c'est l'avènement de la radio numérique. La semaine dernière à Toronto, il y a eu un congrès important à cet égard. C'est un des rares moments peut-être où il y a un projet conjoint entre les radiodiffuseurs privés et la radio publique, et nous en bénéficierons tous, que ce soit en termes de qualité du son ou en termes de possibilités, en termes de programmes.

NICOLAS D. LOMBARD
DEPUTY DIRECTOR
SWISS RADIO INTERNATIONAL
BERN - SWITZERLAND

Swiss Radio International programs eight languages, four of which are our national languages (German, French, Italian, Romansch.)

We have the task of making the link between the past, which is shortwave, and the future, which is satellite. We do both, at double expense. That is why we are short of money, as are several of our colleagues.

We are now trying to take a big step into the 21st century. I have the same schizophrenic feeling as Derek White from Australia because I am also in charge of television. We have a very small outfit, we produce Swiss World which is a program we co-produce with Euronews, so it is produced in five languages.

Otherwise we are a normal radio station of international broadcasting.

ALAN L. HEIL JR.
DEPUTY DIRECTOR OF PROGRAMS
VOICE OF AMERICA
WASHINGTON, D.C. - USA

VOA this year is celebrating its 52nd anniversary of broadcasting. We send our programming via satellites, relay stations, and leased facilities to all areas of the world. We broadcast around the clock in 46 languages. Since the last RCI "Challenges" meeting in Quebec, we've attempted to confront the radical changes in global communications on a variety of fronts. We have:

· Extended our network in placement, or rebroadcasting, to more than 2,000 affiliates worldwide. We reallocated existing budgets to set up offices of Affiliate Relations and Telecommu nications.

· Inaugurated simulcasts, both TV and radio in Ukraine, with a surveyed viewership of 20% of its adult population.

· Restructured our language broadcasting effort by creating a new division for Central Asia, and reorganizing the European Division into separate North and South elements. We inaugurated Tibetan, Somali and Kurdish services, and greatly expanded Serbian and Croatian.

· Expanded our global newsgathering capability to augment our Moscow bureau, re-open our Hong Kong office with both central news and Mandarin service reporters, and substantially increase regional news and reportage by creating language rotating correspondents in the Arab world, Central Asia, Kiev, Prague, Kinshasa, Warsaw and Budapest.

· Created additional economic reporting capability by expanding both the news and current affairs economics/trade desks.

· Continued to build our international training center which now has organized workshops for more than 5,000 journalists from more than 130 countries since its inception a decade ago.

· Begun the complex planning process - with RFE-RL - for U.S. International Broadcast consolidation. In a few weeks the President is expected to sign into law an act bringing VOA, RFE/RL, Radio Free Asia, Worldnet TV and the Cuban broadcast entities under a single Board of Governors within USIA.

· VOA continues to explore direct broadcasting via satellite, digital programming/production operations, and on January 31st, began making its central news and current affairs available on Internet. In our business, history truly is on fast-forward...and we are striving to capture each frame and master its contents in the service of millions of listeners worldwide.

SEMION PROTODIAKONOV
CHAIRMAN
YAKUTIAN NATIONAL TV-RADIO COMPANY
YAKUTSK - SAKHA REPUBLIC (YAKUTIA)

I represent here the Republic of Sakha-Yakutia. It is the largest and northernmost of the national republics within the Russian Federation. Thanks to reforms that have been taking place in our country in recent years, our republic has gained a greater independence in both internal and external affairs.

Our broadcasting system is quite particular. To begin with, we are one-way listeners of all "voices", radio stations, starting with the Voice of America. We have no international broadcasting, even though the territory of our republic is huge - over 3 million square kilometres. We broadcast in six languages, i.e. in two official languages, Yakut and Russian, as well as in Chukchi, Even, Yukogil and Evenk languages.

Our republic is rich in natural resources. We have diamonds, gold, tin, natural gas, furs. For this reason, our neighbors, Asian countries such as Japan and China, have been showing great interest in our republic in recent years. This interest is mutual. We have also been increasingly co-operating with the nongovernmental organization The Northern Forum. Its latest meeting took place in our capital Yakutsk some time ago. It was chaired by a US Senator from Alaska.

CHAPTER TWO

INTERNATIONAL BROADCASTING AT THE CROSSROADS

PART I - THE UPS AND DOWNS OF POST-COMMUNIST TRANSITION

Editors' Note:

A major transformation in the character and content of international broadcasting took place with the ending of the era of the Cold War and the fall of the Berlin wall. In our previous two conferences, CHALLENGES focussed directly on the effects and consequences of the end of this era and, specifically, on the emergence of new regimes and new forms of communications in the former Soviet Union. The first part of this Chapter provides a continuing "update" and analysis of the emerging realities in that part of the world.

The second part of this chapter addresses the emerging new realities in Asia. In many ways, the transformations in this part of the world may not appear to have been as dramatic, or as "close to home" as those of Central and Eastern Europe. However, the long term effects of the new economies, new state systems and new patterns of communications in Asia are likely to have an overwhelming impact upon all of us over the next decade.

ELZBIETA OLECHOWSKA
MANAGER, EUROPE SERVICE
RADIO CANADA INTERNATIONAL
MONTREAL - CANADA

We regret very much that Kevin Klose was unable to attend. He would have provided the key dimension of Radio Free Europe and Radio Liberty, stations whose full success meant for them the end of the road and a radical change of existence.

To other stations broadcasting to Eastern Europe and the former Soviet Union, the difficult process of post-communist transition brought a change of direction and a re-definition of their mandate. Non-broadcasting activities became possible, direct contacts easier and desirable. Placement of programs, re-broadcasting and, linked to it, gifts of equipment, were progressing rapidly and so was training of staff abroad, various visits of experts, recruiting of staff for large stations and their European services directly in the target countries. Production of special series of programs to be run in the target countries on their national networks and on the new commercial stations was initiated with topics considered important for the new-born democracies; topics such as business, environment, foreign languages, in the form of documentaries, teaching courses or skill-experience sharing programs of various format and nature - as simple as language lessons and as complicated as drama productions.

Besides providing radio programming, international broadcasters are reacting to specific needs of stations in Eastern Europe by offering assistance and expertise in re-organizing state radios, in starting private stations, in providing models for legislation on broadcasting, for media accountability and journalistic ethics. Such expertise and assistance are usually welcome in Eastern Europe. Governments of western democracies are quite willing to fund such additional projects despite a general and unfortunate tendency to reduce budgets.

The newly acquired freedom of media in Eastern Europe and growing access to many sources of information and entertainment bring into play a whole range of issues, some of them perceived as negative.

Governments, whether communist or post-communist, don't seem to like to relinquish their control over the media. Different levels of government fight over this control: parliaments, presidents, ministers.

Within media organizations, fights over policies, structures and power continue. Privatization, partial or full, is advocated in many Eastern European countries. Foreign investments are often sought after. Lack of funds, sometimes desperate, forces public radio to try different ways of generating income through commercials and sponsorships, sale of properties, or any other available means. State radios, although already smaller in size, are still largely inefficient. Financial expertise is often inexistent. First attempts at bringing organizations to a manageable size were usually mishandled and did not go far enough.

Competition from the fast growing private sector is not countered properly. Qualified staff are leaving and going to work for private stations where the pay is better and the future looks brighter. That's where most of the foreign investments go. Lack of political stability and disappointment over the duration and pain of the transition to market economy, create resentment and a certain longing for the "good old times".

For this session, we have invited people who are now living this experience. They will share their points of view with us, ranging from a successful private radio station in Moscow to the national Latvian Radio, Radio Moldova and the state radio of Ukraine. Then Arthur Siegel, formerly of Radio Canada International and now professor at York University, will provide a Canadian perspective to this discussion.

SERGUEY KORZOUN
REDACTEUR-EN-CHEF
RADIO ÉCHO DE MOSCOU
MOSCOU - RUSSIE

Journalisme à l'époque post-communiste.

Bien que je ne sois pas de la famille des grands diffuseurs internationaux - je représente une radio privée, commerciale, qui n'est entendue que dans une seule région, celle de Moscou et de ses environs - le passage de l'époque communiste à l'époque post-communiste, nous l'avons vécu, nous l'avons ressenti.

Prenons mon exemple personnel. J'ai travaillé pendant 12 ans à Radio Moscou International, la grande maison-mère pour beaucoup de petites radios privées qui existent actuellement à Moscou et en Russie. J'ai fait 12 ans dans le service français de Radio Moscou International. J'ai rompu définitivement avec la radio internationale et la radio d'État en premier lieu. Ce passage, je l'ai ressenti sur ma propre peau.

A l'époque communiste, les moyens d'information étaient en pleine sécurité économique pour ce qui était des salaires des gens qui travaillaient. Mais il est bien connu qu'il existait l'emprise politique presque totale de l'État, et même totale dans certaines conditions.

L'époque post-communiste peut être caractérisée par la disparition de l'emprise politique et idéologique de l'État, par la diminution des pressions que l'État exerce sur les moyens d'information. Mais cette époque post-communiste se caractérise aussi par la totale absence de sécurité, au point que l'avenir même des "mass média" est toujours remis en question dans mon pays, en Russie.

Quand je parle des pressions qui demeurent, ce sont pour la plupart des pressions économiques et financières. Je dirais que l'époque post-communiste en Russie, pour les moyens d'information, c'est l'époque pré-capitaliste. J'explique pourquoi: il n'y a plus de communisme comme seule et unique idéologie en Russie et c'est la liberté de parole qui est apparue après la "glasnost" annoncée par Gorbachev en 1985. La plus grande liberté de parole existe dans la presse écrite. Les quotidiens expriment tous les points de vue possibles: politiques, économiques, et points de vue des différentes minorités vivant en Russie.

Pour la radio et la télévision, c'est une question plus compliquée puisque ce sont des médias techniquement plus difficiles à conduire. Avec le monopole que garde l'État sur les moyens de télécommunications, en la personne du Ministère de télécommunications de Russie, les nouveaux canaux de télévision indépendants de l'État, les nouvelles radios, ont beaucoup de difficultés d'ordre matériel et financier.

Par exemple, le coût d'un émetteur de 10kW en FM, à Moscou, est de l'ordre de $15,000 à $20,000 par mois. Je sais que ce chiffre, dans les pays développés, représente quelque chose comme $3,000 à $6,000 par mois. C'est le prix que demande le Ministère de télécommunications.

La question sensible ici c'est le monopolisme qu'il exerce sur le marché en Russie, un marché quasi inexistant pour le moment.

Si on revenait au journalisme, les moyens d'information qui existent actuellement en Russie peuvent puiser dans toutes les sources possibles. Un exemple de ma propre radio, Radio Echo de Moscou: Tous les ministres de l'actuel gouvernement, à l'exception de deux, le Ministre de la défense et le Ministre des affaires intérieures, ont été hôtes de nos studios pour les "shows" en direct, pour les "talk shows" en direct, sur nos antennes. Donc, l'ouverture des échelons supérieurs du pouvoir en Russie est très grande.

Il existe quand même quelques tendances bien négatives qui inquiètent beaucoup les journalistes, aussi bien russes qu'occidentaux à Moscou. Cela a peut-être rapport avec cette première phase de capitalisme dans laquelle nous entrons. Dans certaines administrations, administrations d'État en premier lieu, on demande de l'argent pour certaines entrevues. Il existe beaucoup de cas de ce "raquet" de la part des administrations de l'État. Il est parfois difficile d'avoir l'information dans les instances officielles mais quand même, je crois que ce sera surmonté. C'est tout-à-fait surmontable.

Encore un point que j'aimerais mentionner, c'est le rapport avec les gros diffuseurs internationaux qui émettent sur la Russie en langue russe. Il y a deux ans, j'étais presque persuadé que la grande diffusion internationale était très près de sa fin. J'avais surtout en vue la diffusion en langue russe, qui était une diffusion politique et idéologique qui servait les idéaux de l'humanité démocratique.

Je vois que si, à Moscou, à St-Petersburg et quelques autres grandes villes de l'ancienne URSS, la situation avec la diversification de moyens d'information est assez bonne, la Russie est quand même un pays très immense et il existe de vastes régions où la diversité des moyens de communication, surtout électroniques, n'existe pas. C'est pourquoi, jusqu'ici, le rôle que les grands moyens de communication internationale jouent pour mon pays demeure grand. Je crains sérieusement que ce rôle ne diminuera pas dans les années à venir, vu toutes les difficultés que rencontrent les réformes politiques et économiques en Russie et d'autres pays d'Europe de l'est.

Pour en revenir au paysage audio-visuel, le paysage de la radio dans mon pays, je dirais que j'ai vu, hier je crois, à la télévision francophone ici, une émission sur Pablo Escobar, sur la Colombie. Un sénateur colombien a dit de Pablo Escobar, que la seule loi qu'il n'ait pas transgressée dans sa vie, c'est la loi de l'offre et de la demande. Chez nous, en Russie, il y a beaucoup de lois, de très bonnes lois. Mais la seule loi qui n'est pas respectée pour le moment, c'est justement cette loi de l'offre et de la demande. C'est pourquoi je caractérise l'époque actuelle, l'époque post-communiste, de pré-capitaliste et j'attends de sérieuses difficultés pour le journalisme en Russie et sur le territoire de l'ancienne Union Soviétique.

ARNOLD KLOTINS
DIRECTEUR
LATVIJAS RADIO
RIGA - LETTONIE

La commercialisation des programmes.

Quant aux problèmes de cette transition au post-communisme dont nous parlons aujourd'hui, ils sont nombreux naturellement. Mais je n'en considèrerai qu'un seul, celui de la situation nouvelle provoquée par la commercialisation des programmes.

En rejetant l'idée d'un programme audio-visuel comme valeur idéologique communiste, on le traite chez nous parfois, tout simplement, comme une marchandise, c'est-à-dire en qualité d'un produit comme les autres, qui doit se soumettre à la loi de l'offre et de la demande. L'idée est acceptée en Europe de l'Est avec un enthousiasme étrange de néophytes. C'est bien compris les cas des radiodiffuseurs ou télédiffuseurs commerciaux, mais pas seulement qu'eux. Et donc l'expansion des radiodiffuseurs et télédiffuseurs commerciaux est pour le moment, dans notre pays et dans les pays voisins, presque incontrôlée.

On a oublié aujourd'hui en Europe de l'Est et même partout dans le monde, l'opinion britannique des années '60, et notamment le fait que, en créant la première radio privée et indépendante et la première chaîne de télévision privée et indépendante, on avait édité un cahier des charges si sévère que durant les deux décennies qui suivirent, on n'a connu en Angleterre qu'une radio privée et qu'une seule chaîne de télévision privée, une forme hybride d'ailleurs puisqu'elle était à la fois commerciale et du service public, d'où les hauts niveaux des émissions du Royaume-Uni de Grande-Bretagne jalousées par la suite des autres nations. Cette opinion est malheureusement oubliée aujourd'hui, même en Angleterre où, selon les mots du directeur général de la radio autrichienne, le modèle britannique s'est fortement détérioré.

Par la suite, si la production et la diffusion d'oeuvres audiovisuelles sont aujourd'hui traitées comme des produits de consommation courante et rémunérées comme tel, la volonté de toute radio ou télévision qui se veut un service public et croit en sa vocation d'informateur, d'éducateur, d'animateur, perd son sens. Dès lors les critères des contenus spirituels se trouvent éliminés au profit du seul critère d'attractivité. Il ne faut pas oublier qu'une marchandise, pour le producteur, doit coûter le moins cher possible tout en attirant le plus grand nombre possible de consommateurs.

Dans ce cas, comment la production d'une radio de service public étrangère à ce critère commercial, peut-elle jouer la concurrence? Nécessairement plus chère, elle ne peut, en effet, puiser sans limite dans la mine d'or que représente la redevance.

Vraiment, le problème est important. On sait que les grands diffuseurs privés de l'Ouest ont porté plainte devant la Commission de l'audio-visuel et de la culture de la Communauté européenne, dénonçant le caractère anti-concurrentiel du financement des chaînes publiques. Sans le savoir probablement, des radiodiffuseurs privés de notre pays, ont déjà protesté eux aussi contre le financement budgétaire de la radio et de la télévision du service public. Ces radiodiffuseurs commerciaux semblent oublier qu'ils existent aussi grâce aux subventions de leurs maisons de commerce et du produit de leur publicité.

L'argent qu'une maison de commerce se permet de dépenser pour la publicité ou pour subventionner la radiodiffusion privée n'en est pas moins prélevée sur les fonds publics, donc sur l'ensemble des auditeurs, au même titre que les sommes mises à la disposition des radios du service public, par l'Etat.

Mais il faut aussi se poser la question d'une autre manière. Dans quel but l'argent délivré aux radios privées s'oppose-t-il aux objectifs des sommes mises à la disposition des radios de service public? Pour moi, il s'agit là d'assurer un partage du revenu national en faveur de ce qui plaît au détriment de ce qui est nécessaire. La trivialité est favorisée parfois par comparaison à la responsabilité.

La diffusion audio-visuelle dont le seul but est de plaire pour faire gagner de l'argent à son producteur est un phénomène occidental d'aujourd'hui que nous, les Européens de l'Est, voulons traiter comme un bien de la société démocratique. Il nous revient la tâche essentielle de défendre ce bien et maîtriser cette déviation de l'audio-visuel.

La question est plus profonde encore. Vers quelles valeurs spirituelles, éthiques, esthétiques, nous oriente cette diffusion audio-visuelle dont l'unique objectif est de plaire ou de distraire. Nous savons que quant aux valeurs éthiques, l'époque du devoir et de l'obligation qui caractérisait toutes les sociétés patriarcales ou religieuses et dont le dernier symbole reste l'impératif catégorique d'Emmanuel Kant semble bien définitivement révolue.

Mais de même, notre siècle d'individualisme touche à sa fin et ce n'est pas seulement une question de calendrier puisque nous constatons tout le temps des crises de l'individualisme comme de la morale individuelle.

Pour l'Europe de l'Est, je pourrais dire que le moment de rejoindre l'Europe de l'Ouest est fort mal choisi, l Ouest connaissant une crise morale sans précédent. Le post-modernisme vulgaire qui règne à ce propos sur l'antenne commerciale propose un plein relativisme de la morale, une perte de la dimension de l'absolu. Ce relativisme n'a rien de commun non seulement avec l'impératif catégorique mais également avec cette force de volonté dans l'initiative d'une morale individuelle. C'est pourquoi l'homme post-communiste dont la volonté et l'initiative ont été affaiblies par la prise du totalitarisme communiste, qui cherche une nouvelle orientation dans le système des valeurs des pays occidentaux, ne la trouve pas. Le relativisme de la morale, tellement aimé à l'Ouest et tellement propagé sur les antennes, ne peut servir à définir de nouvelles orientations dans nos pays, ne peut qu'approfondir la crise post-communiste que nous traversons.

C'est toujours une drôle d'idée que de faire la morale, ce que je fais en ce moment. De plus on peut objecter qu'à toute époque, même dans une société patriarcale, un être humain aimait la distraction et préférait s'échapper à ce qui était nécessaire. Oui, donc c'était des situations plus ou moins rares et même ritualisées, une situation de carnaval, de taverne, d'auberge. De plus, autrefois c'était souvent l'église qui se trouvait à proximité de l'auberge. Dans mon pays natal du moins, l'auberge et la tour de l'église formaient un ensemble dont l'église semblait s'affirmer comme symbole de la dimension de l'absolu. Maintenant la situation en cause se retrouve sur les antennes, c'est-à-dire qu'elle est présentée chaque soir en permanence dans les foyers.

La question se pose et on la reposera toujours: les moyens de communication de masse électroniques sont-ils des instruments de sous-cultures, de dévalorisation des valeurs? La diffusion sur satellite est-elle une question de technique et de technologie ou bien si elle offre aussi la possibilité d'une diffusion de systèmes de valeurs? N'en sommes-nous pas responsables? Nous pouvons sourire d'un sourire narquois à la vue d'un début d'interdiction dans quelques pays de rediffuser des programmes relayés par satellite. Mais je n'ai pas envie de sourire sur le fait qu'il existe en général des programmes qui gagneraient à être interdits.

Grâce à l'audio-visuel commercial, on n'a jamais tant proposé à l'humanité un relativisme des valeurs aussi drôle qu'aujourd'hui. L'humanité est-elle prête à cela? C'est probablement une poignée de philosophes post-modernistes qui le sont, mais non toute la planète. Par conséquent, grâce au code réglementaire de désordre de l'audio-visuel privé, surtout dans les pays post-communistes, la propagation du relativisme des valeurs morales est devenue une excellente affaire qui se trouve accélérée de surcroît par les mécanismes du marché.

Voilà en ce moment, le principal défi auquel tant les radios nationales que supranationales doivent faire face: sur le plan national, il s'agit de sauvegarder et protéger culture nationale et régionale en tant que richesse de toute l'humanité. L'automne dernier, le monde entier devenait le témoin d'un combat mené par l'Europe pour défendre la sauvegarde d'exception culturelle dans le cadre de l'Accord général sur les tarifs douaniers et de commerce. Autrement dit, on a protégé les droits de ne pas soumettre au principe de libre concurrence, les biens culturels, précisément parce qu'ils constituent des valeurs inaliénables. On doit souhaiter que dans les pays post-communistes soit mise en place rapidement une législation qui évite de tels éléments.

A titre d'exemple, en France, pays de grand potentiel économique et culturel, la participation étrangère dans une société de type "joint venture", ne peut dépasser 20% dans le domaine de la communication. Mais en Lettonie, petit pays dépourvu de moyens, en outre de moyens législatifs, on crée sans la moindre contrainte, des sociétés de radiodiffusion privées avec une participation de capital étranger atteignant les 50%.

Il y a aujourd'hui, dans les champs de la radiodiffusion, de très sérieux affrontements entre les partisans de trivialité au nom du profit et ceux qui veulent rester fidèles ou sauvegarder la responsabilité d'un précieux outil culturel ou bien inaliénable de la société. Certes, il est impossible de définir dogmatiquement la proportion optimale de distribution des heures d'antenne entre ce qui plaît et ce qui est nécessaire. Mais nous pouvons définir plus ou moins précisément ce qui n'est pas nécessaire et de quoi on peut, ou l'on doit, se passer. L'exemple de la lutte anti-drogues n'est-elle pas significative à ce propos?

Pour terminer, dans le domaine audio-visuel, nos sociétés pourraient, et doivent trouver la force et les moyens de renoncer à l'inutile. Et c'est par l'intermédiaire d'une législation attentive à la préservation des valeurs supérieures de l'humanité, même si cet inutile est la source de grands profits.

ALEXANDRU DOROGAN
DIRECTEUR
RADIO MOLDOVA
CHISINAU - MOLDOVA

Le passé et l'intérêt public.

Je représente la République de Moldova et notamment son poste de radio national. Mon pays est récemment apparu après le démantellement de l'URRS. Nous étions toujours conscient du fait que le monde ne nous connaissait pas, mais après le 27 août 1991, lors de la déclaration de l'indépendance de la Moldova, nous nous en sommes convaincus définitivement.

Le but de ces conférences est de nous faire connaître réciproquement. Je pense que les postes internationaux de radio existent notamment pour que nous puissions nous faire connaître dans le monde. Ceci dit, je voudrais profiter de l'occasion pour vous présenter les phénomènes politiques, socio-économiques et spirituels qui ont lieu dans mon pays, dans la période post-totalitaire.

Quelle était l'importance des trois premières années d'indépendance pour la Moldova? Sur le plan politique cette période a été marquée par les nombreux efforts faits pour essayer de transformer la province soviétique en État civilisé. Dans la même période, la Moldova a abandonné le système monopartiste pour accéder à celui pluripartiste. Il a fait tomber dans l'oubli la domination de l'idéologie communiste pour obtenir le pluralisme de visions et des options politiques. L'élection du 27 février dernier peut servir de confirmation. Les observateurs étrangers l'ont qualifiée de premier pas vers l'affirmation de la démocratie dans mon pays.

Toutefois je dois vous faire remarquer que ce processus se déroulait sur l'arène de la confrontation entre le stéréotype laissé dans la mentalité par l'ancien système politique ressenti parfois d'une façon très aigue, et les aspirations à la modernisation de la vie politique ainsi que le désir de ces gens de se manifester dans la politique autant que dans le "business".

Les années d'indépendance ont coincidé avec l'aggravation de la crise économique qui a améné les gens à la paupérisation évidente. La récession remontait à la stagnation du système économique socialiste mais aussi elle a été catalysée par la désintégration économique de l'espace ex-soviétique, destruction provoquée par l'ambition de certains leaders politiques.

Comme les autres républiques, la Moldova a ressenti un beau jour le blocus économique quand les autres voulaient exercer sur elle une pression politique. Ces conditions économiques l'ont rendue incapable d'instaurer de nouvelles relations, le processus de réorientation étant de longue durée. Comme le monde ne nous connaissait pas, surtout notre potentiel économique, la Moldova n'a pas bénéficié au moment opportun du soutien de la communauté européenne et mondiale. A présent la situation change en bien.

Sur le fond de difficultés en Moldova à démarrer la réforme économique, le pays se trouve à une époque de transition vers l'économie de marché. Le patrimoine d'État cède à la privatisation. Les gens deviennent propriétaires. Ce sont également des processus péniblement acceptés en raison de l'inertie de la pensée ainsi que de la résistance de certaines structures ou dignitaires qui ont bénéficié des résultats de la gestion socialiste.

Un des éléments essentiels du processus concerné est la transformation produite dans la psychologie même, à savoir, pour l'homme privé de propriété pendant des décennies, le retour aux valeurs qui sont inconnues ou oubliées.

La période dont je parle est marquée également par la renaissance nationale non seulement des autochtones mais aussi des minorités nationales, et par l'écroulement des idéaux qui ont constitué autrefois les bases de la société.

C'est de cette façon que je pourrais expliquer l'origine des conflits apparus en Moldova et souvent qualifiés par les medias dans le monde, de conflits inter-ethniques. Je suis d'avis que ces conflits reposant sur la confrontation des idéaux ont scindé la société. Poursuivant des buts politiques, certains leaders leur ont attribué un sens d'affirmation nationaliste, les autres les ont interprété comme violation des droits de l'homme.

Je n'ai esquissé que quelques conditions qui j'espère caractérisent justement la situation dans Moldova. Il en résulte qu'il est très difficile d'élaborer maintenant une politique lucide, afin d'avancer facilement vers la réalisation des idéaux de notre jeune État. Notre espoir est liée dans une grande mesure aux effets de la participation de la Moldova à l'activité des organismes internationaux, à la collaboration directe avec les pays du monde dont l'expérience se révèle d'une réelle utilité. C'est pour cela que j'explique notre bonne volonté de collaborer avec tout le monde sur les plans multiples, économiques, scientifiques, culturels.

Évidemment les processus politiques, socio-économiques et spirituels ont également influencé la radiodiffusion. D'un élément de système idéologique d'endoctrinement de la société, la radiodiffusion de Moldova devient au fur et à mesure, une institution publique d'information. Dans ce contexte je voudrais reprendre une idée que j'ai exprimée lors d'un séminaire organisé par le BBC: la radio et télévision soviétique était autrefois la plus indépendante au monde.

Elle ne se subordonnait qu'à une seule personne, le secrétaire général du Comité central du Parti communiste de l'Union soviétique et était tout à fait indépendante des téléspectateurs et auditeurs. A l'heure actuelle, la radiodiffusion de Moldova est en train de passer de l'indépendance à la dépendance de ses auditeurs. C'est grâce à toutes ces conditions de l'affirmation de la transparence, du pluralisme d'opinions, des transformations démocratiques qui se sont produites dans la société, que cela est devenu possible.

Mais il n'est pas facile de devenir un poste de radio d'intérêt public. Dans la mentalité des employés de la radio ainsi que dans celle de notre auditoire, il persiste toujours l'empreinte du passé. Nous continuons à éprouver des difficultés à être équidistants dans les situations conflictuelles qu'affrontent notre société, à tolérer les opinions et les options différentes des nôtres, à nous placer aux positions vraiment démocratiques. Nous réalisons ceci en collaborant avec différents postes de radio du monde. Dans cet ordre d'idée, Radio Canada International est un exemple éloquent bien que nos pays, le grand Canada et la petite Moldova, soient séparés par une grande distance. Et malgré une situation si différente, nos postes de radio ont établi de très bons rapports. Nous diffusons régulièrement le Panorama canadien, les cours d'anglais réalisés par Radio Canada International, le cycle de musique canadienne. Nous pratiquons d'autres modalités de collaboration.

Je suis certain que dans un avenir proche, la Société Radio-Canada diffusera des programmes sur la Moldova. Dans l'espoir d'avoir été explicite afin d'éveiller votre intérêt sur la vie dans mon pays, je tiens à vous remercier de votre attention dans le cadre de cette session et à vous inviter en Moldova en vue d'une meilleure connaissance réciproque.

VICTOR NABRUSKO
DIRECTOR & VICE-CHAIRMAN
UKRAINIAN STATE RADIO & TV COMPANY
KIEV - UKRAINE

The Role of Media in Post Communist Societies.

I will try to provide a short description of the mass media in Ukraine and, in particular, the electronic media as well as to examine some problems that, I am sure, are typical of all post-communist states.

Changes in the system of values that the world has experienced in recent years have also given rise to specific features which govern the functioning of the mass media, especially in post-communist states. My colleague Sergei Korzoun has provided a general description of the processes which have been taking place in the states of the former Soviet Union. He defines this period as pre-capitalistic. Of course, this is a very general definition. I think no modern sociologist or philosopher is in a position to provide an articulate, intelligible and precise definition of what has been happening in our countries in reality. These are very complex problems, I would even say, global problems that involve economic relations, political and social structures, culture etc. They also determine the role, a very important role, that the mass media have to play in post-communist states.

The first specific feature, or rather a group of problems, which I find to be typical of post-communist states today pertains to the emergence and development of the press, the mass media as a "fourth power" in a democratic state. The problems we have been experiencing prevent us, however, from finding a clear definition of the range of the operating conditions which the press should use. Of course, the problems the press has to face now, first and foremost economic and financial problems that my colleagues have already identified here, as well as some ideological problems related to stereotypes which are extremely difficult to get rid of, - all these problems do affect the role played by the mass media and prevent them from establishing their status in the system as the "fourth power" in the new states. This is an extremely complex problem which individual states have to face. On the other hand, it is this set of problems that determines the entire spectrum, the whole structure of relationships that are being established today in post-communist states.

The next specific feature, a very serious and important one, pertains, in my opinion, primarily to the new states that have emerged after the disintegration of the former Soviet Union. The role of the mass media is related here to specific problems of the state system and structure. Even though Poland, Romania, or Bulgaria belonged to the socialist bloc, they were, nevertheless, able to maintain their individual state systems. In the case of Moldova, Belarus or Ukraine, these are practically new states. They have emerged and try to establish themselves in new historical environment. These states do have their own history, roots and heritage. And yet it is today's environment that determines their absolutely new status. The mass media have an extremely important role to play in our new states. They should assist people in recovering their national historical memory, their national consciousness. They should guide them in their search for historical and national roots. This is a very complicated task and the Ukrainian mass media are doing their best to accomplish it. They are fully aware of their responsibility. The grave economic crisis has affected the publishing business in Ukraine. Newspaper publishing has become a serious problem. Under these circumstances the electronic media have been playing an increasingly important and vital role.

Problems of the state system and structure have a bearing on our next objective which is as important as the one identified in the above paragraph. This function can be defined as the task of forming a new citizen of a new state. Probably many of the colleagues participating in this conference do not fully understand these terms and the circumstances in which our mass media have to function for the simple reason that these conditions, objectives and problems have absolutely nothing in common with those they have to cope with in their countries which have had a proven historical background and an established system of values. This difficult task of formation of a new citizen who looks for directions in the economy, searches for motivation in cultural and moral values constitutes an extremely complex ideological problem. In this respect the mass media can play a positive role in post-communist states in the process of creation of conditions for an integration of these states into the international economic and cultural community.

The objectives and specific features which I have identified determine the following guidelines and requirements for the mass media, in particular in Ukraine. They involve an obligatory intellectualization of programs which I believe should provide a certain amount of analysis.

I disagree with my colleagues who try to limit the role of the post-communist mass media to a mere provision of facts. In order to establish a new system of values, to form a new citizen we do require to supply at least some analysis in our programs. The mass media have to play a positive role in the post-communist transition.

I would like to identify here another specific feature which is typical of post-communist states. I am sure that it should be a subject of a special discussion. Today there is practically no post-communist state that has a national state ideology. As a result, there is no national theory of journalism as well. In their turn, these problems generate a number of new obstacles which hamper the integration of former socialist countries into the world community.

ARTHUR SIEGEL
PROFESSOR
SOCIAL SCIENCE AND MASS COMMUNICATIONS
YORK UNIVERSITY
TORONTO, ONTARIO - CANADA

Radio Canada International and the End of the Cold War.

I'm going to look at the other side of the question of broadcasting interaction between western countries and the former communist countries. The title of the session is "International Broadcasting at the Crossroads". February 25, 1995, Radio Canada International will be celebrating 50 years of broadcasting and it seems to me that we've always been at the crossroads. We've never moved much from there and that's not unique to Canada but I think it's characteristic of international broadcasting generally. It comes from contradictions. The notion of one nation speaking to another nation, of creating friendship, is a very romantic one but the reality is that international broadcasting has really been, for most of its history, mischievous. It was born in the war, it was born in sin, contributed toward political intimidation and propaganda, and even Radio Canada International was created in World War II under the War Measures Act. So there are no pure, holy, systems in this area.

Another contradiction that we find is a clash of culture between the journalist and the diplomat. In international broadcasting, when nations try to project their national image or point of view, this becomes especially important, this clash of culture. In Canada, we're quite paranoid about freedom of information and I say that with a certain pride that we try to keep the official hand of government out of broadcasting. It's taken us 62 years to come to the point where we are now insulating broadcasting from government and political interference. We are continually adjusting this mechanism to maintain what we call the democratic ideal and the notion of freedom of the press. This was a very problematic area, the clash of journalist and politician in the era of the Cold War.

Canada itself was not enthusiastic about becoming involved in Cold War broadcasting. We started broadcasting to the first Eastern European country, Czechoslovakia, when it was under German occupation, and it was to bolster the spirit of resistance. We got into broadcasting to communist countries when Czechoslovakia turned communist. It was not by intent but more by default. It was at the urging of Britain and the United States that we began broadcasting in Russian in 1951.

At the same time, the British Foreign Office and the State Department urged us not to broadcast in Ukrainian. They felt that would be playing a dangerous ethnic and secessionist card. But for internal political reasons, Canada started broadcasting in Ukrainian, and shortly afterward in Polish, then after the Hungarian Revolution we started broadcasting in Hungarian.

This was a difficult period for Canadians abroad, for RCI, because the democratic idea, the notion of truth, was in contradiction to the ideal of the battle for man's mind. We didn't stay long in this game. We weren't very successful at it because we had more emphasis on even-handedness than trying to fashion news and commentaries for certain ends. By 1960, a very short period, we began to decompress, to get out of the Cold War game. It took about five years because the system had developed a momentum of its own, its psychological warfare. It took about five years to fully detach ourselves from the problems of Cold War broadcasting.

What I'm saying is that we got out of Cold War broadcasting some 30 years before the disintegration of the communist word. Steps toward normalizing relations were taken. We entered into exchange programs, particularly in sports and hockey. Hockey was the equivalent for us of the American ping-pong diplomacy with China. When these exchange programs developed a momentum of their own, the CBC national service took them over, took them away from the international service.

Then RCI developed television programming. When that developed enthusiasm and success of its own, the national service took that away. RCI created a recording industry in Canada. When that became highly successful, the national service encroached on that. So we have a history of success of international broadcasting and when it gets too successful, it gets taken away.

As we get out of the Cold War, we experience a number of difficulties. If there was no political reason for RCI, diplomats thought, that maybe we should do away with it. Lester Pearson who was one of the godfathers of Radio Canada International, wanted to give it away to the United Nations. In 1967, just after the Expo in Montreal, the government thought it would close down Radio Canada International. So Radio Canada International has had its share of difficulties while maintaining its dignity.

What I am getting at is that Radio Canada International was well prepared for the end of the Cold War. We got out of it long beforehand. It opened up new windows, new directions, as it prepared for international broadcasting, exchange agreements, windows to Asia. It has had to dig into creative broadcasting, creative financing. During the great budget cuts in the current recession, in the early '90s, RCI was virtually declared dead by the government, but RCI is a ship that will not go down. The President of the CBC, after making these incredible cuts, has expressed great admiration for the creative dimension of RCI.

I am suggesting that broadcasting to Eastern Europe became the reason of the very existence of RCI and yet with the disintegration of the communist system, RCI was fully prepared, years ahead, to continue a dynamic operation, cutdown by budgeting, cutdown by the dropping of language, but nevertheless a persistence in continuing international programming.

CHAPTER TWO

INTERNATIONAL BROADCASTING AT THE CROSSROADS

PART II - BROADCASTING TO AND FROM ASIA

ALAN L. HEIL, JR.
DEPUTY DIRECTOR OF PROGRAMS
VOICE OF AMERICA
WASHINGTON, D.C. - USA

Introduction.

A recent report by the Media Studies Center at Columbia University in New York City, describes our topic best. It is entitled: "The Unfolding Lotus: East Asia's Changing Media." We'll try this afternoon to capture the essence of that change. In no other region of the world, perhaps, is the communications revolution moving at such a dizzying pace.

--There is the sustained influence and, yes, expanded reach, of shortwave radio and rebroadcasts in the region by all of us.

--There is the phenomenal growth of satellite television, within and across national boundaries.

--There is the looming potential of digital in its countless forms, and the marriage of digital and TV in ways we can only dimly perceive.

Each of these "petals of the unfolding lotus" has a particular lustre in the satellite communications age.

I'm reminded of the story of a film crew from a private foundation which recently went to Tibet. The crew visited a Monastery near Lhasa, determined to record authentic footage in one of the relatively few remaining sanctioned Buddhist orders in the ancient kingdom. There they were, the monks in saffron robes, stirring hot tea in a huge black cauldron, in the center of the cavernous kitchen. The film crew conscientiously recorded the ritualistic Tibetan chants. All the out-takes were brought back to Washington, and screened before an audience of foundation executives and a member of VOA's Tibetan service staff. At the solemn moment of chanting, he burst into uproarious laughter. It turned out that the monks were intoning, in union: "This is the Tibetan service of the Voice of America - coming to you from Washington".

Indeed, that thirst for information...about what is going on in Asia, and what is going on in the world, remains of consuming interest in unexpected places...despite the incredible explosion of media choices for the peoples of Asia. Are the choices whetting appetites for even more information?

In a yearend interview last December with Patrick Tyler of the New York Times, the U.S. Ambassador to China said that widespread access to outside sources of information in China is now better than it ever has been - despite jamming of some foreign boradcasts. He noted that there are hundreds, perhaps thousands, of faxes, telephone links, satellite dishes, and cable systems criss-crossing the land. This explosion of the media, Ambassador Roy observed, "has fundamentally eroded the ability of the authorities to maintain a closed society."

Less than two weeks ago, we saw a vivid example of that. That same New York Times correspondent, Patrick Tyler, obtained a statement by seven Chinese intellectuals calling for an end to repression of free speech and a release of all political prisoners.

Within hours, international broadcasters beamed news of the appeal via satellite and shortwave back into every city and hamlet in the world's most populous nation. As correspondent Tyler reported from Beijing: "Official Chinese news organizations have not yet reported the appeal, but its existence is likely to become widely known here through foreign broadcasts to China."

We see examples of this phenomenon far beyond radio, far beyond shortwave. We see accounts of it in the literature of our trade, in the spring of 1994.

--Katren tribesmen huddled around their sets in the mountains, watching the BBC.

--A Japanese bond trader at an election night party, arguing that political reform in his country would be accelerated if there were a Japanese-style Larry King Show live.

--We know that central Chinese television draws on CNN and NHK for some of its foreign news, and that it reaches 500 million viewers.

--We know that the Australian international TV service will be relayed for the first time very soon to eight million cable subscribers to the Guangzhou TV and Radio Corporation in Southern China.

The multimedia age truly is at hand.

We can look ahead, and view the faint outline of what this means in rapidly-changing media environments. Asia may be an important part of this sharpening image. Excerpting from the Economist's Global Survey of Television last month:

"Computers and television are coming together. Digitization dictates that, in the past two decades, PCs, VCRs, satellite dishes and camcorders were all dismissed by skeptics. They then went on to change millions of lives, in ways large and small. Each did so by liberating consumers, to manipulate the information they receive, to have a bit of control over mass entertainment. Television will also liberate, as it incorporates elements of all these technologies." The Economist concludes: "As the universe behind the TV screen expands, it will (increasingly) be the people in front (of it) who shape the soul of the new machine."

It is perhaps in that longer range context that we should consider broadcasting to and from Asia. Nine in ten households now own television sets in Hanoi and in Ho Chi Minh City. Among satellite systems speckling the Asian skies, Asiasat and Indonesia's Palapa are soon to be joined by Apstar, PAS-2, Intelsat, Rimsat, and others. With digital compression, the channels between broadcaster or editor and media consumer (the listener, the viewer, the reader) are blurring beyond belief. That is the challenge to all of us in international broadcasting in a satellite age.

DOUGLAS BOYD
PROFESSOR AND DEAN
DEPARTMENT OF COMMUNICATIONS
AND INFORMATION STUDIES
UNIVERSITY OF KENTUCKY
LEXINGTON, KENTUCKY - USA

Star Television.

Let me first say this is my third Challenges conference. There are many old friends, and some new ones here. I cannot thank the organizers enough for allowing a few obscure university professors to come. It's probably the equivalent of being politically correct to have us around.

Also today, while I was sitting at the back listening to the morning session, I came to the realization of why it's a good idea to have a few university professors here. We too are always talking about money problems and restructuring. Maybe American universities, at least research universities, and international broadcasters have something in common.

One of the things we can do as university professors, when we approach the classroom, is to take a bit of a theoretical approach, which I assure you I will not bore you with this afternoon. Alan is right. For the most part my geographical area of interest has been the Arab World and to a certain extent, Europe. I had the pleasure, because of the Japanese connection with Kentucky, to spend a couple of weeks in Japan in 1991 and then again in 1992 and just recently in Malaysia and Hong Kong. I've also just come from the educational part of the National Association of Broadcasters' meeting, held annually in Las Vegas. So what I'd like to spend a few minutes on today, that you probably know more about than I, is Star Television.

I do not plan to talk of Star Television. I really thought I'd say a few words to follow what Alan has said. One of the great changes which has happened in the last decade, certainly the last five years, is that it is now impossible for an authoritarian government, or one predisposed to limit information, to do so. There are just too many phones, faxes, too much satellite television, too much medium wave and international broadcasting that many of you are involved in, for information not to get around. It's only those who really don't want the information that don't have access to it now.

I admit to being somewhat fascinated by Star Television. As you know, it operates out of Hong Kong. It has received a great deal of publicity. They were one of the first, if not the first, organizations by satellite to distribute very widely BBC World Service Television.

As I was in my hotel room, travelling as I do with my Sony digital radio, and finding on my television set not only CNN but also BBC World Service television, I found the medium wave service, the rebroadcast and the BBC World Service English language on radio to be somewhat less attractive.

From a kind of theoretical perspective, one of the things I've talked to you about before is the idea that no longer is there just a radio audience. I certainly agree with Dr. Mytton and Alan Heil that shortwave broadcasting is very much alive; it is far from dead. But, to a certain extent, what the potential radio listener faces now is other things to do, so to speak. For example, increased local quality of radio and television. In many countries, governments and private organizations that had a kind of monopoly or quasi-monopoly over local broadcasts understand that international broadcasting in terms of radio or television now come in and provide competition for them. To a certain extent, production values, news accuracy, broadcasting days and new channels have been added in order to counter, to recognize that kind of competition.

I made two trips to Star TV. It is an amazing technical facility to witness, both in terms of the satellite uplinking and downlinking, and the production facilities. I told a group of people at our broadcast meeting in Las Vegas, primarily educators, the four criteria for young Hong Kong based Chinese to work in the production facilities of Star Television: fluency in English, being a graduate of a higher educational institution and to have a good work attitude, and they will not hire anyone in their technical facilities, production facilities, who has any television experience. They don't want to have to unlearn what someone else has taught them. They want to start fresh.

So Star Television, whether it comes directly to apartment houses in India, through cable systems throughout Asia, is being pirated by people in Israel and the Gulf and provides that one measure of competition for international medium and shortwave radio that will continue. Whether it's VCRs, whether it's pirated movies, it is a very busy media world, Asia, which is increasing in economic importance. More disposable income, less leisure time.

In conclusion, it's very clear that what many of you do very well, broadcast in and to the area, will never disappear but in my opinion, the competition will become increasingly keen.

MASAOMI SATO
DIRECTOR GENERAL
RADIO JAPAN NHK
TOKYO - JAPAN

Asian News to the World.

I am delighted to have the opportunity to speak at this conference. As Radio Japan is one of the Asian broadcasting stations, I will speak from an Asian perspective.

In Tokyo, at the beginning of this month, a thought provoking symposium was held for those of us who engage in international broadcasting. The title of the symposium was "How television is covering issues in other countries". Many issues concerning television reports from Japan and the United States were raised at this symposium.

What astonished us most in Japan was the large information gap between Japan and the United States. Over eight and a half months, between 1992 and 1993, five networks each from Japan and the U.S. conducted a survey analysis of news content. Results showed 33% of international news on Japanese television dealt with the U.S. and Japan-U.S. relations, or 36 hours and 54 minutes, while the U.S. network coverage of Japan and its relations added up to only 3%, or 3 hours and 5 minutes.

It has been known for quite a while that more news information about Europe and the United States appears in Japanese media than information about Japan appears in European or U.S. media. But this was the first time that fact was shown so obviously.

It is Radio Japan's role and duty to let the world know about Japan. The symposium in Tokyo asked what should Radio Japan broadcast to the world? To coincide with this symposium, we at Radio Japan studied a trial program. We decided to exchange the top news of the day with Asian broadcasting stations and we rebroadcast them to the world under the title of "Today's top news from Asia".

We think that much of the Asian news reported through Western radio services is based on the viewpoint of developed countries. We expressed our wish to convey Asian news based on the Asian perspective to Asian broadcasters and we eventually received favourable responses for news exchange from five broadcasters, including KBS, Korea and Voice of Vietnam.

Also, starting in April, Radio Japan is going to strengthen the Asian service by increasing by four hours its broadcasting in several languages, including Chinese, Burmese and Vietnamese.

More Asia and the Japanese news to the world, news exchange and expanding our Asian services, turned out to be some of the answers from the symposium in Tokyo.

It is also Radio Japan's responsibility, however, to extend our service to specific regions of the world, as well as to defineour role to the world.

During the Japanese general elections last July, we knew the result could be a turning point in Japanese politics and we reported about ballot counting in both English and Japanese, as well as in Chinese and Korean. We also included news specials. This measure was taken because China, North Korea and other east Asian countries are particularly interested in Japanese politics.

Needless to say, this flexible programming has become possible thanks to the advanced technology, including satellite transmission and overseas relay transmissions. Radio Japan studied overseas relay transmissions in 1979 and today we transmit our programs with six overseas stations.

Domestically, we have 300 kW transmitters and we haverenovated Radio Japan's operations room, for the first time in 20 years, introducing the latest in computer and digital technology. These renovations made it possible for us to greatly expand our Russian service last year. We have to admit however, we have not yet introduced our satellite data service and rebroadcasting which most major international broadcasters have already done. There are many reasons for this, but one of the biggest is the fact that NHK is reliant on fees paid by television viewers in Japan.

Radio Japan is a public radio, subsidized by the government but there is a common belief that since the overseas section of NHK has obtained a certain level in its world service, it should be geared to providing visual service to the world.

We are in the midst of keen competition among the world broadcasters. We hear there are more than 500 million shortwave receivers in the world today. Although there are certain shortcomings in shortwave broadcasting, we believe it still plays an important role in international broadcasting. On the other hand, developments such as digital audio broadcasting are going to be even more attractive means of audio transmission for international broadcasting.

Whether these technological improvements will be truly meaningful or not remains to be seen.

QUESTIONS

(For Radio Japan):

Two years ago, NHK was pursuing a project called GNN, the Global News Network. This project was suddenly abandoned when the President of NHK resigned. I know there were discussions about the pros and cons of this project. I would like to know why this project was abandoned by the people of NHK?

Masaomi Sato:

I just want to add that GNN was a project where they wanted to have 24-hour broadcast, of which eight hours would have been produced by NHK, eight hours by a European broadcaster and eight hours by a North American broadcaster. That would have been in competition, in a way, with BBC or CNN maybe. The GNN is not stopped completely. It is just on hold. GNN's plan is now progressing in a slow manner. We've already started a GNN project in the United States and Europe, in total 15 hours of broadcast combined between Europe and the United States. The prerequisite is a sort of worldwide cooperation. If that materializes, we would like to start a 24-hour broadcast in the future. As I touched upon a bit in my speech, we'd like to start the visual service in Asia in the near future. I really agree with the point you mentioned, that of the competition between CNN and BBC World TV Service. I'm sorry to say that at this point I cannot say when we are going to start the TV service in the Asian region.

Richard McClear for Professor Boyd:

When you talked about Star Television and being able to communicate without censorship. I understand that Star Television is now thinking of dropping the BBC World Service television because of objections from the People's Republic of China, or at least fear they won't be able to penetrate the market of the People's Republic of China enough and they are replacing it with a movie channel. Also, when I was sitting in Albania, I was not able to watch the Larry King interview with Jerry Adams because of British objections if CNN carried that program. So, the objection of one government, in the case of China, is wiping BBC World Service television off of Star Television, the objection of one government in Europe was able to wipe out the entire Larry King show from broadcast all over Europe. Do you see this as something that will be a continuing problem or do you see that these problems will be overcome? Will the market forces of a large market create this type of censorship in the future?

Douglas Boyd:

I think your point is really an excellent one. Aside from my very broad comments about it being almost impossible to restrain the flow of communication and information now, you are right, there are instances where, for commercial purposes or political objections in the cases you mentioned, there can be at least one channel shut down. The situation with Star and World Service Television is a complicated one. There are people here from the BBC that are more up on this. I know that within the next few days, there will be a court case in London involving the fact that BBC World Service Television may come off of Star. There is wide speculation that the relatively new owner of Star Television, Mr. Murdoch, probably from an economic perspective, would like to place a Chinese movie channel on the transponder. Mr. Murdoch's decision is largely an economic one, not one of information, whereas the original owner, Mr. Lee, was very interested in having World Service television on at the beginning. Yes, there are ways of temporarily stopping information. Ultimately though, if you wanted to see that interview or hear what it was, you would have caught it in the International Herald Tribune or on other stations. One brief event that happened this morning that you may not have seen will probably be in the Wall Street Journal tomorrow. I caught it on CNN this morning. An announcement and a proposal advanced to the Federal Communications Commission, the American regulatory agency, to the effect that Microsoft, teamed up with McCaw Communication which is the largest cellular operator in the United States, for project 2001. They are proposing a worldwide system of satellites where each individual will have access via satellite communication to voice data and phone information. I offer that not as a Star Wars perspective on communication but the fact, riding on what Alan said, that increasingly there is a marriage of technologies that will increase at some expense, the worldwide flow of information.

CHEN WEN BING
PRESIDENT
PEOPLE'S BROADCASTING STATION SHANGHAI
SHANGHAI - PEOPLE'S REPUBLIC OF CHINA

Shanghai Broadcasting Amidst the Excellent Situation of Reform and Opening.

Radio Shanghai is one of the biggest regional stations in China. Established on May 27, 1949, it has a history of 45 years. Its broadcasting covers the areas of Shanghai and the Yangtze Delta, with 50 million listeners daily. Radio Shanghai was the first station in China to set up traffic and information, English news and economic sub-stations, having increased its number to eight now.

With more than ten frequencies of 8 AM, 2 FM and 3 SW, Radio Shanghai broadcasts eight sets of 145 programmes with 49 live ones, 128 hours a day, having broken the highest record of its own history.

The percentage of listeners of "990 AM Morning News" in Radio Shanghai has reached 40%, occupying the first place of all the programmes in Shanghai. Compared to "TV Morning News" which covers only 4%, our percentage is much higher. Now Radio Shanghai has a series of popular and well-known programmes on economics, arts and entertainment, sports, science and technology, social education and programmes for children.

Each year, Radio Shanghai receives about 100,000 letters from listeners who regard it as an excellent teacher and friend. From it, they acquire valuable information, knowledge and pleasure.

Radio Shanghai has established extensive contacts with broadcasting stations and corporations of over 40 countries and areas. It has successfully held the Shanghai International Broadcasting Music Festival which is a new attempt at strengthening international cooperation and exchange. Friends from other countries who participated in the Music Festival praised its large scale and its fine organization. They added the Festival has reached the level of international Music Festivals.

Radio Shanghai was first to put on "advertisement" programmes, which have greatly increased its income, enabling it to put on more popular programmes and to embark on its own road of self-development and self-funding.

Radio Shanghai has now accumulated all the funds it needs, on its own. The income from advertisements in 1993 is double that of 1992.

We mention these facts in order to give a concrete example of Asian broadcasting affairs at this conference. We are now facing keen competition from the news media and TV, but broadcasting still has its irreplaceable superiority and potentiality. The key problem is that broadcasting workers must not hesitate to go ahead against competition, challenge, difficulties and failures. They must have the determination to win an excellent and bright tomorrow for themselves. Such a belief has enabled Radio Shanghai to reach the progress and vitality it has today.

As we all know, the broadcasting programmes of any country cannot survive if they do not conform to the politics, economics, and culture of that country. The existence and development of Radio Shanghai is inseparable from the background of reform and opening in China.

China is taking gigantic strides on the road of reform, opening and modernization. Shanghai, one of the great cities of the world, will surely be in the forefront during this historic period of transition and we should see many changes in the next year and even greater changes in the next three years. The reform and opening in Shanghai requires that Radio Shanghai also embark on a road of reform and opening.

We will describe three measures taken by Radio Shanghai on the road to reform and opening:

1. Establishing a series of sub-stations to meet the needs of reform, opening and modernization in Shanghai.

Radio Shanghai has more than ten frequencies, making it possible to establish a series of sub-stations. In October 1992, eight sub-stations put on programmes about news, market & economics, arts and entertainment, music, English news, foreign language teaching, traffic & information, and the Voice of Huang Pu.

The news sub-station is the locomotive of all the other sub-stations. The programmes of news on the hour, especially the "One-Hour Morning News", is the most popular item. The slogan goes: "If you want to keep abreast of world events, please listen to our One-Hour Morning News". The majority of Shanghai citizens listens to the "Morning News".

This programme includes selections from newspapers & magazines, brief news from the most up-to-date foreign newspapers & magazines, sports, financial quotations, detailed news reports, phone calls from listeners, today's forum and the weather forecast. Besides the news programmes, it also broadcasts programmes on art & literature, science & technology and programmes for children, greatly satisfying the needs of people in this period of reform and opening.

The market and economics sub-station was set up for the development of market economy. Everyday it broadcasts 800 items of different kinds of information on economics. "The Latest Stock Quotations" broadcasts the prices of over 100 daily stocks more than ten times, which greatly draws listeners' attention.

The art and entertainment sub-station and the music sub-station put on colourful programmes from Chinese traditional music and operas, and foreign music. Take the music programmes,for example: 50 sets of programmes are produced a week, which is the total of all those of the previous year.

The English sub-station broadcasts news, special reports and music programmes in english and is very appreciated by the officials of consulates, businessmen, students, tourists and English students.

The foreign language teaching sub-station puts on programmes in five languages: English, French, Japanese, Russian and German. Large numbers of listeners call it "The big classroom on the air". Many thanks to Radio Canada International for helping Radio Shanghai set up the "Everyday English" programme, with over 40,000 listeners. More than 3,000 listeners took part in the final exam and 100 of them won prizes.

The traffic information sub-station was set up at the request of the City Government, broadcasting information about city traffic, the arrival and departure times of trains, ships and airplanes.

The Voice of Huang Pu was set up for listeners in Taiwan, to enhance mutual understanding and friendship. Its purpose is to promote the peaceful unification of our motherland.

The above eight sub-stations each has its own characteristics and special assignments. As practice proves, they conform to the world tendency of "narrowcast". Listeners of various strata and requirements may choose whatever they like. The sub-stations have made considerable contributions to the modernization of Shanghai.

2. From "shut" to "open" model.

The success of any broadcasting station depends on the number of listeners it has. Formerly, the situation was "the station broadcasts and listeners listen", with listeners playing a passive role. Instead, they should be made to take an active part in the programmes. An important change is the hosts of live programmes answering hot-line phone calls from listeners. Radio Shanghai now has 145 programmes of which 49 are live ones, broadcasting news, dialogues, service, arts, etc.

"The Hot-Line from Listeners", for example, reflects listeners' requests, worries and our suggestions for solutions. Typical cases are chosen for broadcast. The hot-line received 30,000 calls since its inception a year ago. Listeners have great confidence in the programme and they warmly participate in it.

"The Citizen and the Society" is a programme for the higher stratum of society. Debates on important issues in the news are carried on by the host of the programme and an invited guest, and listeners who respond with phone calls. For example, in January 1993, the Mayor of Shanghai, Huang Ju, carried on a dialogue, broadcast live, with the citizens of Shanghai, about the ten projects to accelerate the modernization of Shanghai and raise the living standards of the people, asking for their opinions and suggestions. Eight vice-mayors and more than fifty district and county officials also did the same with the citizens. More than 260 topics were discussed with more than 2000 people participating in the year 1993. Listeners praised this programme as a bridge to enhance mutual understanding and co-operation between the government and the people.

"Quietly Spoken Words" and "Advice by Well-Known Doctors" are service programmes. Radio Shanghai was the first to start the "Quietly Spoken Words" programme, in the deep of the night, to transmit and exchange scientific topics and to answer and solve problems put forward by listeners in their letters. "Advice by Well-Known Doctors" is somewhat like a "hospital on the air", inviting well-known doctors to the live-broadcast room to advise listeners on their problems. It once received more than 3000 patients in one appointment.

Live broadcasts on the arts and entertainment, with hosts presiding, are of various kinds. Through the hot-line, listeners ask for special songs, talk shows, poems and dialogues in films, and take part in various prize-awarding contests of knowledge. They are greatly interested in and enthusiastic about such programmes.

As you can see, Radio Shanghai, going from a "shut" model to an "open" model, not only wins over a large number of listeners, but also accomplishes its multi-function of transmitting information, educating through entertainment and service to society.

3. Multi-method, multi-form, multi-channel, international exchange and co-operation.

Another important reform measure of Radio Shanghai is to have wide contacts with other broadcasting stations in the world, with peace, friendship, co-operation and exchange as the guidelines.

In my speech at the International Broadcasting Symposium at Montreux, Switzerland, in 1992, I said: "Radio Shanghai is now enjoying wide world contact with its programmes on foreign language teaching (especially the English language), exchange of programmes with the broadcasting stations of more than 30 countries and regions, mutual visits by staff members, co-operation in producing special programmes and the staging of the International Broadcasting Music Festival with its world impact". In recent years, international exchange and co-operation has developed further. In November 1993, we successfully held the Fourth Shanghai International Broadcasting Music Festival. The festival is held every two years with the next one due in November 1995.

Exchange of programmes with equality, mutual benefit and two-way transmission as the guiding principles, is also very active. Radio Shanghai has put on various music programmes. We also transmit music programmes from the U.S., Canada, France, Germany,

Japan, the Netherlands, Singapore, Australia, and from regions such as Hong Kong and Taiwan. At the same time, programmes on music, cross-talks and radio plays by Radio Shanghai are supplied to France, Singapore and others, through various channels.

Co-operation in the production of various kinds of special programmes with the broadcasting stations in other countries is another landmark of Radio Shanghai's widening and deepening of world contact. For example, The Voice of Germany and Radio Shanghai together produced a special scientific programme on "Chinese Acupuncture and Moxibustion". To celebrate the 20th anniversary of twining of between Shanghai and Yokohama, reporters of Radio Shanghai and NHK were exchanged to produce the special programme "A Colourful Bridge on the Air across a Narrow Strip of Water", which lasted three hours.

The number of staff members on mutual visits increased considerably. In 1993, reporters, editors, hosts of programmes, technical management personnel of Radio Shanghai were sent to visit nine countries, totalling 19 delegations with 31 people, while 49 delegations with 148 people of broadcasting stations and corporations of other countries visited Radio Shanghai.

Radio Shanghai and broadcasting stations and corporations of other countries have several times jointly produced large-scale arts and entertainment performances and contests. They are planning to establish an arts and entertainment advisory corporation and a music programme production centre with the objective of further developing the exchange of Chinese and western cultures and the production of music programmes.

In conclusion, we are of the opinion that broadcasting must advance on its own road. Different from newspapers, TV and other media, broadcasting must develop its own superiority. Also, in each country, broadcasting should have its own special characteristics. Radio Shanghai is now in search of a way typical of China, typical of Radio Shanghai.

At the same time, broadcasting as a mass medium and carrier of information has its own regulations and laws of development to be obeyed by all broadcasting stations of the world. So, we must learn from the advanced experiences of the broadcasting stations of other countries in the production of programmes, management and financial matters, and innovate our broadcasting technical equipment.

It is necessary for us to increase exchange with other countries, to strengthen our cooperation and to study and discuss continually the regulations and laws of development of broadcasting, so that broadcasting will forever be invincible in its keen competition with and challenge from other mass media. This is our objective in attending this international symposium and also in holding in October of this year, a large-scale symposium on broadcasting. As the Director of Radio Shanghai, I seize this opportunity to cordially invite all of you to attend the symposium to find ways and means for the further development and thriving of broadcasting.

FREDERICA DOCHINOIU
HEAD, ENGLISH DEPARTMENT
RADIO ROMANIA
BUCHAREST - ROMANIA
(Read by Marian Bistriceanu Deputy Editor-in-Chief)

The Asian Service of Radio Romania International.

Radio Romania International is a special Department of Radio Romania whose purpose is to present developments in Romania as they happen, on a daily basis, to the world. Life in Romania, particularly now when there is a transition period from a totalitarian regime to democracy, from a command economy to a market economy, is quite complex and we think it is most appropriate to draw a fair and objective picture of our country.

Shortwave broadcasts are a reliable source of information for people living in different parts of the world wanting to know what is happening in a certain country at a given time. Since the 1989 revolution, Radio Romania has offered to its listeners an objective presentation of events and RRI's programmes beamed to Asia have the explicit purpose of showing true images of life in Romania. We know that the media in some countries do not give much attention to a medium-sized country like Romania, so that is one more reason to present the political, economic, cultural trade and, why not, sports events in this country, as they happen.

The endeavours of the English department, rejuvenated to a proportion of 55% after 1990, are backed by those of the news and current affairs departments in bringing interesting people to our microphones who have important things to say about events in Romania, about daily life, about political occurrences, about the tourist attractions of the country. Commentaries and brief feature reports on daily events complete the picture RRI projects through its shortwave programmes to the world about the dynamic changes occurring in Romania.

This year, RRI marks its 55th year of existence, when Romania began broadcasting abroad on shortwaves. Today, we have a daily one hour programme for Asia at 14.30 UTC. At the beginning of the Asian service, in the late 50's, a first half-hour programme at 15.00 UTC was started, targeted towards Asia (particularly India and the regions around it). Programme content at that time included a news bulletin and information about Romania, as well as a few minutes of folk music.

At that time, the communist government's interests for propaganda entailed an increase in broadcasting hours so, after roughly ten years of a single half-hour programme beamed to Asia, it was decided to produce two half-hour programmes and, in the late 60's, a second programme beamed to Asia was started, namely at 12.00 UTC. The first half-hour included news but primarily information on topical events. The second half-hour usually included, besides news and a commentary, our regular features which covered a wide variety of topics, from youth and culture related features to economic and entertainment programmes. A few examples are: "Youth Club", "Cultural Artistic Notebook", "Week-end Miscellanea", "Radio Pictures".

Of most interest were the programmes in which listeners could make a direct contribution, such as Listeners' Letterbox and Let's Talk It Over. Questions from listeners varied, of course, but all were related to what was happening in Romania. Over the years, answers were given about Romania's transportation industry, housing, wildlife and how Romanians spend their spare time. Needless to say that until 1989, all answers had to be somewhat politicized, otherwise the answer was not approved by the then Chief-Editors.

For about 20 years the two programmes beamed to Asia conveyed an image of Romania that the communist government wanted to be known abroad. As most of you know, it was rather far from domestic realities. But December 1989 came and with it, the turning point in our lives and in our broadcasts. On the very day of December 22, 1989, the first half-hour for Asia, which was our first English program of the day, could not announce to the world the collapse of communism because the transmitters had been cut off. The first news bulletin which included information about the revolution was beamed to Asia at 15.00 UTC. From then on, the programming at Radio Bucharest changed in content, trying finally to reflect objectively what was going on in Romania.

Those who had tuned in before and after 1989 could sense the huge difference and they wrote to us. Since many listeners living in different countries in Asia had for years requested longer programmes, we finally managed to comply with their request in the spring of 1992 when out of the two half-hour programmes, we created a full hour at 14.30 UTC, thus being able to bring some new regular features and to extend some of the existing ones. Before, our Asian service never had full musical programmes due to the two half-hours.

Now, our listeners can enjoy Romanian art, folk and pop music for about 11 or 12 minutes every other day. The "Cultural Artistic Notebook" now covers 25 minutes, "Youth Club", 20 minutes, "Letterbox" and "Radio Pictures", 11 minutes each. The first half-hour brings many two or three minute long reports on topical events, commentaries, press reviews, a daily guest who might be a foreign visitor or a Romanian personality. On Saturdays we have introduced many new features such as: "On the Spotlight" which focuses on different topics like environment, religion, etc,; "Listeners are Interviewing" in which personalities from Romania's president to the gymnast Nadia Comaneci and football player Ghorghe Hagi, are asked questions sent in by our listeners; "Pages of Romanian Literature", highlighting our best known writers, poets and playwrights, "DX Mailbag", "Through Bucharest", ""Along the Centuries", every fortnight, and "Philatelic Agenda". All these featurs had never been broadcast in the Asian Service when we had two half hour programmes. Special mention should be made of the "Romanian by Radio" courde each Friday, which enjoys great popularity and "Women, the Other Force" every Wednesday. As to listeners' response, the greatest number of letters comes from India, Pakistan and Japan.

To conclude this brief outline of Radio Romania International's programmes beamed to Asia, let me stress once more that the broadcasts are aimed at presenting the realities in Romania in a fair and objective manner, stressing all the problems arising from the transition period to the market economy. Until 1989, and particularly in the last ten years, we wondered how anyone could listen to the heavy propaganda we were obliged to transmit. Today we can see, from listeners's reports and letters, that they have a real interest in what is going on in romania, all the more so because shortwave programmes remain the only source of quick and reliable information if you want to learn something sbout other countries, or to learn about Romania from Romania.

LI DAN
DEPUTY DIRECTOR
CHINA RADIO INTERNATIONAL
BEIJING - PEOPLE'S REPUBLIC OF CHINA

Common Problems with Chinese Characteristics.

It's nice to be here - to be here with you, my friends, both old and new. Over the past years our overseas colleagues have shown warm concerns about CRI - formerly Radio Beijing - and its staffers. On behalf of all at CRI I'd like to express our whole-hearted gratitude to you, especially to Allan Familiant from RCI. Without his efforts I wouldn't even have the opportunity to be here to say "thank you".

How do you see CRI and its people? Let me give you a brief picture.

First, the Good News.

1. We have set up CRI's own news-gathering network. CRI's newscasts used to be based on wire stories from the Xinhua News Agency. Now CRI has a nation-wide news-gathering network. It also has established overseas correspondent bureaus in twenty foreign capitals or major cities. At present, some 70 Chinese radio and TV stations, as well as newspapers, have subscribed to CRI's news service, and for that CRI is better known in the country and the project also generates a small income, so that our people now have some pocket money.

2. Program Reform.

Since listeners in different countries tend to have different interests, it's very difficult to provide stories that fit all our 43 language services. So we let some language departments set up special programs for their particular audience. For example, the English service has Current Affairs and Chinese Cooking; the Japanese service has China Reports and Ancient Chinese Jokes, and the Arab service has The Chinese Moslems, to name just a few.

We've also ventured into live coverage of major events in China, such as the parade on National Day, opening meetings and closing ceremonies of the National People's Congress and the Chinese People's Political Consultative Conference, the Beijing Asian Games and the first East-Asian Games held in Shanghai. During major Chinese festivals or festive seasons in target countries, relevant language departments also run special programs to bring holiday greetings to our audience. This kind of programs are among our listeners' favourites.

From time to time, CRI also runs specials with overseas radio stations that require audience participation. These specials have been highly successful.

3. We've opened New Channels for Overseas Broadcasting.

(A)   Improving overseas reception through renting transmitters abroad and entering mutual program relay arrangement with our foreign radio stations.

Reception of CRI signals used to be poor or impossible in Africa, Europe and North America, because most of CRI's programs were transmitted by low-power transmitters with no overseas relay stations. The situation has improved greatly since 1987, when CRI agreed to mutual program relay with radio stations in Canada, France, Spain, Switzerland and other countries.

It also has entered into agreements to rent air time from radio stations in Brazil, Mali, Russia and United States.

(B)   Exchanging programs with foreign radio stations.

Exchanging programs with foreign radio stations is another way to extend our coverage. We have paid special attention to mailing programs to foreign radio stations to be used on their air time, on their AM or FM broadcasts.

In 1992 CRI sent a total of 1400 hours of programs to radio stations in 54 countries and regions.

(C)   Launching domestic foreign-language broadcasts to cater to foreign friends, tourists and businesspeople inside China.

Over the past decade China has seen a big increase in the number of people from other countries who come as tourists, experts or advisors to aid China's development, and businesspeople. In order to make life easier for them and keep them better informed about what's going on around them, CRI launched an English service in the capital area in 1984. Later on other language programs were added, and the program is now relayed to 15 other major cities in China.

4. CRI now boasts Listeners all over the World, with the growing Audience.

Ten years ago CRI received an average of 78,000 letters from overseas listeners a year.

In 1992, the number jumped to 328,000. Last year the number reached 550,000 - a new record. And these letters came from 170 countries and regions. If we follow commonly used letter-listener ratios where one letter represents 300 to 500 listeners, CRI now boasts nearly 200,000,000 listeners around the world. But to tell you the truth, nearly half of these letters were response to a quiz program and most of the letters came from Asian and African countries.

Those were the good news.

Now, the problems, or what do you call it, challenges.

Although we lost the opportunity to hear the speeches at the present conference and share all your experiences, I can almost assure you, for I can imagine, that we do share almost all of your problems, and we have more, more problems. I am not going to list them here, but the difference is almost all those problems or challenges pose a direct threat to the real future of international broadcasting in China or the very existence of our team, CRI.

Unlike other international broadcasting organizations, almost all our foreign-language staffs are trained in China, which usually needs 4 to 5 years' training, and it would need another 4 to 5 years on-the-job training to make them competent. So the work enthusiasm and dedication of these talented people concerns the stability and existence of our team. You can't easily find the right people to fill in their place once they decide to quit and move to better paid jobs or more interesting jobs. As a matter of fact, we lost about 30 of them each year in the past 10 years. The factors affecting their enthusiasm towards shortwave radio broadcasting can be better paid jobs in those new companies, especially joint ventures in the early days of Chinese reform, and nowadays, the rapid development of television, including international TV broadcasting or the satellite television which makes our radio talents lose balance in many ways, as CCTV-China Central Television - and CRI work under the same ministry or work in the same building and in these two organizations people know each other well and very often they were classmates in schools. So what I want to say here is - the seriousness of our common problems is greater, if not vital, when they come to China. Thinking about this, sometimes I say to myself and to my colleagues: these are the common problems with Chinese character-istics.

QUESTIONS.

Discussion.

Derek White:

It's not so much a question but to add to something Doug Boyd said. I think, often in discussions, a lot of stress is placed on Star because it's captured so much publicity for various reasons, not the least being the participation of Mr. Murdoch. I'm glad, Doug, that you claimed him as yours! The development of satellite television in Asia is far wider, of course, than Star and it does have the effect of making greater competition and changing patterns. I think Indonesia is an interesting model. It virtually now has an "open skies" policy. Indonesian citizens can buy for a very modest price, a dish which will give them a range of satellite services. At the same time, Indonesia is rapidly improving its domestic television and domestic radio services, including developing a domestic satellite service which it also intends should carry direct broadcast radio. Simultaneously, it's expanding its shortwave services for domestic purposes. I think the result of this is that while the opportunity for inflow of information increases, it may be that the demand for information will decline and the need for overseas interna-tional broadcasting, in the sense we know it, will decline as those countries develop their own services. There are other societies, of course, which are endeavouring to restrict that flow in different ways. You can't have dishes in Singapore or Malaysia. Singapore is building extensive cable services. It starts next year, and its objective is to cable all of the 7,000 blocks of flats that house 91% of Singapore's population. By that means it will control the flow of information to a very large degree. It will undoubtedly take into its cable services certain overseas broadcasters, I hope. We've had talks about it and Australian Television will be one of them. But it also opens the way of course, for others to to take it or not to take it, if the occasion arises. Malaysia, I think, will try and control the flow of information by selecting the programmes it allows to be retransmitted through its television systems. So, while everything that Doug has said is true, that the sources of information available are increasing all the time, it's at least possible that, as I'm suggesting here, as countries improve their own systems, the demand for information may decline

Douglas Boyd:

I'm thankful that you picked up at my attempt at humour. For those of you who don't know, Mr. Murdoch, originally an Australian citizen, became an American citizen for only one reason, that is to acquire the original Metro-Media radio and television stations in the United States, which have formed the backbone of what is now called "the fourth television network" which is the Fox Network. One's loyalties seem to be oriented toward whatever or whoever you want to buy, something we find rather interesting. I'm afraid, with regard to passport, we claim him as our own.

I absolutely agree with Derek. As a university professor, and one who likes to look at the audience, and one who has lived in several developing countries, as many of you have, I find it is the audience that wants to be in control. We have these ideas, whether we are broadcasters or university professors, that certain things are happening but in fact it's the audience that always seems to seek out a service they believe is useful and credible. Whether is was broadcasting from the U.S. and the BBC to Europe during World War II, whether it was the old Soviet Union seeking out certain broadcasts or those in Asia... It's going to be a very interesting mix of new technology. You're absolutely right that the tendency is for many systems, some of them in the Middle East, to go to the ultimate oxymoron wireless cable, or NBS, or to cable, in order to control information. The other thing that is happening is that the dishes are becoming smaller, the electronics less complicated. Ultimately people who want badly enough to receive information and television being arguably the most powerful medium, will find a way to do it.

I was in Malaysia at the beginning of this year and you are right. Malaysia has joined the ranks of those countries that have stopped people from building satellite dishes. Yet out in the country, they haven't. When I talked to some of my friends of the Arab World where satellite dishes are not permitted, we often share something quite interesting. They find it very difficult to believe that where I live in Lexington, Kentucky, I cannot have a satellite dish because I live in a planned community. When I bought my house, I agreed not to put up a satellite dish. These are the old dishes that people who planned the community thought were rather ugly and they decided we had to go with cable systems. So, I join my friends in not being able to pull down those satellite signals that many of you see.

Graham Mytton:

I also want to react to Mr. Li Dan on what he said about his audiences and his listeners' letters.

I found his address absolutely fascinating about Radio Peking, but we get this old chestnut. I think he said, correct me if I am wrong, Mr. Li Dan, "if we follow the commonly used ratio of listeners to letters". Sir, there is no commonly used ratio of listeners to letters, because there is no ratio. There is no relationship whatsoever between the number of letters you receive and the number of listeners you have, and I can prove it.

One of the nice things about my job is that I do handle all the listeners' letters, and in reference to what Don Browne said, I am also a stamp collector. It's a bit like being an alcoholic in a brewery, it's one of the nicest jobs in the BBC, because I don't do the research, I do all the letters.

And because my department of 60 people, 20 of them engaged in research and 40 of them engaged in listeners' letters, because we have this access to feedback in two different forms in the scientific reliable audience research way, doing the surveys, and also in the handling of the feedback from the listeners, we can compare the two, and the comparisons are quite remarkable.

You would think there would be some relationship, you would think that if you got a lot of letters from one country, that would mean some relationship to the listeners. Or that if you got very few letters from another country, there would be some indication there of the number of listeners. I am sorry, I wish it were true but it isn't. In fact, it is not only not true, it is so untrue, that it makes things very, very, very misleading.

Let me give you an example. Last year the BBC also, like Radio Peking, Radio China International, got about 550,000 letters. They fell from the previous year of just under 700,000 letters. Why? Because our audience was down? Of course, not.

The reason was because of the rising price of stamps. One of the things that the World Bank has done is to insist that Nigeria and Tanzania, and Kenya, and Zambia and a number of other countries stop subsidizing their postal services, so they are making them charge their proper price for the stamps to pay for the postage, so the mail falls.

The largest mailbag we got of all, we have 39 languages, we count all the letters, we log them by country, we log them by language, and we log them by what they write about. Last year we received 550,000 letters. We received 100,000 letters in the Tamil language. The Tamil language is on the air for about 15 minutes a day, we know from research on the ground that it has 1,000,000 listeners.

Now if you got a piece of paper in front of you write these figures down.

Tamil - 100,000 letters, 1 million listeners.

On the next line write Hindi. We know from our surveys that we have about 25 million Hindi listeners, in an average week, 25 million listeners. Last year we received 50,000 letters.

Next line write: Hausa. We know from research in Nigeria and in neighbouring Niger and in neighbouring Ghana that BBC audience in Hausa is about 9 million weekly. Last year the mail fell because of the higher price of postage to about 18,000 letters.

And I leave you lastly with Swahili. We know from recent research in Tanzania and in Kenya that there are about 7 million Swahili listeners weekly. Last year, because of the rising price of postage and because of the low level of literacy in Swahili in Kenya, it's much higher in Tanzania, but even so only 10,000 letters in Swahili.

So you can see there is absolutely no relationship.

CHAPTER THREE

TOWARDS A NEW IDENTITY: EDUCATION, TRAINING, STAFF/PROGRAM EXCHANGES, CO-PRODUCTIONS

Editors' Note:

One of the ongoing themes to have emerged from previous CHALLENGES conferences has been the important role to be played by international broadcasting in education. In searching for a common purpose among international broadcasters from far flung parts of the world, one of the most common refrains may be found in the words "education" and "training" and "exchanges" and "co-productions". As international broadcasting emerges into a new era of more openness, the possibilities of closer collaboration and the forms of co-operation become increasingly vital and urgent. This chapter offers some explorations of those issues and prospects.

BERT H. STEINKAMP
DIRECTOR, PLANNING AND DEVELOPMENT
RADIO NEDERLAND
HILVERSUM - THE NETHERLANDS

Introduction.

Our subject for this session is, I would say rich, if not overflowing. The general title is "Towards a new identity" for international broadcasting, or external broadcasting. It's then subdivided into four points of view: education, training as a specific form of education, staff and program exchanges between broadcasters, and co-productions. The notion of co-production clearly refers back directly to any identity, old or new, because as broadcasters here know, it's tempting to define a boundary line between the identity of the one party in a co-production and the identity of the other. That is precisely why some attempted co-productions never come about, because the co-producers cannot agree to what extent they are going to give up elements of their identities.

To give you their points of view, we have an equally rich panel.

Most of us are very much aware that in the 1920's and slightly later, broadcasting almost sprang up from a cradle called "education". The very first broadcasting programs were educational programs in ages when we thought of increasing the knowledge of the masses. If you hear such old programs insofar as recording still exists, it is a classroom tone which applies to such programs. Teachers speaking to pupils.

Entertainment came later, but education was at the very roots of broadcasting. Therefore, I think we are now in a very good position to see where this almost natural link between two disciplines, education and broadcasting, could bring us with the help of new technologies and new forms of co-operation, into a new era for broadcasting in general and in particular, into a new era for external broadcasting.

ALEXANDER PICHA
DIRECTOR
RADIOZURNAL, CESKY ROZHLAS
PRAGUE - THE CZECH REPUBLIC

Education and change in Czech Radio.

I think the best experience in education is practical experience. That's why I have decided to describe to you the fresh experience of the BBC course in Czech Radio. I think our conclusions can be generalized for the majority of the public and media in the form of communist countries.

The introduction of the private market into the broadcasting environment in the Czech Republic three years ago has remarkably changed problems of education in Czech Radio. Our private radio stations with various music and news orientation have come into being only in the capital town of Prague. There is a great hunger for well educated radio workers of all professions, especially for our foreign broadcasting department, because of their knowledge of the foreign languages.

During the last three years, more than two thirds of news editors having worked in Czech Radio have left to work for private companies. Under such conditions, Czech Radio has no other choice but to employ people without any practice in broadcasting and often people without journalistic practice. This situation makes new demands on education in the Czech Radio.

Czech Radio employs more than 1,800 workers. Most employees work in Prague. The foreign service and the three nationwide stations also broadcast from there. Our organization has its own seven member department of education. A range of its activities is wide. It provides teaching languages, computer courses of all levels, specialized courses for technicians, training for journalists, and so on.

One of the education forms used in Czech Radio is international education exchange, used especially by editors of the news channel. I have experience with a recent BBC course held in Czech Radio in Prague. The course was organized by the BBC as part of its program to help post-communist countries. At first, a representative for BBC came to Czech Radio to discuss course conditions. Months later, two experienced experts, former journalists, arrived for a two-week course.

Czech Radio prepared for the course 20 young journalists divided into two groups. The first problem arose paradoxically in forming the groups.

There are few young journalists able to understand and speak English. This fact reflects a level of language knowledge in the Czech Republic. Up till 1990, Russian was taught as the only one compulsory foreign language in Czech schools. Nowadays there are some western languages taught at primary and secondary schools but our level of knowledge is still not very good. To be able to run the course, we had to ensure an interpreter for each group.

The second problem was forming two 10 member groups of employees who wouldn't be working for nearly two weeks. Our news channel employs about 20 editors of home, foreign and sport news service. Fifteen people work in the shift and 10 editors in the current affairs section. Because of financial reasons, we only can afford to employ three journal editors. Therefore, we had to include into those groups also several regional editors.

On the other hand, there weren't any material problems. Czech Radio provided accommodations in the headquarters and the technical equipment: tape recorders and machines for the lectures and participants of the course.

The British experts were well prepared. Months before the course, a representative of BBC came to Prague to discuss personally what to focus the training on. Nevertheless many problems appeared during the course which were limiting the efficiency of the training. The first paradox was a journalist's disbelief in the sense of the course. Despite the fact that BBC is considered as a model for us, other journalists believe in the BBC but not in courses. They received the lecturers very warmly but accepted the course only as entertainment.

Czech Radio management promoted the course but from my personal discussions with the editors, it's clear that it didn't have too much effect. The problems come from traditional access to education in our country. The solution will take a long time. Nevertheless, the course removed some very old ways of preparing the news. The lecturers decided to prepare small pieces of news and reports with our editors. The journalists learned how important it is to prepare a frame of an interview in advance, to know what is the main aim of a report, what one has to record and how to work up the recording. Such practical help is very useful for our public radio because our private competitors have the best training experience.

The Czech private radio stations have mostly the capital. That's why they can use experiences from sophisticated western media markets. The experts of the western companies teach editors of joint Czech private radios how to make news more attractive for the audience, how to pick a method as the most interesting and how to take over the editors from the other media.

On the whole we can say that foreign, imported courses are very important for Czech Radio. From other experience with the practical BBC course, we already know that for higher efficiency, close cooperation between educational departments of both broadcasters is necessary. In any case, it's better for foreign lecturers to teach our editors in the Czech Republic. Czech Radio should send an experienced employee to the foreign radio who should get acquainted with the working conditions of the host organization and later supervise the course in the Czech Republic. On the other hand, foreign experts should get acquainted with the conditions of the receiver of training program.

I must say I am glad it's not necessary to explain to other journalists how important democracy and freedom of the press is. However, foreign broadcasters can still give us advice on how to use journalistic craft in regard to efficiency of work and using the latest technology. Our experience with the BBC course in Czech Radio was very pleasant. I think it's good that in the world of competition, public broadcasters help each other.

NATALKA BEREZHNA
DIRECTOR
RADIO ROKS
KIEV - UKRAINA

Commercial Radio in Ukraine.

Radio Roks is a commercial radio combining in its programming information and music. We started our broadcasts only last June. Our short experience suggests that there is a great difference between commercially-driven international programs and broadcasting financed and controlled by the government.

First of all, these programs are international in content and as such they appeal to big audiences. Otherwise, nobody would listen to them.

Second, being a commercial station, all partners share in revenue.

Third, these programs provide information, therefore they should be credible and enjoy the confidence of their listeners.

Each of the above items has its distinct characteristics.

First. Since these programs target big international audiences, there is a need for "hosts" who have been trained to conduct such broadcasts. However, to the best of my knowledge, there are no educational institutions that provide training for would-be disk jockeys or "hosts".

Second. What should be the optimal ratio between international and domestic content of the programs in order to appeal equally to listeners in several countries, including the country from which the programs originate?

And last. How should we incorporate advertisements and commercials in our programs? On the one hand, advertising should not annoy or irritate our listeners. On the other, there is no revenue without advertising. The proper balance is very important in these programs.

Ukraine, our country, has just gained independence. Ukraine is trying to overcome the consequences of the information blockade it has been subjected to. Here again our program combining information and music, has its specific character. It is the way in which information is delivered to our consumers. The program should provide firsthand information about the political and economic situation in Ukraine.

It is no secret that nowadays laws change very often in our country. New laws are enacted and old ones are abrogated. Entrepreneurs from neighboring countries who wish to invest in Ukraine would be able to get information concerning the economic and political situation in our country immediately, the same or the next day. In any case, they would get it much faster than from the press.

Bert Steinkamp:

Radio and television training for the third world has been going on in a number of countries including my own. Canada has seen a lot of such activities, for instance, on the part of Ryerson Polytechnical Institute. In the United Kingdom, there used to be the BBC training for third world countries and for commonwealth countries. In Glasgow, for quite a number of years, the Thompson Institute's specific radio and television training was abandoned about 15 years ago and was resumed in a reduced form in the Thompson Institute in Cardiff.

I could also cite the examples of ENA in France, the training institute of Deutsche Welle in Cologne, and my own organization, the Radio Nederland Training Center in Hilversum, Holland, which started its activities in 1969 and is still going strong.

Originally, all the training of that nature was done in the training country. That changed during the mid-70s when some of the training was transferred to in-country training which is much more effective in many respects, because it takes the trainees away from their regular work for a shorter period, and is easier on program directors or engineering directors hard-put to find qualified replacements.

A second reason why in-country training deserves our attention is that it can be much better geared to local circumstances.

A few things inevitably went wrong.

I am reminded of the pioneering work of a countryman of mine, a director of Her Majesty's Stationary Office, the Dutch version of it. At a UNESCO symposium in the late 1970s, this specialist was invited to talk about his pioneering work of mobile printing vans working in rural areas of countries like Colombia or Indonesia. During the symposium, a rather fashionable Third World journalist working for a group of Dutch newspapers was extremely critical of the pioneering work of the director of HMSO in The Hague. The director listened patiently to the criticisms and said, in his gruffy voice: "If I had not done something, you would not be able to talk about it".

I think that is a lesson to us all. It teaches us modesty. The ideal training situation has yet to be invented, but in many cases we can improve it.

PETER KENYAN-JUI
COMMONWEALTH OF LEARNING
VANCOUVER. BRITISH COLUMBIA - CANADA

Education and The Commonwealth of Learning.

I will speak as an educator who believes very fervently in the power of media and particularly in distance education where print media, in the past, had been the main vehicle of education. I think that, increasingly, the world is realizing that learning can be a pleasure, that learning can be combined with many educational technologies and make the process pleasurable for the learner. This is where we think communication technologies do combine very well with distance education.

I will cite a number of countries where the Commonwealth of Learning has tried in effect to bring together educators and broadcasters. I think this must be one of the challenges, that perhaps we train broadcasters on one side and educators on the other, and we never bring the two together. Yet we say that distance education is best applied where communication technologies are brought in to buttress that particular medium. We have tried that in the Commonwealth of Learning. I will give one example, in Namibia, a young country where they believed very powerfully in the use of the Namibian Broadcasting Corporation. Through the Commonwealth of Learning and through the Department of Communications here in Canada, we brought in a trainer to train educators from the Ministry of Education and broadcasters from the Namibian Broadcasting Corporation. To me, if you want people to work together, you begin by training them together. In a way, the suspicion that has been there before is wiped off because you are bringing these two groups of very important people in any development, together. I would say perhaps we need more of that. Even in a meeting such as this one, perhaps you should have more educators than broadcasters, or at least maintain a balance.

Let me also say that particularly in developing countries, where the power of radio is yet to be taped, there is still need for more training. We still need to rediscover radio. This might be the second challenge - rediscover radio to combine with other media, TV, print, journalists, to try and bring education and training to our people. I think we must look at what exists locally and try to understand which media people are more comfortable with. In our societies in Africa, we believe more in the word that you hear than in the one that you see in print. Many people actually learn through what they hear. We are not a reading society by and large. We are an oral society. This is why we have found that radio is a very powerful medium. And because of the level of technology that is required, radio is capable of reaching many countries, including the rural areas.

Let me also say here that we have experimented with rural broadcasting. Again, where you produce programs locally, right in the rural areas, and field recording units are now available, and with a little bit of training, people can record programs where they are actually happening. I would say perhaps we need to bring more trainers locally, where the people are and where programs can emanate from the people involved in development.

QUESTIONS:

Richard McClear:

I had some of the same experience when I was in Tirana having people come in for two weeks, do workshops, then leave and seeing what response they had and or didn't have. Now I am in the position of having to make recommendations to my funding agency about ways to do further training. I was there for an intermediate term residency and I was perhaps able to get a few things accomplished. But I'm wondering what your thoughts are about the idea of having journalists do longer term residencies, six months or more, doing training on an every day basis on site, rather than workshops? Or, an alternative, and I've talked with the Peace Corps about this in Albania, and they are actually doing it experimentally, having some people who are teaching English, and also have journalistic backgrounds, mid-career people or end of career people who are in the Peace Corps, working two or three days at the radio doing journalistic training, developing a relationship over a two year period. Do you think those are possible other scenarios for doing journalist training?

Alexander Picha:

I think it is possible but I prefer to have all courses and lectures in our environment because I notice that our journalists are not able or they maybe don't want to accept and adopt the results of the experience of other journalists.

What we need is practical experience. We need professionals who can teach us how to be able to compete with private radio stations. What is very serious is the decline of audience ratings in comparison with private radio stations. I don't think that it could be useful to create mixed international work teams. I think the best is to cooperate with other radio stations, get to know how they work and then use practical knowledge.

FRANÇOIS DEMERS
PROFESSEUR
UNIVERSITÉ LAVAL
STE-FOY, QUÉBEC - CANADA

Quatre thèmes de la radiodiffusion internationale.

Il y a deux ans, à Québec, pour approcher le phénomène de la radiodiffusion internationale sur ondes courtes, je métais donné ce que j'ai appelé: 4 grilles de lecture. Revoyons les à la lumière de ce qui s'est passé depuis.

Mais faisons d'abord un bref détour par le thème de l'atelier: Nouvelle identité. Je choisis ici de comprendre ce thème dans le sens du marketing, dans le sens du repositionnement des acteurs. Pourquoi est-il nécessaire, à ce moment-ci, qu'ils se repositionnent? Sans refaire la liste des facteurs que nous avons identifiés il y a quatre ans à Waterloo et il y a deux ans à Québec, on peut résumer à l'aide de ce lieu commun: il y a une espèce de tourbillon qui a saisi le monde de la communication internationale, il y a une espèce de coup d'accélérateur très visible, il y a tous les jours des nouvelles qui témoignent de la bousculade des changements.

Ainsi, tout à l'heure, quelqu'un parlait de la toute dernière, ce projet d'un filet de 840 satellites autour du globe que concoctent conjointement Microsoft et McCaw Cellular Communications. Nul doute que la face du monde en sera changée dans un futur qui est déjà là d'une certaine manière.

Au nombre des autres éléments-clés, il y a eu bien sûr l'onde de choc de la fin de la guerre froide. Il y a eu aussi la délégitimisation morale des frontières et leur ouverture plus ou moins profonde un peu partout à travers le monde. Tout cela a provoqué la bascule, sur la scène internationale comme c'était déjà le cas sur la scène nationale, de centre de la gravité du système des médias vers l'auditeur, vers le consommateur, vers sa capacité de choix. Cela a incontestablement provoqué chez les radiodiffuseurs internationaux un nouveau souci de l'auditoire. Dans certains cas, il s'agissait de définir un marché commercial pour pallier au retrait des États comme bailleurs de fonds; les limites de cette avenue sont vite apparues. Dans beaucoup de cas, il s'agit plutôt de répondre aux États at aux gouvernements qui demandent avec insistance: "Est-ce que vous parlez à ces gens? Est-ce que vous envoyez vos ondes dans les airs, comme ça, sans savoir s'il y a des appareils pour les capter et des gens pour les écouter?"

Ce qui a changé, c'est qu'avant, on pouvait présumer que le rideau de fer créait un besoin d'information alternative dans les populations sous contrôle communiste. On pouvait postuler avec crédibilité que le devoir de prêcher la démocratie qui animait les politiciens et artisans de la radio internationale allait automatiquement à la rencontre de l'immense besoin de vérité des populations cibles. Ce qui a changé, c'est bien sûr que la radiodiffusion sur ondes courtes n'est plus la seule à offrir ce service;le commerce s'en mêle maintenant.

Mais surtout, ce qui a changé, c'est qu'auparavant, les radiodiffuseurs internationaux avaient le temps de se construire un auditoire. Ils pouvaient miser sur un processus de lente pénétration. Leurs bailleurs de fonds étaient prêts à les soutenir longtemps sans résultats palpables. Un exemple remarquable en ce sens, c'est celui de la présence de Voice of America en Chine communiste. J'ai reçu il y a quelques semaines un texte sur le comportement de Voice of America (VOA) dans le cadre de l'affaire de la Place Tien An Men. C'est le dernier numéro de *Journalism Monographs* intitulé *The Voice of America and China* - sous-titre *Zeroing in on Tienanmen Square*. Ce travail montre bien que la construction d'un auditoire significatif pour VOA s'est faite sur 30 ou 40 ans. Rendu au milieu des années 80, elle pouvait apparemment compter sur plusieurs millions d'auditeurs réguliers et un fort niveau de crédibilité en Chine continentale. Alors, quand est arrivée l'affaire de la Place Tien An Men, elle a vraiment pu jouer son rôle de source d'information alternative pour les Chinois.

Aujourd'hui, les pressions diverses faites sur les Etats bailleurs de fonds poussent ceux-ci à raccourcir les délais: pour continuer à opérer, il faut déjà pouvoir présenter un auditoire comptabilisé ou pouvoir en définir un qu'il paraît possible d'atteindre très très rapidement.

Chacun se cherche donc une nouvelle niche. Le spectacle que je vois deux ans après la réunion de Québec, ne me permet pas vraiment de parler d'une seule nouvelle identité mais de plusieurs nouvelles identités. Certains font des contrats de retransmission avec des FM, d'autres vont du côté visuel, certains revoient la liste des pays qu'ils visent. Toutes sortes d'opérations sont faites par les uns et les autres, poussées à la fois par cette offre devenue abondante sur le marché de l'information internationale, mais aussi par les gouvernements bailleurs de fonds qui comptent leurs sous et qui demandent de plus en plus de justifications.

Conclusion d'ensemble à ce chapitre: la nouvelle identité de la radiodiffusion internationale est déjà plurielle. La réorganisation de la radiodiffusion internationale dans l'après-guerre froide ne se fait pas selon un modèle unique.

Revisitons maintenant les lieux sous l'éclairage de mes quatre grilles de lecture de 1992:

La première regardait les choses sous l'angle de l'État-nation et des relations internationales, entre les nations. Cet éclairage permettait notamment de rappeler le lien entre la naissance et le développement des radios internationales et les situations de conflits entre États, ou de volonté d'influence de certains États sur d'autres. Sous cet angle, la donnée principale était alors sans conteste la situation de guerre froide qui a dominé le paysage jusqu'à la fin des années 80. Depuis, les radios internationales comme plusieurs autres institutions ont dû entreprendre de renégocier leur place et leurs liens avec les États-nations.

Sous l'angle de la relation fondatrice entre les États-nations et les radios internationales, il est devenu évident au tournant des années 90, que le sort des radios allait être suspendu à la vigueur de leurs États-mères. Ainsi, on ne peut pas dire que l'existence des radios soutenues par les États français ou allemand aient vraiment été menacées, malgré les réorientations et ajustements qu'elles ont dû subir, qu'elles sont en train de subir, dans l'après-guerre froide. Tandis que d'autres, tel Radio Canada International ou Voice of America, ont été davantage soumises à des coupures sombres ou inquiétées.

Mais la fin de la guerre froide n'est qu'un aspect du changement d'environnement international qui a marqué les récentes années. En effet, s'il faut en croire des théoriciens des relations internationales comme l'américain Roseneau, le français Badie et les australiens Camilleri et Falk, un deuxième monde de relations internationales s'est imposé de plus en plus en-dehors de l'emprise des États-nations. Le domaine des communications serait l'un des territoires de ces contacts transfrontières sans contrôle autre que celui du marché, un marché d'ailleurs caractérisé par la guerre commerciale entre des blocs et la prolifération des conflits ethniques, religieux et civils.

C'était d'ailleurs là ma deuxième grille de lecture: le marché privé des communications internationales. Il y a quelques années encore, il n'y avait que les réseaux de communication interne des multinationales, les grandes agences de presse, et les radios-internationales qui parvenaient à se soustraire plus ou moins à la légitimité des souverainetés nationales. Aujourd'hui, les mass-médias se sont évadés eux aussi, que ce soit par le biais des satellites, comme CNN ou TV5, ou par leur intégration dans les réseaux de propriété transnationale, notamment en Europe de l'Est.

Cela veut dire entre autres qu'en matière d'information alternative, c'était là ma troisième grille de lecture, les radios internationales sont appelées à se fondre dans un paysage mondial où elles ne sont plus ni les seuls ni les principaux fournisseurs. Sauf dans le cas d'urgence, quand une frontière se ferme pour une raison ou pour une autre, alors que les ondes courtes peuvent encore être appelées à jouer le rôle de circuit de dépannage.

C'est sans doute ce repositionnement, à côté des réseaux privés et en particulier à côté des réseaux de télévision, qui explique que certaines radios diversifient leurs activités. Certains diffusent aussi sur le FM en plus des ondes courtes; d'autres développent un volet image: par exemple, Radio France Internationale dans le cadre d'accords de partenariat, ou Deutsche Welle et la BBC par exemple qui ont introduit la télé dans leurs studios. Dans ce contexte, la concurrence avec la télévision par satellite est devenue forte. En matière de contenu, la radio internationale est incitée à se spécialiser, sinon bien souvent à se replier sur un rôle plus étroitement lié à l'affirmation culturelle de l'État-nation qui la fait vivre: promotion de la langue et vitrine de modes de vies nationaux, à la manière de Radio Japon ou de Swiss Radio International.

En fait, l'ouverture des frontières et la légitimation de la circulation des informations à l'échelle mondiale ou régionale rend secondaire ou marginal le rôle des radios internationales dans cette fonction d'information alternative qui est prise en relais par les réseaux commerciaux. Un exemple qui résume et préfigure ce changement peut être trouvé dans l'affaire du Chiapas au Mexique alors que les médias d'ailleurs sont débarqués en légion dans cette zone et ont ainsi empêché l'État fédéral mexicain de se soustraire au regard international. Un autre exemple, c'est le soutien direct de l'organisation française de défense des journalistes Reporters sans frontières dans la parution du quotidien de Sarajevo.

Une autre conséquence de cette concurrence croissante en matière d'information alternative à l'échelle mondiale se trouve du côté des normes et standards journalistiques pratiqués par les radios internationales. L'attitude du comportement de Voice of America dans le cadre de l'affaire de la Place Tien An Men est encore une fois révélatrice. Les auteurs concluent en effet que VOA a utilisé les standards journalistiques normaux et courants dans les grands médias anglo-américains, ce qui a notamment facilité la reprise des ses informations par les autres médias.

Ce qui est remarquable dans ce cas, c'est que les standards de VOA apparaissent tout à fait alignés sur les normes du journalisme ordinaire anglo-américain. VOA se situe légitimement sur le même terrain que les autres entreprises journalistiques et non plus sur le terrain de la propagande brute. Cela ouvre un autre champ d'expertise et d'éducation dans lequel les universités et les radiodiffuseurs internationaux peuvent collaborer, celui des débats sur les normes journalistiques "internationales". Cette expertise devient d'autant plus pertinente que dans les ex-pays communistes, on est avide d'apprendre les meilleures façons de faire du commerce et les meilleures façons de faire du journalisme qui soient compatibles avec le commerce.

Ma quatrième grille était relative à la culture. Elle nous ramène à la question de la souveraineté nationale et du protectionisme culturel et linguistique. Samedi, en attendant l'avion je voyais dans le quotidien Le Devoir la ministre québécoise de la culture, madame Liza Frulla, qui déclarait *Avec les nouvelles technologies, la planète peut facilement devenir anglophone.* Une déclaration qui réfère directement à cette problématique.

Mais la question de la culture peut aussi nous conduire sur le terrain de l'interculturel, là où les radios internationales, paradoxalement en raison de leur mandat de propagande, ont développé une expertise certaine. Leurs journalistes devaient maîtriser une ou plusieurs langues étrangères. Ils devaient aussi étudier la culture des pays cibles pour s'assurer un minimum d'efficacité de leurs messages. D'autre part, les radios internationales étaient un des lieux privilégiés d'accueil et d'intégration d'intellectuels réfugiés ou dissidents. Ces deux démarches en ont fait des centres d'accumulation de connaissances sur les autres, sur les étrangers.

Parce qu'il s'agissait d'influencer, il fallait comprendre la culture des récepteurs. C'était là le niveau particulier de souci de l'auditoire, marketing marqué par la recherche débridée de l'auditoire peu coûteux à atteindre, c'est-à-dire pour l'exprimer brutalement, d'un auditoire déjà capable de comprendre l'anglais et déjà fasciné par la consommation à l'occidentale!

Non sans ironie, je souligne que, à Vancouver, nos hôtes officiels sont d'une part un professeur de science politique, de l'autre un professeur de communication. Le premier nous renvoie au cordon ombilical de la radio internationale avec l'appareil de l'État et le corps diplomatique. Le second nous rappelle l'insertion de la radio internationale dans le monde des médias. Manifestement, il manque la troisième source des activités de la radio internationale, soit les langues et les études culturelles.

Cette image me permet de revenir au thème central de ce panel: la formation. Avec l'anecdote suivante: la faculté des arts dont je suis le doyen a signé l'an dernier un accord de coopération avec China Radio International. Je souligne que les négociations à cette fin avaient commencé avant Tien An Men et ont été signées avant la nomination d'André Ouellet aux Affaires étrangères. Cette entente prévoit la venue chez nous par tranches de six mois de membres du personnel de China Radio International pour premièrement, perfectionner leur français, secondairement étudier les standards journalistiques nord-américains et troisièmement nous informer sur leurs activités, l'information internationale et le journalisme en Chine, dans un perspective comparative. En contrepartie, des membres de notre personnel pourront séjourner pendant six mois ou un an à China Radio International dans le rôle d'experts étrangers en français. Une première stagiaire chinoise est d'ailleurs arrivée il y a quelques jours.

Je cite cet exemple parce qu'il me semble illustrer à souhait les portes qui se sont récemment ouvertes, en matière d'éducation et de formation professionnelle, pour des institutions comme l'Université Laval, en matière de radiodiffusion internationale.

Avant, nous pouvions offrir une formation en science politique, en langues, en histoire ou en technologie des communications.

Maintenant, nous pouvons aussi offrir un enseignement des normes, standards et pratiques journalistiques, en voie de devenir les mêmes pour tout le monde.

Mais si nous pouvons ainsi aller à la rencontre de ce qui se passe dans le monde de l'information internationale, c'est aussi parce que l'Université elle-même est travaillée par la mondialisation. Un autre exemple en ce sens: un comité étudie depuis septembre - il doit remettre son rapport le mois prochain - le projet de création d'un diplôme de 2e cycle en journalisme international: un an d'étude, un an de perfectionnement. Il s'agit d'un programme conjoint avec l'Ecole de journalisme de Lille en France qui prévoit des stages auprès des institutions internationales (OTAN) et de la Communauté Economique Européenne (CEE), dans des médias de pays francophones d'Europe et du Canada ainsi que dans des centres d'études sur les médias à New York et à Washington.

Ce programme devrait aussi servir de fer de lance pour inciter les candidates et les candidats en journalisme à la maîtrise d'une troisième langue, par des ententes à venir avec l'Espagne et le Mexique. C'est dans ce cadre que la faculté a participé il y a une quinzaine à la mise sur pied d'un réseau de l'enseignement du journalisme dans les pays francophones, le réseau Théophraste, basé à Lille. Peut-être sommes-nous, nous aussi, inspirés par les craintes de la ministre Liza Frulla relative à la place du français!

Un autre exemple de cette ouverture sur le monde, c'est le séminaire sur les médias et la démocratisation que nous avons tenu récemment et dont le clou était la présence de quatre journalistes chevronnés de la télévision de quatre pays d'Europe de l'Est, par ailleurs stagiaires pendant un mois à l'Université Laval et dans des médias québécois. Notre conférencier vedette était un journaliste mexicain.

Je vois ici mon collègue Gaétan Tremblay de l'Université du Québec à Montréal (UQAM); je sais qu'eux, ils ont une entente de coopération avec une école de journalisme en Roumanie.

Bref, les universités prennent elles aussi le virage de l'internationalisation sur un terrain, celui des communications, qui est nouveau pour elles. De votre côté, il s'agit d'un terrain sur lequel vous avez une incontestable longueur d'avance mais où votre place est aujourd'hui devenue problématique. Peut-être pouvons-nous nous entraider un peu plus, un peu mieux?

Bert Steinkamp:

When this session was being organized, it was described to me by Elzbieta Olechowska as having the following general scope: "In search of new objectives, international broadcasters have begun to focus on the powerful and positive role played by international broadcasting in the education process of nations. Distance learning using the airways for education objectives, sharing information, co-production in programs, are just a few concrete efforts in the redefinition of international broadcasting. Further, a new internationalism is permeating the practices of international broadcasters. The exchange of people, the lending of technical expertise, the training of technical and program staff, programs especially designed to fill voids of knowledge or democratic tradition, are all further examples of the re-orientation of the field."

We've heard broadcasters' views from Eastern Europe, academicians views from Canada, now a broadcaster's view from Canada, the Executive Director of the host organization, Radio Canada International. I would like to put this question to him: How does one organize such a heavy "cahier de charges" for one's own organization?

TERRY HARGREAVES
EXECUTIVE DIRECTOR
RADIO CANADA INTERNATIONAL
MONTREAL - CANADA

Broadcasting to target audiences.

I think I'll get into the sorts of things we do, in our own relatively small way. Others do very much more, some similar, some not so similar.

Let me touch on the general question of identity first. I think we must understand or expect that the identity, of each individual broadcaster stems from your individual reasons for existence. The individual mandate you've received from your country or your organization - from that stems what you do, how you serve the audience. But before you decide how you will serve the audience, the audience you want to get, obviously the reason for your existence is the starting point. In our case, our main role is to tell the world about Canada.

I guess it was a simpler world, politically and in a broadcast sense, when the Wall was up and, with all the good and bad of that. Everybody sort of knew where they stood. But with the wall down, a state of flux developed in many countries and rapidly changing political situations. In addition the fracturing of the methods of delivery of the message with the addition of international television, with more satellite for radio and television, cable, all of these. This has made the fairly simple and straightforward role of shortwave radio as it used to be, much more complicated. It's now a less settled environment. This increased competition is a good thing because it makes us rethink our existence and our way of doing things. I think the two go together. The technical means have changed and at the same time. I'm not saying the only reason we existed was to broadcast beyond the wall but that was a lot of it for a lot of people. In other parts of the world it was a more settled environment in broadcasting terms internationally.

I want to speak about what we do and how we are trying to meet the challenges as I've outlined them and as I believe them to be. We do exchanges of staff. One of the things that hasn't been mentioned, perhaps unintentionally, is that when there are exchanges of staff, of training, there seems to be an unspoken assumption, and I hope it's not just my sensitivity, that people are doing this and it's good for the recipient-period! It's also very good for those who are initiating it, the donor if you will, because certainly in our case, when we exchange staff with Radio Ukraine or Radio 1 in Moscow, it's not just a matter of "helping them out", it helps us out. It brings the linguistic skills of our people in that language unit up to current level of slang, colloquialism, and so on. It immerses them in the society that they are serving. So it is certainly not a one-sided thing. It's as valuable to us as it is to them.

There are other things we've done to try and expand the methods of bringing the message to the target country. We started distributing Canadian pop music. We send out pop music to about 300 stations around the world each month. We do try to put a bit of control on this, and I'm sure others have their own methods, but every second or third month it's accompanied by a card that asks the broadcaster in Santiago, Chile, or wherever, "Have you used it? Do you like it? Do you wish to continue receiving it? If you don't answer, you are off the list." If they don't answer, they're off the list. That way we aren't sending it out pointlessly.

Secondly, classical music. We've started an initiative a while ago of classical music performed by Canadian artists and orchestras. Radio Orphée in Russia carries a program every Sunday night on their FM stereo network, from Radio Canada International, which is all Canadian artists and the Canadian music scene. Similarly in Radio Latvia, Mr. Klotins tells me now, I think twice a week, which is also appreciated. The same thing will happen in several cities in China, in Santiago, Chile, in Buenos Aires and a few other places. We think that is useful for getting across the Canadian experience. Again, that's the reason for our existence.

We've been very active in the field of language lessons. English language lessons in Russia presently play in 25 cities across the country, from Anadyr in the Arctic Circle across Alaska through to Stavropol, and many others. Fifteen cities in China, in Moldova, in Kazakhstan on the national network, in Ukraine, on the national network, in Estonia, Latvia, Lithuania. We did give Namibia some help and put together a series of English lessons in eight native languages there. These are all things that are not enormously expensive to produce and place. Obviously, they must be attractive to the recipient and useful. We try to tailor them that way. For instance, we've now started a weekly program which we send by courier, not by satellite or anything, on Canadian business activities in China. It's played in four cities in Mandarin and one city in Cantonese, that's Guangzhou of course. It's also in Beijing, Shanghai, and in Xian. This is useful, valid information for the local audience. It helps them understand more about Canada and the role Canada is playing in China, and the role immigrants of Chinese origin are playing in Canada. We think that's valuable too.

We are also putting together - this is something the BBC has been more active in - a series of what we call "self-help programs" in Russian and, subsequently, in Ukrainian. We give short lessons at the family level, if you will, on democracy, entrepreneurship, and the environment. When I say democracy at the family level, it's not arguments about clauses in the national constitution, it's a matter of "the garbage wasn't picked up last week - how do we organize to get City Hall to do something about it"? Not that we always do it perfectly here in Canada but we share our ideas with you and take what is best.

In addition, we do special programs for our peace keeping forces overseas.

I will finish by saying that re-broadcasting, or placement broadcasting, or whatever you wish to call it, on local stations in target countries, is a very valuable and useful tool. However, this can end tomorrow in any one of those countries if the national authorities or the local radio stations say "Sorry, Hargreaves, that's very nice but this stuff is not as good as it used to be and we have something better from somebody else, and you're finished." Or, it could be a political decision for political reasons, in which case if you wish to continue to have access to that audience, then you still must be on shortwave because they can try and keep it out but obviously it's not as easy, as the last 40 years have shown us. It's something we must all keep in mind - that placement rebroadcasting, satellite service to local stations, are instruments, but are not a replacement for some of the things we've been traditionally doing.

The other point I'd like to make is that over time, some countries have found that after 1989 or 1990, speaking of Eastern Europe generally but other parts of the world too, that there was an attractiveness in taking a program from RCI, from Voice of America, from the BBC, there was an attractiveness in its uniqueness, in its originality, one hopes in its production values and its content. That may continue. It may also spawn over time, depending on the material that is used, a reaction which is not a totally unknown one in this country of concern about the degree of foreign influence that is there. Not to say there shouldn't be available material from other countries and outside influences but there has to be a balance in any nation as to how much they take these and how much they produce of their own. I think that will be a factor that will arise from time to time. I think it is one we will have to be sensitive to, as international broadcasters. We have to expect it and take it into account as we go along.

QUESTIONS:

Discussion.

Peter Kenyan-Jui:

When it comes to print materials, we have found that internationally, there are some materials that are transferable with hardly any modifications. There are certainly some subjects that are valid anywhere in the world. Chemistry is chemistry. Mathematics, to a certain extent, is mathematics, etc. And if then, through print materials, we are able to transfer sometimes whole courses from one place to another and have the modern versions done or used in the same way you would use a foreign text, why don't we do so, with broadcast media?

I'm saying that many countries have such lack of good programs that even an example of a good program produced in Canada or wherever, is a good thing for the local producers, to see clearly the level of excellence that they have to aspire to. To me, if such local producers don't have a vision of what makes a good program, they will go on doing mundane programs in the old way.

Let me give an example. A month ago I came from South Africa and great things are happening there in the field of education. Some of the programs they have been producing are very poor but nobody told them that because they were not broadcast outside South Africa. Some of the distance education materials produced by such renowned universities like UNISA, the University of South Africa, are about 20 years out of date and nobody told them because, of course, they were only looking inwardly. After April 27, perhaps the world will change in South Africa and they will no longer be closed in. We certainly now would like to have more examples of what the rest of the world has been aspiring to, both in print and in broadcast media. Certainly the South African Broadcasting Corporation is going to undergo tremendous change but we must also bring in some of the best programs from wherever. I think South Africa will be prepared to look at whatever programs there are.

Let me just mention the case of Canada. I would say that some of the Canadian programs can go anywhere because I have used them. I have used their radio forum in my own country, in Kenya, almost without any modifications. What I am saying, really, is that perhaps some of those programs we really need to rediscover.

I have just mentioned the case for South Africa because I think, in the whole area of distance education and communication technologies, South Africa will need a lot of help. In the whole area of training, they will need now to start retraining even their own producers and programmers and educators, to really have a wider vision of what education is all about. I say they are about 20 years behind the times. We certainly are not going to lag behind because the whole world is now focusing on what South Africa is going to be able to do. And they need a lot of help.

Also in the area of training, let me say that you are not going to make much difference unless you are able to produce a critical mass of experienced people locally. I agree all the training that has been done by Thompson Foundation, by BBC, and elsewhere, has been good in itself, but they haven't done enough. They never produced that critical mass of good educational broadcasters in each country to sustain the programs. What happens when two or three are transferred to another Ministry? Or they are promoted? You leave the whole radio station in a quandary. We have not trained enough. You can never overtrain in this whole area.

Donald Browne:

Some of you with whom I've spoken during this conference, know that one of my pet projects right now is to look at indigenous language broadcasting by Maori, by Australian aboriginals, by native Americans, and so on. In doing that, a question has arisen. I'll pose it to anybody who wants to try to answer it. It'll start as remarks or observations but I think you will see the question flowing out of it.

I think generally speaking, moste of us in this room would conceive of broadcast journalism as an interesting and attractive activity for younger people to want to embrace as an occupation, as a profession. But in some of my investigations of indigenous broadcasting, I find that is far from the case. It is not easy for a lot of these stations to recruit people who want to be broadcast journalists, for several different reasons. Some of them have to do with the perception on the part of young people - and François Demers and I were talking about this at lunch - that radio is no longer worth bothering with. The other media are more important and more interesting, so why does anybody want to get involved with radio?

A second aspect would be what might be called the "tallest flower in the garden" syndrome. That is to say, if you go on radio as a journalist and start covering local affairs, if it's a local station, you can look to be shot at by other members of the community, sometimes quite literally shot at. So it can be dangerous. Some don't want to place themselves in that kind of risky situation. That's part of the problem. People who won't go into journalism for various reasons and might otherwise be well qualified.

There is another side to this however, and that is the feelings on the part of some of the people working in indigenous broadcasting that people coming into broadcast journalism have the wrong motivations for doing it. The one is the motivation tied in with the kind of theme that attaches to being in this position without any sense really of responsibility or of really trying to help an audience. Another which is far worse, but far rarer because perhaps people won't confess to it, is the possibility of earning money off this. In a very direct way of being in a position where people will pay you to say or not to say certain kinds of things. A sort of checkbook journalism.

I don't know how widespread this is, but I hear enough talk about it nowadays to wonder and therefore propose to any of you who want to make remarks upon it, just how difficult is it to get good people interested in radio broadcast journalism nowadays?

Terry Hargreaves:

Just in general terms about recruiting people, I know what you say about television being more attractive. People see you and if you're good looking, it's even better, and so on. Back in the 50s, everybody said radio was dying or dead and we're still there. I think it also has something to do with the degree of sophistication of the programming that is produced in the country, the network, the place that people are looking to work. There are local commercial stations in Canada with very low resources and the same in the United States, where a major newscast is 2 minutes and 45 seconds long and there has to be 14 items in it, so some of the nuances are inevitably lost. There isn't anything else at all except the local murder or traffic crash or weather forecast.

For anybody with any sensitivity or ambition, obviously that is not an attractive place to work, in any event.

So I think it depends on the organization and what they are doing, if they have that breadth of programming that would attract somebody to say "this is something I could get my teeth into and be part of and it would be useful."

Insofar as the comment about the taking of money. I wouldn't call it "checkbook journalism". It sounded like bribery to me. Some may find it's a fine line, but I always thought checkbook journalism was a fairly straightforward sort of exchange where you paid somebody to give you a story and the story would be the same whatever you paid, whereas the bribery you're speaking of is, of course, something totally different. That again, is up to the control mechanisms you have in your hiring policies and your training policies. I think it may be a difficulty and part of it for international broadcasters may be, as we heard from many today, that we are not all in a huge growth mode. In fact, rather the reverse. There's not that many openings. And even if there is an opening, you say "Would I want to join an organization that looks like it's gradually disappearing?"

But there are obviously some values in being in radio over television. I've worked in television for many years and I've enjoyed it, but I much prefer radio. I think the ego factor is a very strong one. Obviously we don't want shrinking violets. People who are afraid to talk are not very much use in radio.

Peter Kenyan-Jui:

Two points. One about the new identity for radio. I think domestic broadcasters just about everywhere do suffer from what I call "country cousin syndrome". I'm sure with the challenges that the international radio broadcasters face today, this syndrome perhaps will catch on with the international broadcasters as well. If that is the syndrome you find yourself at least caught up with, what is it that radio can do better than perhaps television, and that too particularly in the context of the developing world?

In my view, what radio, both at a domestic and international level, can do better than television is information. I don't think television can beat radio in terms of its efficiency in bringing news more frequently and more cost effectively to people.

Education! It is very predictable of me coming from the Commonwealth of Learning to advocate the use of radio, but I do so on the basis of my personal experience of using radio quite effectively to teach foreigners over a number of years. Also, lately, my experience of doing the same thing in a number of developing countries in the Commonwealth.

The other point. You mentioned the training of broadcasters. The earlier training was to bring the broadcasters from Third World countries to developed countries, the Thompson Foundation, Radio Nederlands and several other institutions. Then the training was reversed where you took the trainers for in-country training. If you look at the advancement, the rapid expansion in the broadcasting field, a study that I associated with in my own country, in the educational broadcasting field alone, it was our estimate that about 11 million people would be working in the educational field in one way or the other, in India, by 1997. There is another study done by the Asian Mass

Communication Research and Information Center where they have predicted thousands and thousands of people who need training in the area. Now these conventional methods of training, bringing people face to face, interpersonal communication situations, all very effective and perhaps part of it inevitable, I think it is important we think of other modes of training broadcasters themselves. I know that not many people may have faith, but it is possible to train broadcasters using distance education mode and we are in touch with the HFS Institute for Broadcasting Development to do just that. We are thinking of developing multimedia packages - here I am using the word "multimedia package" not in the computer sense of the word but a mixed media mode - to train broadcasters using distance education techniques.

Terry Hargreaves:

One quick comment on comparing audiences. I'm not suggesting Dr. Kenyan was meaning it in this way but there is nothing new about that. Obviously we want to maximize our audiences but the fact is that television is there. I guess as international broadcasters, we have to say, in the sense that it's a new phenomenon, a new challenge that we have to face. Domestic broadcasters have faced it for years within the Canadian Broadcasting Corporation.

Back in the early 60s and into the 70s, there were dramatic changes in the way programs were produced, the networks were run, and feeling our way as to what we could do that television couldn't do. Because earlier we were the television of that time, or the entertainment fount. Then we had to find a new role. Within the Canadian experience, the domestic side of CBC has done that very well. Internationally we have to do that as well. The television challenge is there but I think it's probably, in a way, a good thing to have to look to our laurels and find out what the new identity is and how we have to face the new competition and deal with it.

Graham Mytton:

This is an old chestnut which comes up all the time about the difference between radio and television audiences. Within any disrespect to the speaker, it's a meaningless question. Are you talking about radio and television worldwide? Because if you are, obviously there are more radio listeners then there are television viewers. If you are talking about China, there are more television viewers than radio listeners. If you are talking about India, there are more radio listeners than television viewers. If you are talking about Kenya, there's far more radio listeners than there are television viewers. If you're talking about Botswana, there's no television viewers at all. It all depends on the country. World wide, television audiences are growing fast but radio still reaches more people. Even where you have 100% penetration of both television and radio, radio still plays an important part. It has a different role. It's listened to at different times of the day, for different things. You don't tend to watch television when you're driving your car. A lot of the conversation and discussion we had about radio versus television is really rather shallow and unsubstantiated. We shouldn't be talking about radio and television being in direct competition when they are doing different things.

The remarkable thing though is how, in some parts of the world, radio has slipped a lot. Particularly in Asia, China, Japan, the Philippines to some extent. Radio has slipped much further as a medium than it has in Europe. If you look at the health of radio in Europe, to some extent in the United States and Canada, it's still a very strong medium, it's not listened to any less now than it was 30 years ago. In some areas, it's listened to more. Why? Because it's portable. You can listen to it in the car, you can do things with radio that you can't do with television.

You can even, if you're fed up with the proceedings here this afternoon, listen to the radio here in the room at night. Let's remember radio is a very different kind of medium. It has always been different from television and will be increasingly as the media become differentiated.

CHAPTER FOUR

THE ECONOMICS OF INTERNATIONAL BROADCASTING:

STRIVING FOR EXCELLENCE AND EFFICIENCY
BROADCASTING TO YOUR OWN CITIZENS
PUBLICIZING OF INTERNATIONAL BROADCASTING

Editors' Note:

International broadcasting exists in an ever-changing context, both national and international. International broadcasters, hence, have two sets of realities to which they must pay very close attention. They must ensure sufficient support, both financial and political, from their national governments while at the same time they must seek sufficiently large or relevant support from their international audiences.

Previous CHALLENGES conferences have addressed these issues. The problems and pressures seem not to have abated over the years. In this chapter, these ongoing dilemmas are explored from a variety of perspectives.

DEREK WHITE
GENERAL MANAGER
ABC RADIO AUSTRALIA
MELBOURNE - AUSTRALIA

Before we move to the topic today, I just crave your indulgence to pursue briefly yesterday's discussion on broadcasting to Asia and the future of radio and perhaps, finally to get Graham Mytton excited! I don't think anyone suspects that radio doesn't have a future. It's shortwave radio that's of concern and by a coincidence, to my distress, yesterday when I got back to my room, there were some faxes from Australia with the latest developments in Asia. The T&T Turner Network cartoon and film channel will go into Asia in the very near future, first on Palapa and then on F-Star One and F-Star Two. If you're not aware of it, F-Star Two has a footprint from Tasmania to west of Moscow, which is an incredible footprint. So, that will join Turner's CNN 24-hours a day to the region.

Home Box Office is now available through Palapa and will extend to other areas. Perhaps more importantly, ESPN, the sports network, reveals the latest trend in broadcasting - I'll just read you a little extract: "With little fanfare from its regional headquarters in Hong-Kong, the world's largest network, ESPN, is spreading its services throughout Asia and the Pacific. The network's 24-hour service can already be watched by millions of cable and satellite viewers in 18 countries in the region, via Palapa. There are special services for China and Taiwan, with Mandarin and Cantonese in Hong-Kong." They are only the start. Those regional languages of ESPN's move plan to regionalize both the content of the service and the languages in which it's broadcast.

I just wanted to give a little picture of the sort of developments that are taking place and the competition that shortwave radio will face in the future. I think that really sets the tone for today's discussion on the economics of international broadcasting: Striving for excellence and efficiency - because when the competition gets tougher, governments are going to need more evidence of the efficiency of the broadcasters.

The Economics of International Broadcasting

In her note to me on the topics for this session, our conference organizer said "International broadcasting has remained relatively distant from the process of commercialization which appears to be symptomatic or synonymous with the proliferation of media and the freeing of media from state control".

International broadcasting as radio, perhaps, is free of commercialization, although I note that Radio Moscow, from a BBC report, is offering to carry advertising internationally. But certainly television, even pristine public service broadcasters like the BBC and my own ABC, have gone commercial for television, if not for profit, at least to defray costs. And, if the Australian government had changed at the last election, I'm sure Radio Australia would have faced lower government funding and an imposed choice: cut the service or chase advertising, probably disguised as sponsorship, simply to maintain or expand the service. For a broadcaster, that would seem to me to be no contest. Any broadcaster is going to go off down the commercial trail as fast as possible to maintain their service!

I wonder how many here face that choice, or might have to face it? I know of no public broadcaster which is not under funding pressure despite statements, I think, by Radio Nederlands and Deutsche Welle in the last day or so that their funding is to be preserved, despite cuts. The BBC's cut, of course, equals my entire administration's budget for a year, so I can't have too much sympathy.

All of us are fighting to maintain the quality, diversity and reach of our product, while achieving efficiency and cost reduction, under the rule of economic rationalism. If governments continue to question the funding of public service broadcasting, what, if any, are the alternatives? I doubt that it's advertising. My recent experience of trying to sell time on television suggests that marketing managers are not men or women of great charity. Rather they look to invest in those hard audience measures difficult to obtain for international broadcasting.

Moreover, we may have a philosophical conflict. Our aim, in many cases, is to reach people who might not otherwise receive news, information and service or training programs. They are the people least likely to have the spending power sought by the advertiser.

The same argument applies to the concept of listeners' fees. Leaving aside the mechanics of collection, who among us would be the first to suggest that we should charge, particularly Third World listeners, for what critics might see as the cultural imperialism of the affluent?

Let me address one model of fiscal salvation: to lift one's identity domestically, to promote at home and thus win recognition from public and government alike, to broadcast internally as well externally and to concentrate on your own nationals abroad. I suspect that one of our panel, Juhani Niinistö of Radio Finland, will diagree with me, but I cannot help wondering whether such a national approach, useful as it has been and still is, will not be overtaken by events?

In an age where the need for national propaganda has decreased, a new breed of trans-national broadcasting might develop - CNN without the American accent, BBC World Service without the British! Or single language radio channels shared by different broadcasters. Perhaps it's not just the international radio broadcasters who feel threatened by change. I note that a suggested topic for the next Commonwealth Broadcasting Association conference, which will be held here in Vancouver later this year, is "The survival of domestic broadcasting in an era of global competition". I suppose we should ask why must we all be so defensive, feel so nervous? Perhaps our panel can find ground for optimism?

HÉLENE ROBILLARD-FRAYNE
DIRECTRICE DE LA PROGRAMMATION ET DE LADIFFUSION POUR LA RADIO DE LANGUE FRANCAISE SOCIÉTÉ RADIO-CANADA MONTRÉAL, QUÉBEC - CANADA

Radio Canada et Radio Canada International.

Je représente la "radio domestique" à ce colloque de radios internationales. Ce n'est d'ailleurs que depuis environ quatre ans que je connais l'expression "radio domestique", expression qui, de façon évidente, fait partie de votre vocabulaire usuel, mais non du nôtre.

Il m'intéressera de savoir quels sont, dans vos pays, les modes de collaboration entre radios domestiques et radios internationales.

Pour le moment, je décrirai ici les modes de collaboration actuels entre la radio de Radio-Canada et Radio Canada International.

Radio Canada International diffuse en sept langues, dont le français. Pour ce qui est de la programmation, Radio Canada International diffuse certaines émissions de la radio de Radio-Canada:

- des bulletins de nouvelles
- des émissions d'analyse de l'actualité
- un magazine scientifique
- un magazine société/culture
- une émission d'auto-critique des médias
- des émissions relatives à la vie quotidienne dans des grandes villes
- une émission rediffusant les meilleurs extraits des émissions diffusées au cours de la semaine.

En termes de programmes, il y a donc une collaboration entre la radio de Radio-Canada et Radio Canada International.

Pour ce qui est de l'exploitation à présent: Même si en termes d'exploitation la collaboration est moins étroite maintenant qu'il y a quelques années, il subsiste néanmoins une certaine interaction entre la radio de Radio-Canada et Radio Canada International:

- Depuis octobre 1993, Radio Canada International a sa propre régie;
- Il est légitime pour un organisme de radiodiffusion de vouloir être prioritaire. Or, à la Maison de Radio-Canada à Montréal où se trouvent les têtes des réseaux AM et FM français de Radio-Canada, des stations régionales de CBC Radio et de CBC Stereo ainsi que le service du Québec Nordique, Radio Canada International n'était pas et ne pouvait être la préoccupation unique ou même principale et a donc eu recours à ses propres installations.
- Néanmoins, il y a une certaine collaboration qui persiste en termes techniques entre la radio de Radio-Canada et Radio Canada International. Certains branchements sont encore possibles entre l'édifice où est Radio Canada International, la Maison de Radio-Canada et d'autres centres de diffusion.
- Il subsiste aussi une collaboration technique en termes de consultation et de formation.
- De plus, en cas d'évacuation de la Maison de Radio-Canada et afin d'éviter l'interruption de la diffusion, Radio

Canada International est d'accord pour nous donner accès à ses locaux et à un studio.

- En mars dernier, nous avons fait une émission en direct de Pékin et Radio Canada International nous a donné accès à son circuit.
- Radio Canada International est un "client", au même titre que les divers services programmes de la radio de Radio-Canada, sur le circuit permanent de la radio de Radio-Canada entre Montréal et Paris.

Voilà pour ce qui est de l'aspect technique. Maintenant voyons d'autres aspects de l'exploitation mais qui ne sont pas techniques:
- Radio Canada International a sa propre discothèque mais peut recourir, sans frais, à celle de Radio-Canada.
- Jusqu'à il y a deux ans, existait à la radio de Radio-Canada un service des annonceurs et Radio Canada International y avait recours à l'occasion. Maintenant que ce service n'existe plus à la radio de Radio-Canada, Radio Canada International doit trouver ses propres annonceurs de relève.

La collaboration entre la radio domestique et la radio internationale s'étend à d'autres domaines:
- Lors de coupures très importantes subies par Radio Canada International il y a quelques années, la radio de Radio-Canada a intégré certaines personnes.
- Une publicité en ondes à la radio de Radio-Canada fait connaître les services de Radio Canada International.
- Lors de visites de visiteurs étrangers, nous intégrons souvent aux visites de nos visiteurs une rencontre à Radio Canada International et vice-versa.

Comme on le voit, même si en termes d'exploitation, Radio Canada International est maintenant moins dépendant de la radio de Radio-Canada que dans le passé, il existe encore néanmoins une certaine collaboration entre la radio de Radio-Canada et Radio Canada International.

La radio de Radio-Canada et Radio Canada International ne sont pas en concurrence. Ce sont deux organismes autonomes qui s'entraident et qui trouvent leur intérêt mutuel dans un certain niveau de collaboration. A mon avis, nous n'avons d'ailleurs pas pleinement exploité toutes les possibilités de collaboration. Peut-être ce colloque pourra-t-il faire découvrir de nouvelles pistes à cet égard.

Derek White:

Most organizations do try and achieve some collaboration even if by exchange of programs. I certainly believe it's important where possible, for the external broadcaster to have a distinct type of material used on the domestic service. Sometimes it's not easy, to quote our own example. Radio Australia sees itself as having a particular expertise in Asia, through our Asian language broadcasters. Yet, try as we might, we find it very difficult to have the domestic service draw on the expertise of those language broadcasters. They would rather go around the corner to the university - with apologies to all academics here present - to find an academic who may not have visited the country in question for 20 years but who reads books about it rather than go to language broadcasters who are in constant touch with their country of origin and really follow that country's events with particular interest.

ANGUEL NEDIALKOV
DIRECTOR
RADIO BULGARIA
SOFIA - BULGARIA

Bulgarian National Radio in Transition.

International broadcasters from what is now referred to as "the eastern bank of the post-communist swamp" tend to stress the uniqueness of the political, economic and editorial problems they encounter in their activities. This may well be the case. Yet, when the word goes out to slash financial funding for their institutions they join the chorus of their counterparts from all over the world . So what is so different and yet common in our efforts to achieve excellence and efficiency from the perspective of a medium-sized international broadcaster in a post-communist country like Radio Bulgaria?

It is now generally recognized that the former eastern block countries are experiencing a political and economic crisis and that is obviously true. Yet this fact, in itself, cannot and must not serve as a general excuse for the inability to work out clear strategies, editorial policies and for taking proper managerial decisions, especially in public radio services in the post-communist countries. The private radio stations already operating there have proved they can and are successfully overcoming these problems.

One of the problems we encounter is taking pragmatic decisions in a highly politicized environment. An attempt at reducing excessive expenditures could, and often does, end up being labelled as politically motivated. It requires much courage, strong reasoning, vision and I should say even a touch of self-sacrifice on the part of the top and senior managers to go ahead with such unpopular decisions. It's not easy and therefore it has been my observation that reforms in many institutions in the ex-communist countries have boiled down to the replacement of the old guard by the new breed, of the "bad guys" with the "good guys", without probing deeper and downsizing the excessive, overgrown and overstaffed managerial, administrative and editorial structures, which are bringing this system to suicide. Therefore the old ways of achieving efficiency and excellence may be reduced or abolished but are not replaced.

In the case of Radio Bulgaria, the complex multi-level structure designed to execute censorship rather than to serve managerial purposes was completely dismantled. A new structure was introduced. It scraped duplicating managerial levels and reduced senior staff from nearly 30 to 7.

We realized that difficult as it may be, that step towards efficiency, should necessarily be combined with the introduction of a new labour contract with the staff who, under the previous system, were used to and enjoyed the benefits of legislation that virtually entitled them to a life contract with the employer. The system of short-term contracts and renewal of the contract, depending on managerial performance or editorial excellence and contribution, which was employed by Radio Bulgaria, helped create the basis of a new staff motivation and a standard tied to performance. It will in the long run effectively reduce payroll expenses.

But here we begin to face other challenges. The top managers must clearly outline their editorial policies and must set clear cut rules concerning all technological or editorial aspects of the output of the radio station. And, these rules should be communicated to every staff member and serve as a basis of assessment of his or her editorial or managerial preformance.

This is not an easy challenge in view of a completely demotivated staff. I believe that many of my colleagues from the eastern European countries also inherited this problem. Radio Bulgaria faced the challenge and reduced its overall staff from nearly 230 to 175 without labour conflicts or accusations of political bias.

The third challenge was for us and I believe for many broadcasters in the ex-communist countries, to provide a rationale for the choice of broadcast languages and target areas. Under the communist regime, this was controlled by the party rather than by the station. International broadcasters served primarily to promote the communist ideology and interests during what is now referred to as the post Cold War period.

During the stage which saw the collapse of the communist states, the emergence of new ones, the re-emergence of old feuds and new friendships, it proved very difficult to obtain from the politicians any coherent policies with regard to international broadcasting.

The Board of Directors of the Bulgarian National Radio submitted its ideas to the Parliamentary Committee overviewing radio and television. Since politicians prefer to be confronted with solutions rather than problems, the project was unanimously approved.

So in the final analysis, against the background of political upheavals, of economic distress and shrinking funding, Radio Bulgaria managed to maintain its program output within a well reasoned scope, and even to add new target areas to its activity by resuming broadcasts to Japan, to East and South Asia in English, to North Africa in Arabic. We made a more rational use of transmitting capacity and slashed down transmitter expenses by a third. We opened broadcasts for ethnic Turks in Bulgaria on FM; provided financial resources for opening Russian and Romanian services in the near future - the Russian service will go on the air this fall. We prepared grounds for a monitoring service and for expanding our transcription services. In doing so, we believe we have come a step closer to the opposite bank of the swamp, to being ready, together with the other international broadcasters, to meet the present and the future challenges that we came here to discuss.

QUESTIONS & COMMENTS:

Bert Steinkamp:

I'd like to make a few observations on the degree of cooperation with domestic services. I think we should distinguish quite clearly between countries like Australia or the United Kingdom where the broadcast in the national language can also serve for a worldwide audience, including expatriates of either Australia or the U.K. In the situation we have in the Nederlands, we cannot use the domestic broadcast in Dutch, for any other purpose than serving expatriates. This makes an enormous distinction between the possible degree of cooperation. Nevertheless, you invited comments on situations in some countries. A fairly recent development in my country is a result of the growing success of domestic regional broadcast. It has taken about a third of the domestic radio market, which I think is quite a job. Each of the 12 provinces basically has a regional radio broadcaster. They were hard-put to obtain foreign news in a proper journalistic manner on their minimal budgets and we are happy to provide that for them. It resulted in what is called RNC, Radio News Center, in which regional, national and international broadcasters are cooperating. It happens to be housed within the precincts of Radio Nederland, so it's on our ground. It's fairly young, less than a year old. It's having a bumpy ride as a result, but one need not be too optimistic to believe it might become something worthwhile.

Another development I should like to draw attention to is that for the first time in our history, and as a result of our restructuring, we are now negotiating with eight public domestic national broadcasters to come to an agreement where we would have free use of those programs from domestic broadcasters which we would find sufficiently interesting for our international expatriate audiences. This will come up before the NOS Board in April and I think it will come through. We shall only pay the additional costs involved like rights or extra production funds. News is deliberately not involved in that because the approach to news of an expatriate in Indonesia, to events in the Netherlands is so much different from that of a Dutch national living in the Netherlands, that the use of national news for international purposes is ruled out.

Derek White:

I might just add to what Bert just said. Again, I think all organizations succeed when they try to find areas of mutual benefit. One of the peculiarities of the Australian Broadcasting Corporation is that it's had a national newsroom for its domestic service in Sydney which processes overseas material and a newsroom for Radio Australia in Melbourne which, of course, stresses overseas material. We are trying to address that at the moment and it's possible the Radio Australia newsroom will become the overseas news handling center for all of the ABC when we move into our new office which will co-locate the Victorian branch of the domestic radio and Radio Australia. So it's that sort of cooperation which can have great benefit in the same way Bert was describing.

JUHANI NIINISTÖ
HEAD OF EXTERNAL BROADCASTING
YLE RADIO FINLAND
HELSINKI - FINLAND

**Broadcasting to your own Nationals,
PR for external broadcasting.**

In Finland, the external broadcasting network, Radio Finland, is an integral part of the national (domestic) broadcasting YLE. In recent years, external broadcasting has been contributing to the creation of an increasingly valuable competitive edge of YLE: facing competition from around fifty commercial local stations, YLE is nevertheless the only major service available to Finnish nationals in domestic languages outside the country's borders.

Parallel to foreign language external services in English, German, French, Russian and classical Latin, YLE maintains extensive services in Finnish and Swedish. Listeners in Europe are able to receive a full-fledged service, 24 hours a day, with some alternatives available. The service comprises simulcasts or reruns of the domestic networks as well as custom-made programming. For listeners outside Europe, a more traditional external service programming is offered. At this point I should remind you that in Finland, all external broadcasting - be it in the domestic languages or in foreign languages - is based on normal YLE revenue. No governmental subsidies have been available for decades.

The increased "formatting" of domestic FM networks has made the unedited use of those networks more difficult. Instead of direct simulcasts, compilations or pickups have become more common. It should be possible, of course, to provide various formats parallel to each other. The cost factor prevents us to offer this level of service.

The domestic appeal of external broadcasting.

In Finland, external broadcasting is available domestically, as well, in various formats: the service for Europe on the AM dial, the satellite audio channel on cable networks or as direct-to-home reception. YLE maintains an FM channel as a special service for listeners in the area of the nation's capital (Capital FM) as the third domestic outlet of the external service.

In addition to YLE programming in English, German and French it provides relays of major international stations such as Voice of America, National Public Radio, Radio Australia, C-Span, the BBC, Deutsche Welle and Radio France Internationale. All these services have contributed to an increased public awareness of external broadcasting in Finland over the past three or four years.

In the process, it has been proved as well that some of the journalistic qualities of external broadcasting have a certain domestic appeal. It turned out that the longer-than-domestic lifespan of news in external broadcasting (due to serving different time zones) and the odd hours of airing prime time news shows satisfied a certain demand in Finland, and thus an audience emerged for a local AM station.

Listening to the AM had been completely defunct in Finland since the early 70s. Interest in the news-oriented programming of the Helsinki AM outlet of the external service meant a kind of very small revival for AM as a medium. The station was then nicknamed Capital AM to benefit from the image of the popular Capital FM (featuring foreign stations and YLE). The appeal of this type of external programming domestically is close to that of all news channels in major cities. Actually, the Capital AM and FM are being advertised with the slogan "More news than on any other station".

The main elements of Capital AM are now also available on the Eutelsat II-F1 satellite (audio). Although it is not intended for domestic consumption, several cable networks in Finland have made the satellite channel available to their listeners. The main reasons being the availability of YLE foreign language services in Hi-Fi and the additional news services.

Popularizing shortwave.

The need to know how to tune in and to use a schedule with frequencies and time zones is often a major obstacle for listening to shortwave. In Finland, as in most countries of western Europe, listening to shortwave is not common domestically. Thus Finnish tourists who had purchased radios to get programming from home on their holiday abroad often failed in their efforts.

During the winter of 1992-93, a special campaign was conducted by YLE to promote awareness of shortwave and the availability of receivers.

Spots on YLE TV channels were used, as well as brochures about receivers and programming. According to a survey carried out after the campaign, some 80% of those polled were aware of international radio. In the campaign it was also pointed out that the external service was available free of charge, as part of the services rendered by YLE for the price of the television licence fee, a "must" for an owner of a television set in Finland, and in many other European countries. The campaign also gave external broadcasting higher visibility and profile within the corporate culture.

To conclude, I think the developments in Finland - the importance of serving your own nationals and of being present locally - are indicative of the current trend in Europe. That is, the demarcation lines between domestic and external broadcasting are vanishing, external broadcasting organizations work domestically, if it is administratively possible, and find new ways of using their expertise. If you are planning an all-news channel, before investing in costly new operations, it is worth taking a look at your local external broadcasting for, possibly, a more economical solution.

QUESTIONS & COMMENTS:

Juhani Niinistö:

Our unique Latin broadcast is a gimmick that has given us much publicity worldwide. It was created by the Head of our cultural programs and people laughed at him at first. Even the Washington Post published our frequencies free of charge. *Newsweek* published a picture of the Pope listening to a shortwave radio with a caption "He's listening to the news in classical Latin". I don't think he did, but...

Derek White:

You can't get a better endorsement than that. So for people who want to start a Latin program, there's the model. It does raise a question however. How much of your budget goes to publicity and promotion? I suspect that for most external public broadcasters, it's not very much. In our case, I must say it's minimal. I'd welcome any comments on how you make two dollars seem like two million in publicity terms because publicity for external broadcasters is surely more difficult than for domestic broadcasters. You have a much more diverse audience to try and reach and your every effort is reduced by the competition. You're one voice among many, to the audiences you are trying to address.

Nicolas Lombard:

Of course, you are aware also of the fact that it is highly important to get to be known within your own country because the taxpayers are the ones who pay your license, who pay the budget. However, inside the country we found one gimmick that is rather interesting. We sort of piggy-back when there are big exhibitions like the Kunstmesse, where there are big exhibitions in Zurich, in St-Gallen, in Geneva, and there are TV studios. The TV studios of the region always attract a lot of people. Nobody's interested to see a radio producer producing a program somewhere. But TV stars that are explaining TV to their own public and then Swiss Radio International with their public relations manager coming along and explaining what Swiss Radio International does within the country but above all for the listeners outside. We met with a lot of interest and we have done that now for three consecutive years and we find increasingly that people are getting to know Swiss Radio International. I think that is one of the very important aspects of international broadcasting.

Derek White:

I'd certainly like to also back up what Nicolas has said. ABC, for its own domestic reasons, is trying to convince the government that it should continue to keep its funding. We have had a series of open houses involving private radio and domestic television personalities around Australia. We've tagged on those and that has been a very effective way, a very cheap way, of getting lots of people going past our door to take our program guides and our information, and also to meet broadcasters of other nationalities who they would not normally come in contact with.

WALTER SCRAGG
PRESIDENT
ADVENTIST WORLD RADIO
SILVER SPRINGS, MARYLAND - USA

Changing Technologies and Objectives for Religious Broadcasters.

I regret that there are not more religious broadcasters here. It's quite a large sector of the international radio industry and I'm sure that if there were more here, you might find them interesting people to work with. I thought that because of the fact that there are really only two of us here that represent that particular sector of international broadcasting, that I would first of all just describe to you the economics of religious broadcasting as far as international broadcasting is concerned.

These are my observations and I'm not going to name any organizations. There are some types of religious broadcasters who are funded by the parent organization. In other words, there are some pockets somewhere that provide for a station or purchase time and that's that. But that isn't true of them all by any means. There are a number of religious international broadcasters who represent a kind of consortium where different people with different religious interest agree to get together to broadcast. There is yet another kind of religious broadcast which is a kind of commercial international religious broadcasting where facilities are put up by an entrepreneur of some kind and then time is sold to various denominations and other people that have religious interests. You're probably familiar with all three of those.

International religious radio is, at the present time, a growing industry. By no means is it retreating though it is being reshaped. It sent shock waves through this particular sector of the industry when one of the catholic orders in America decided to purchase four 500kW transmitters and located them in Alabama. That shows what the thinking of some religious broadcasters is. It isn't a day to get out of it, it's a day to use it more widely. Our own church has recently had its own little shock wave when one of its former pastors and now a dissident decided to purchase the Christian Monitor facility in Maine and is now operating from there, or will be by the end of this year, using their 500kW transmitter there. That's something that's of interest to us as a church.

As far as Adventist World Radio is concerned, for me personally, it's very important. I was one of those who made it begin to work back in 1971 and after a period in church administration, I was invited to come back and head it up once more, after 15 years away from that. You can imagine I found things very different. New technologies, many things happening that are completely different.

At the present time we are organized with a central office in Washington, D.C., or rather Silver Spring, just outside of Washington. If you want to look at efficiency of operation, the head office is operated by myself, an administrative secretary and a part-time clerk to help us with various office duties - that's it! We hold an enterprise together which has offices or activities in Guam, England, Germany, Italy where we operate two sats, in Guatemala, Costa Rica, Ivory Coast, Russia and Slovakia. That is held together by means of fax and E-mail. And while I'm here, if you walked by me you may have noticed that I've got a computer program that I'm working with and usually when I'm doing that, I'm handling administrative matters that have to do with AWR. We keep it together that way. That's it! We are an organization that is built around modern communication technology without which we wouldn't survive. That may very well be something for those of us who are in international broadcasting to think about. We are very familiar with the broadcasting technology. There are also management efficiencies that can be affected by use of similar technology, if we're willing to make full use of them.

The programming concept of AWR is what I really want to talk to you about. As far as the financing of AWR is concerned, the church provides the facilities. It's up to our local church operations in different countries to provide the programming. That of course gives us a somewhat interesting approach. There are about 50 studios in different parts of the world that contribute programs to AWR. These programs, at the present time, are accessed by our stations via air mail and other ways, such as carrying tapes from certain countries where it wouldn't be possible to mail them for political reasons, and various other things.

The Economics of International Broadcasting

The demands of operating an organization of that kind are perhaps unique but they are certainly cost effective. If you are interested in automation and digitalization and how that can work in the assembly of radio programs in different languages, I'd like to invite you, if you're going through Germany, and Frankfurt, to visit our AWR Europe office just south of Frankfurt.

Come and have a look at the automation we use to handle over 20 languages, and putting together programming blocks for release throughout various facilities. I'd think you'd be fascinated by it. It's a fully automated operation and at night time, we set it up and it runs for several hours without anybody even worrying about it.

We operate with one hour programming blocks and we transfer our programming from cassette to DAT-cassette and produce program units of two to four hours which are then released through our stations on an automated basis. We try to automate quite efficiently.

Our own view of life, as a church, makes us interested in some things which are important to us. I don't know how much you know about Seventh Day Adventist but let me just tell you this. Health is very important to us. Some of you may be aware of our Stop Smoking programs and that kind of thing. But did you know that both corn flakes and peanut butter were invented in the kitchen of a Seventh Day Adventist hospital? I don't know whether that's a blessing of the Lord or not, but it's one of those things that is true about us. There is a historic interest in health within our church.

All of our language programs, the 34-35 of them that we operate at the present time, include health sectors in their one hour programming block. This has led us to establish a central resource office. Again we are using modern communications technology in order to distribute those resources. It's located at our college in England. We provide resources on floppy disk to some 35 of our studios. I have wondered to myself if international broadcasting has every really got into this area of sharing of resource development, which might be something that could be looked at by various organizations who would be interested in that.

Religious radio is changing rapidly. Audiences are shrivelling as shortwave shrivels in certain parts of the world. This has led religious radio also into national broadcasting to look at rebroadcast and relay of its programs. Adventist World Radio, at the present time, is looking at that particular possibility, especially as more and more stations in different parts of the world, AM and FM, are accessing religious broadcasting from satellite. This is becoming a phenomenon in our industry as in other parts of the industry. We perceive ourselves as having a future in that part of the industry.

Finally, perhaps I'd like to touch on publicity. It seems to me that here we are very much like you are. We are very interested in publicity that keeps our church members and those who control the budget that gives us money, aware of what we are doing and supporting what we are doing. A lot of our publicity is directed at making sure that those who support us are going to continue to support us. I'm sure that's true of other religious broadcasters. However, we too have looked into this particular area at ways in which we can publicize the presence of our programs in different parts of the world. It is a difficult thing to do. We do try to make use of the shortwave journal, the various journals that are available, and have also carried advertisements in newspapers. We've found that effective, particularly in countries where the cost of newspaper advertisements is not very high. The idea of some radio program guide put together internationally, that could be readily available to those who might be listeners, is also attractive to religious broadcasters.

In conclusion, I would like to say that in the area of efficiency, Adventist World Radio does use the research tool and we are in cooperation with the BBC, through an organization that we are a part of, in accessing information on our audiences. Thanks to Graham Mytton and his group, we've discovered recently that AWR is the most listened to broadcast in Russia. That made us feel real good. I want to pay a tribute to the research facilities which the BBC makes available.

Derek White:

There are very interesting points that you've made about the use of automation, in particular as a cost-saving area. For those broadcasters who face penalty or similar rates for their 24-hour operation, then the use of automation in various ways can be a substantial cost reduction factor. Radio Australia has gone to a system of digital recording and editing which has saved us substantially and does allow much of the 24-hour operation to be handled with minimum number of staff, and that's been most effective.

WAYNE PETROZZI
PROFESSOR
RYERSON POLYTECHNICAL UNIVERSITY
TORONTO, ONTARIO - CANADA

Avoiding the Tower of Babel: Inter-Cultural Communications in International Broadcasting.

As I am not active in international broadcasting, it is important to emphasize my comments are those of an outsider. I hope what I am about to say contains little of the hubris of the academic and enough of the humility of the curious observer. I am interested in particular in one aspect of your world - international broadcasting as cross cultural communication.

Before proceeding to this discussion it is necessary to character-ize its context. Remarkable and fundamental change is the hallmark of our time. On one hand, the map of the world is constantly in the process of being redrawn. At no other time in this century has the work of cartographers been so appreciated or in such demand! Many traditional nation-states have fragmented or are fragmenting. By some estimates, should all current irredentist movements succeed, United Nations membership would increase by a third. Not only are there more states - there are more and diverse states jockeying to be seen and heard on the world stage.

On the other hand we live in a world that is shrinking. Advances in communications and increasing contacts are turning the globe into a village. The globalization of the economy means that in economic terms borders are becoming more and more permeable, less and less significant as people's economic well-being becomes more interlinked.

Paradoxically these two sets of forces, as opposite as they seem, produce a similar effect on people - an increasing need for people to have and to share a sense of belonging and community - to share an identity. This is the context within which I wish to frame today's remarks.

My own understanding is that in a world so diverse and with so many states, international broadcasting can be the means whereby societies project an image, an understanding of themselves for others to come to know. We can agree that because we are so many and so diverse, our need to understand has increased proportionately with the changes of the past five years.

It is not as clear, however, that our understanding has increased likewise. There are valid reasons for this lag. Many of these new states/societies have not projected an image or understanding of self onto the international scene. In turn, there are reasons for this having to do with inadequate finances or technical resources or expertise or access. A great deal of collaborative work in the international broadcasting community is aimed at overcoming some or all of these impediments. Conferences such as this try as well to develop strategies or solutions to overcome these limitations.

A second reason is the past history of international broadcasting which to an extent haunts the present and impedes the possibility of a different future. Previously, some international broadcasting had an aggressive, imperial character. We projected an image of ourselves outward not as part of a process of mutual understanding since we weren't interested in receiving others' images. We were rather interested in imperial outreach.

The politics of the world have changed, however and this rationale no longer is as relevant. But that past means many societies still do not trust entirely the medium, still suspect that international broadcasting may be a metaphor for imperial broadcasting. In turn, that suspicion becomes an additional impediment to the continued development of international broadcasting.

Undoubtedly, international broadcasting can provide opportunities for states/societies to develop the capacity to place their image on the world stage. It also can provide programming that facilitates cross-cultural understanding. However when we think about international broadcasting it is important to consider that the word "international" doesn't denote either a process or a space. What does this mean? Well, if all that the word "international" means is a stage or a highway (a use now as ubiquitous as highways themselves) where every image has a space or alternatively a process whereby every state projects an image outward what would be the result? International broadcasting defined in either of these ways would be little more than a high tech version of the Tower of Babel - multiple images and voices only able to talk past one another, where transmission never becomes communication.

Instead, we need to think of the concept of "international" as referring to an outcome rather than a process or a space. Perhaps I can clarify what this means with a couple of examples from my own world experience.

The Economics of International Broadcasting

Universities are organized around disciplines. Each discipline has its own history, its own way of seeing the world, its own method, and often even its own language (certainly its own concepts). In these regards disciplines employ many of the same demarcation criteria that states/societies employ. Notwithstanding the interaction between and among disciplines, they are quite able to proceed in isolation from each other and most of the time they do.

Yet the most exciting and stimulating intellectual work occurs when the boundary lines get set aside by a work that draws its insights, its genius from a number of disciplines - such a work is interdisciplinary. It is not the process or any specific space that the work occupies that leads us to characterize the work as interdisciplinary but rather its actual content. More specifically such a work resonates with some or other of the profound questions that help define a discipline and speaks to a larger set out of issues which extend beyond the discipline's boundaries.

International broadcasting, at its best, is analogous to such indisciplinary works. It manages at once to offer something to many and diverse audiences. It speaks to their specific needs or interests while offering them insights about others and their world. More to the point, international broadcasting weaves the thread of a common humanity, that nevertheless, accepts and respects our diversity. The "inter" in international refers to the content of our communication and its transparency for audiences.

It is important to reemphasize the nature of these considerations. Cross-cultural understanding is your business in many ways and I would not propose to tell you how to go about it. Perhaps, though, I might share with you another of my experiences in the hope that it will clear up any remaining uncertainties about what I take international broadcasting to mean.

Ontario, Canada's largest province, is also its most diverse. The Metropolitan Toronto region is the most populous urban area in the province. In the province and in Toronto, in particular, the government of Ontario faces its own challenge of cross-cultural communications. The clients of Ontario public services in the Metropolitan Toronto area speak upwards of one hundred languages. The people who constitute Ontario's public service represent nearly as broad a range.

I was involved in the delivery of a course on inter-cultural communications to members of the Ontario public service.

The aims of the course were to enable the Ontario government to better serve a diverse citizenry and to enable public service managers to better manage a diverse work force. The challenge is not unlike yours. On the one hand, we have to provide people with the practical knowledge and techniques required for interacting successfully with diverse clients and employees. On the other hand, we have to provide people with an understanding of the underlying ethos of inter-cultural communications - that is, we all have experiences that are worth sharing and from which we can learn - that is the source of the "inter" in inter-cultural communications.

In an increasingly diverse world inter-cultural communication and learning are of ever increasing importance and necessity. To your credit, international broadcasters are taking up various aspects of the challenge. At this conference and at earlier conferences we have heard about some of the types of interaction occurring - co-productions, sharing of training, local sourcing of productions are examples that readily come to mind. These are profiled elsewhere in this volume. My own hope is that we will learn about other such enterprises in an ever-widening circle of participation. As that occurs international broadcasting will advance its outcome - the mutual understanding of countries' images.

QUESTIONS & COMMENTS:

Discussion.

Je m'appelle Saïd Ben-Slimane. Je suis journaliste d'origine tunisienne et il m'est arrivé aussi de travailler à Radio Canada International. Je crois même avoir fait tout le parcours du journalisme en commençant par les reportages de base, passant par la caricature politique, ce qui est un pléonasme, et je me suis retrouvé à Radio Canada International au moment le plus percutant je pense pour tous les journalistes ici présent, c'était la guerre du Golfe. De par ma position en tant que Tunisien, en tant qu'Africain, Musulman, Arabe d'origine et puis Néo-Canadien, je me suis aperçu que la guerre du Golfe est un détour très important dans la radio internationale et qu'elle a signalé un hiatus, un fossé énorme entre les attentes des uns et des autres. Moi je pourrais parler au nom des auditeurs qui viennent du Sud, de ceux qui vraiment ont vécu autrement cette guerre-là et ses répercussions politiques et militaires. Je ne parle pas de Radio Canada International puisqu'à l'époque je me suis intéressé à tout ce qui se faisait ou se disait à propos de cette région du monde. Il y a vraiment un fossé énorme. Plus nous allons vers une perfection technologique, moins nous communiquons alors qu'il y aurait un intérêt extraordinaire de donner l'autre point de vue et d'arrêter, pour une fois, de diaboliser, de déshumaniser l'autre. Pendant des années nous avons vécu, entre guillemets, en croyant que les Soviétiques sont des diables. Or, il aurait été intéressant de montrer le Russe ou le Soviétique dans sa vie de tous les jours, de réfléter son propre point de vue. Je ne voudrais insulter qui que ce soit mais je suis certain que 70 à 80% des auditeurs américains ou autres ignorent même qu'il y eu des alliés arabes parmi eux, ignorent même qu'on vit normalement de l'autre côté de ce nouveau rideau de fer. J'étais très frustré de constater le monopole de fait qui a été instauré par CNN et Peter Arnold alors que c'est à nous, journalistes, d'être les premiers journalistes, comment dire, planétaires. Ne pas laisser ce monopole aux nouvelles technologies qui sont très réductrices en fait.

Derek White:

Thank you for that perspective. It actually links with something that I was about to say in response to Wayne's remarks. The difficulty for all of us is to reach a diversity of audiences with a diversity of viewpoints. I referred earlier to the new television services to Asia and regretably, I think, in Asia and, perhaps, less so in Europe where I heard this morning Belgium has rejected the Turner Film and Cartoon Network as having not sufficient European content.

There were no such restrictions in Asia on satellite television. I suspect the effect of the broadening of satellite television will be not so much an increase in cross-cultural broadcasting as a dominance of the American ethos perhaps illustrated by McDonald's. It's not a prospect we should necessarily welcome because it represents to some degree the disappearance of many of the differences in cultures which should be preserved. I'm wondering whether today we have addressed the sort of questions that were posed by Elzbieta when she wrote to me about this session. "If profit is not the justification for international broadcasting, what should it be? Should the state, in the name of public interest, continue to support financially international broadcasting? Should there be a new equilibrium established for the support of international broadcasting? Who pays? Why and how?" I would be very interested to hear any suggestions from this conference as to how or what the alternatives to finance international broadcasting might be. Should the broadcasters pay or should the listeners? I'll address that briefly.

I find it difficult to consider the listeners as payers. What can and should state-financed international broadcasters do to justify their existence in a changing world? We've heard some various viewpoints and attempts to do this. Proving their excellence and efficiency is the obvious thing to do. But how? I suspect we could be as effective and efficient as all, but unless we can prove we have an audience, then our reason for being ceases to exist.

Walter Salmaniv:

My name is Walter Salmaniv. I'm a program listener and not a broadcaster and I'm glad that you raised that point. As far as efficiency is concerned, I'm surprised no one has mentioned relay exchanges. Obviously I'd like to hear Finland for instance but on the west coast of North America, it's just a bit too far away and it's a difficult catch. Therefore, unless I'm a DXer, I'm not going to bother to listen. But it seems to me a very efficient way would be more extensive use of relay exchanges. A number of broadcasters do that and you don't have to be a large broadcaster.

Derek White:

Thank you. I think we have that lesson to a degree in the use that many of us have made of what I regard as the adventurous world radio network system where, in place of the difficult to receive shortwave signal, there is a satellite delivery which is being rebroadcast in various ways. I think pending what I hope will be the development of direct satellite to radio high quality broadcasting, that at least offers the chance to overcome the shortwave problem.

Donald Browne:

Just a moment ago, Derek, you asked about cases where people have to justify their existence and it surprised me that at this conference we have a whole body of international broadcasters whose ranks I thought would have been decimated at the end of the Cold War. That is the many broadcast operations that have been set up in Eastern Europe precisely for the purpose of fighting the Cold War. And when the governments all changed, such operations might very well have been thought to be obsolete, to have disappeared. So, I'd be very interested to hear from some of our colleagues from Eastern and Central Europe how you, to paraphrase Madonna, rejustified your existence if not your love? Who did you have to fight with? How did you convince them that you're worth supporting in this new era, especially with the tight budgets you all have?

Kim Elliott:

I can find a justification as a listener. I work for VOA but I'm speaking as a listener again. I did listen quite a bit to the stations from Central Europe during the transitional period: Radio Prague and as many of the others as I could hear. They were a valuable source of information about those countries during one of the most interesting periods of time in those countries. If the stations of Central Europe, of the former communist countries, are looking for justification, there are a few of us, a very small minority in the United States and Canada, who were there listening and tuning in as much as we could to find out what was going on, not just politically but culturally and economically. Some of the broadcasts, I have to say, were very good. Just in the period before the downfall of communism and then during the transition itself, and just after the New Year's Eve of 1989 going into 1990, was really a fascinating night to be a shortwave listener because the stations of those countries who had just switched from communism to the transitional period had some very interesting things to say. Getting back to your point about economics and funding. I'm surprised that public international broadcasters have been so shy about advertising as a means of revenue although perhaps there are statutory problems there. Those of us who listen to international radio, we don't pay licence fees to the countries for the privilege of hearing those broadcasts. We don't pay taxes to those countries for the privilege of hearing those broadcasts.

So maybe it's not too much to ask for us to listen to a few brief tasteful advertisements for products representing those countries. In fact that would be killing two birds with one stone, it would be promoting trade and tourism with that country and paying for the international broadcasting effort at the same time.

Graham Mytton:

The answer to Don's question has been given in the various presentations that have been made so far, including Mr. Nedialkov's this morning. The survival of international broadcasting in Eastern Europe has been at a much lower level than before. Radio Prague used to be a major international broadcaster and is now a very minor international broadcaster. I think the answers are fairly easy to understand. I wonder if I could refer though to the question that our Tunisian friend just referred to. He expressed his concern about the way in which news gets reported and he mentioned CNN. I do want to kill this myth that CNN was such a big player, such an important news medium in the Gulf War. It was important, of course, but it's tremendously put out of proportion. CNN broadcasts in English and I don't have to remind people in this room that not everybody in the world speaks English. So the influence of CNN broadcasting in one language will always be limited, and nowhere more so than in the Gulf region itself. Throughout the Gulf crisis, immediately after the Iraqi forces invaded Kuwait, we were doing research in the area, in Egypt, in Saudi Arabia, in the United Arab Emirates. We did research continuously from August through the following May, so we were able to research and follow the audience behaviour during the period of and immediately after the invasion, during the outbreak of the air war in January and the outbreak of the ground war shortly afterwards, and when the war came to an end. It's clear throughout that period that radio took pre-eminence even in households where people had television. The choice tended to be for radio rather than for television to get news of what was going on. People first heard about the news from radio. The vital thing about this, and it refers to what our Tunisian friend is suggesting, is that it provides people with tremendous alternatives. In the Middle East you do not have a great deal of choice in television. You have the national broadcasters and you have CNN in some areas, and World Service television in Arabic as well, and there are other satellite services. There's actually still very limited choice but that limited choice does not apply to radio.

Those of you familiar with the book we produced last year, there's a chapter in there on what happened during the Gulf War. If you look at the number of radio stations the people listened to, listening to international radio went up enormously during the Gulf War, particularly for the BBC, Monte Carlo, Radio France Internationale and Voice of America. It's quite striking the number of stations that people listen to. In fact, it's quite normal for a person to regularly listen to four, five or even six radio stations then choose between them what he or she chooses to believe. I could just end with a quote. We did some qualitative research in Egypt after the war was over and I'll just quote to you from what some of the Egyptians said: "Credibility is achieved when several stations give the same news. You determine the credibility of a station by comparing it with actual events and with other media. You must also use your own thoughts. Media can make you hate someone when you don't even know them." People talking about the media as if they are autonomous. We must not assume that media somehow create a reality which takes over in a person's mind. People are still autonomous. They can listen to the BBC or the Voice of America and disagree with everything. People form a reality, their interpretation of the world they live in, by switching, by listening to different stations, by reading newspapers and magazines, by listening to friends and discussing matters.

All of us here are part of an international democratic debate. I think that is all we can ever hope to do. I do wish we would stop talking about it as if we were creating a kind of reality which takes over for people, some kind of imperialism involved. Of course there are aspects to that whereby certain countries are more dominant in this business than others but let us never forget the autonomy of the individual in making his or her mind up as to what they want to believe.

Derek White:

I think that also is in part an answer to Don's question that the reason for being is to produce the diversity which makes that process of decision-making possible.

Juhani Niinistö:

Someone mentioned that listeners in target areas don't pay taxes or licence fees. I can tell you that we have considered that if YLE starts a 24-hour satellite service in North America, we would encourage the subscription trick that American public radio stations are using. That money will be accepted!

Derek White:

Concerning Kim's point, perhaps the majority of publicly funded broadcasters are nervous about taking advertisements. We live in a highly commercial environment. In most cases, the most successful media are commercial. Perhaps the pristine public service broadcasters have to rethink their position.

Richard McClear:

I'd like to comment on three things. First of all what Graham said. Before the Gulf War, radio listening in our community of Sitka, Alaska, was down about 30% and we lost most of our listeners to people using CNN or MTV as they used to use radio. So radio listening started declining. As soon as the Gulf War happened, our radio listening shot up. It's what convinced us to start carrying the World Service and CBC. That increase in listening has held for two years. It's just started to decline now. What helped our increase was the fact that we had BBC World Service, we had CBC radio and to some extent, other world broadcasters available to us, that we could immediately put on and people could hear a diversity of sources.

Secondly, to talk about Dr. Browne's question. Before I went to Albania, I was one of the people writing letters to my senators saying "public broadcasting domestically is terribly underfunded; we can't cover all of Alaska. Why do we need to provide money for Radio Free Europe/Radio Liberty or Voice of America? Let's spend that money domestically on our service." And as many other public broadcasters, we tried to whip up sentiment among our listeners to do that too because there is that competition happening.

Thirdly, after being in Albania for a while and seeing the impact of international broadcasters on improving the quality of domestic broadcasting there and looking at our overall foreign policy, I'm rethinking that and writing retraction letters. But there needs to be some way for international broadcasters, especially in a place like the United States where VOA has no domestic presence, to get that message across, and they've made an absolutely dreadful job of it in the United States.

The Economics of International Broadcasting

Derek White:

I do think that's an important question in terms of the point Don raised, that it's not a one-sided argument. One has to question - as is being questioned in Asia at the moment- the need for a Radio Free Asia or whatever it is to be called. It's already producing objections from certain governments.

Bert Steinkamp:

I'd like to come back to the question of why are there so few relay arrangements. Although there are quite a few between the more affluent international broadcasters the speaker is absolutely right, there is a limited number between smaller broadcasters. But the reasons for that are sometimes very funny. A few years ago we got a request from Radio Japan and I'm sure Sato San will be agreeable to my speaking about it. His predecessors are here anyway. Could we exchange something on our transmitter site in the Nederlands, giving hours for Radio Netherlands on Yamata in Japan? We could not because Dutch law forbade it. Foreign broadcasters were not allowed on Dutch territory. We are a fantastic democracy as you know, extremely open-minded and tolerant, but it could not be done. The law is being changed at the moment so bidders are welcome. The unfortunate thing is that the hours on our transmitters which other broadcasters want happen to be our prime time hours so the thing falls through. I think that's the most practical reason why there are so few relay arrangements between the small broadcasters.

Terry Hargreaves:

First on the relay. We do quite a few and as Bert says, you look at your schedule and say there are lots of hours free but they're not the hours the other fellow wants. In addition, perhaps Holland might do what the Japanese did when we asked for our first relay agreement with them and Japanese law forbade foreign broadcasters from broadcasting from their territory. I guess the Japanese really wanted to do the exchange because they put a bill through the parliament and they changed the law so that we could broadcast from there and others do now.

To go back a bit on the funding question, I think in a way maybe we skate around it or maybe it's just so self-evident that it hasn't been discussed. The reason for the existence of most of us is because there's a national will on the part of governments and understanding of the necessity or the need for international broadcasters for a variety of reasons: some are prestige, some have geopolitical reasons, selling of foreign policy point of view, of reflecting the national culture, of increasing trade or whatever. I think we all go in with some sort of mandate as to what we do, however narrow it may be. For instance our mandate is primarily to reflect Canada to the world and make people interested in it.

Well some people, no matter what you do, won't be interested and you have to live with that. We wouldn't be fulfilling our mandate or being terribly useful to the people who are paying the bills if we said: "Well, more people would listen if we didn't talk about Canada and we talked about the rest of the world in a completely neutral way". That's all very well but the benefit to the funding agency is rather minimal in that case. I think we have to face the fact that government priorities change from time to time and we have to live with it. Some people seem to suggest at some of these meetings, that it's an abstraction, that they're funded and just doing good to the world. Let's get serious. If some government puts in 15 million as in our case, or several hundred million in other cases, they're not doing it just out of good will. I'm not saying that their purposes are evil but they have a reason for doing it and the mandate reflects that.

CHAPTER FIVE

THE ECONOMICS OF INTERNATIONAL BROADCASTING:

MEASURING EXCELLENCE AND EFFICIENCY
AUDIENCE RESEARCH

Editors' Note:

One of the ongoing and vexing problems related to international broadcasting and, indeed, all forms of media, is "who is the audience". Fortunately, the CHALLENGES conferences have always devoted a significant amount of time to an exploration of audience research. Indeed, in previous conferences the sessions devoted to audience research have provoked some of the best presentations and discussions.

The chapter which follows brings together some of the very finest and most accomplished audience research specialists in international broadcasting. As new global realities are unfolding, the questions "who is listening to international radio and who is watching international television " assume increasing urgency. Of particular interest in this chapter is the presentation of some vital data on television audiences by CNN and the comparisons presented by other broadcasters from various parts of the world.

GRAHAM MYTTON
HEAD, AUDIENCE RESEARCH & CORRESPONDENCE
BBC WORLD SERVICE
LONDON - U.K.

Introduction.

We will concentrate on how we measure performance, both in quality and in quantity, and how we report our research activities to our respective managements, and how this information is used in strategic planning, and used in changing what we do.

I often get asked: "How do you do audience research for international broadcasting?" People understand the need and the way in which audience research is done here in Vancouver, in Toronto or New York... but wonder how we do it internationally. It's no different really. The same methods. There's no mystery about it. It's just that whereas my opposite number in BBC radio and television has just the United Kingdom to cope with, I've got all the other countries to cope with.

I was commissioned a few years ago to write a handbook on the methods of audience research, by UNESCO. I have one here. (If you are interested, copies are available through UNESCO.) It describes the methods used in audience research both for television and radio. UNESCO is starting a series of regional seminars on audience research, starting in Nairobi this August, and probably in Singapore in November.

Often during this conference I've heard references, particularly in the opening sessions, to listeners' letters. It is important, of course, to receive letters from listeners. It's a reassurance that somebody out there is listening. I've said this before at Challenges conferences. Letters are a notoriously unreliable, incomplete and even misleading source of information. You can only find out who is listening by doing more systematic, more thorough, more reliable forms of audience research. But how do we know who is listening? How do we know what the consequences are of that activity?

NICOLE BEAULAC
PREMIER CHEF DE RECHERCHES
SOCIÉTÉ RADIO-CANADA
MONTRÉAL, QUÉBEC - CANADA

La recherche sur l'auditoire à Radio Canada International.

Radio Canada International, à l'instar de plusieurs radiodiffuseurs internationaux, se préoccupe de mieux connaître ses auditoires. Toutefois, la mesure de l'efficacité pour tout radiodiffuseur international est tributaire de sa taille et des budgets qu'il peut y consacrer. Les besoins en recherche de RCI sont assurés par la Direction de la recherche de Radio-Canada, laquelle dessert l'ensemble des constituantes de la Société Radio-Canada, soient les télévisions et radios nationales ainsi que RCI.

Rappelons brièvement les objectifs de RCI pour ensuite décrire comment sont orientées les recherches:

-RCI s'adresse à un auditoire international via les ondes-courtes;

-RCI s'adresse aussi aux Canadiens à l'étranger en rediffusant des émissions produites par les réseaux nationaux de radio de la CBC et de la SRC;

-Depuis la fin des années 80, RCI a diversifié ses moyens de rejoindre les auditoires en rediffusant certains de ses produits sur les radios locales dans plusieurs régions du monde.

Comment la recherche appuie-t-elle RCI dans son mandat?

En plus des informations sur l'environnement médiatique des pays sondés, les recherches sont utilisée par RCI pour estimer prioritairement la taille de ses auditoires selon les régions-cibles et les langues de diffusion.

A titre d'exemple, lors des coupures de budget substantielles de 1991 qui se traduisirent par une réorganisation importante des services de RCI, la recherche - confrontée aux scénarios de coupures - dut soupeser et analyser les estimations d'auditoire par régions-cibles et par langues afin de rationaliser les choix difficiles mais rendus nécessaires par la conjoncture budgétaire.

Mais en 1994, qui écoute RCI?

D'après la vingtaine d'études récentes dont nous disposons, le profil de l'auditoire régulier de RCI via les ondes-courtes est nettement plus masculin que féminin; cet auditoire a un profil d'éducation plus élevé que la moyenne et est dominé par les auditeurs d'âge moyen.

Nous sommes actuellement à refaire une estimation des auditoires directs réguliers de RCI, c'est-à-dire les auditeurs qui ont écouté une fois ou plus par semaine RCI en diffusion directe selon les régions-cibles. Ces estimations d'auditoire par région-cible sont parcellaires puisqu'elles ne rendent compte que des auditoires obtenus en diffusion directe via les ondes-courtes.

Nos premières estimations d'auditoire de RCI, principalement via les ondes-courtes, sont à la baisse en 1994 comparativement à l'estimé réalisé en 1989 dans la moitié des régions-cibles desservies, soient en Europe Centrale et de l'Est, aux États-unis, en Europe de l'Ouest ainsi qu'en Amérique Latine. L'auditoire estimé de RCI est relativement stable en Afrique et aux Antilles.

Ces baisses de l'auditoire direct de RCI suivent en cela le mouvement de l'ensemble de l'écoute des ondes-courtes qui, comme on le sait, sont à la baisse dans plusieurs régions du globe, particulièrement en Amérique Latine et en Europe Centrale et de l'Est.

Les principales raisons évoquées pour expliquer ces baisses sont:

- La progression des ondes FM dans divers pays alors que plusieurs radiodiffuseurs nationaux utilisaient auparavant les ondes-courtes dans leur propre pays;
- La libéralisation des régimes politiques dans plusieurs pays, laquelle libéralisation a entraîné un plus grand accès à l'information;
- L'avènement des chaînes télévisuelles spécialisées en infor mation telles CNN, BBC, etc...
- Et RCI a évidemment perdu une partie de ses auditoires par l'abandon de la moitié de ses langues de diffusion.

Par contre, elle en a conquis de nouveaux! Au Moyen-Orient par exemple, où on note un auditoire substantiel pour notre diffusion en arabe. Dans cette région, nous avons pu estimer - en plus des auditoires directs de RCI - ceux que l'on rejoint également via les ondes moyennes diffusées par Radio Monte-Carlo.

Nous ne sommes pas en mesure d'estimer les auditoires rejoints par RCI en Asie, particulièrement en Chine où depuis 1992, RCI diffuse en mandarin entre autres, par les ondes-courtes.

Nos estimations de l'auditoire rejoint par RCI sont incomplètes parce qu'elles ne rendent pas compte des auditoires rejoints par rediffusion. En effet, dès 1987 RCI a commencé à diversifier ses sources de diffusion, soit par des cassettes d'émissions ou par ses cours d'anglais, afin de rejoindre encore plus adéquatement ses auditeurs potentiels.

Mentionnons à titre d'exemple les efforts déployés par RCI notamment en Amérique du Sud, dans l'ancienne URSS et en Chine.

Ainsi, par la rediffusion sur les chaînes locales en ondes moyennes, RCI devrait pouvoir rejoindre davantage des publics différents.

Actuellement, faute de temps, de ressources et aussi parfois face à l'impossibilité d'obtenir des données d'auditoire dans certaines régions, nous ne pouvons rendre compte de l'auditoire de nos émissions en rediffusion. Ce que l'on sait cependant, c'est que nos auditoires sont grandement sous-estimés. Je citerai à titre d'exemple les données recueillies par la BBC en Jordanie où RCI obtient, via Radio Monte-Carlo, trois fois plus d'écoute que ce que l'on mesure dans un autre sondage obtenu via la BBC sur les radiodiffuseurs internationaux.

Notre prochaine démarche en recherche sera d'évaluer ces auditoires non seulement en radiodiffusion directe mais aussi en rediffusion, puisque RCI est de plus en plus présent dans de nombreux pays via ce mode de diffusion. Nous devons rendre compte de ces auditoires additionnels non seulement pour justifier les ressources actuelles et futures de nos services mais aussi pour évaluer notre rendement et pouvoir ainsi prioriser nos efforts.

S'il est illusoire pour nous de vouloir rendre compte de tous les nouveaux auditoires de RCI en rediffusion indirecte (pas de sondages existants, manque de ressources pour acheter et colliger toutes les données,...) nous tenterons d'obtenir, à titre d'exemples, des données en radiodiffusion indirecte dans certains pays où il existe des sondages et ce, pour chacune des régions-cibles où RCI y accorde beaucoup de ressources, soit en Chine, dans l'ancienne URSS et en Amérique du Sud.

Je voudrais enfin rappeler que l'estimation de l'auditoire des radiodiffuseurs internationaux demeure un exercice incomplet pour de multiples raisons. Ainsi, la capacité de mesurer adéquatement l'auditoire de ces diffuseurs est inversement proportionnelle à l'écoute de la radio via les ondes-courtes. en effet, l'écoute des radios ondes-courtes est justement plus importante dans les pays où l'on ne peut mesurer adéquatement les auditoires, pour des considérations de régimes politiques. Dans de nombreux pays, on note également l'absence de moyens de sonder les gens (populations nomades en Afrique, en Inde, etc...), ce qui rend impossible non seulement la mesure des radios internationales mais aussi la mesure des radios locales.

L'utilisation des ondes-courtes est-elle toujours justifiée?

Je terminerai en citant ici des données publiées dans la revue *Time* du 14 février dernier. Quand le mur de Berlin est tombé en 1989, plusieurs ont cru que la liberté se répandrait partout dans le monde.

Ce n'est malheureusement pas le cas, selon "Freedom House", un groupe de New-York qui s'occupe des droits de l'homme. Le nombre de pays ne respectant pas les droits de l'homme a progressé l'an dernier, de 38 à 55, ce qui rend selon leur catégorisation, 41% de la population mondiale "non-libre". Pourquoi cette progression? Les rivalités ethniques et le fondamentalisme islamique étaient cités comme facteurs importants. Toujours selon Freedom House, 72 pays étaient considérés "libres" alors que 63 autres étaient catégorisés "partiellement libres".

Ainsi, les restrictions que vit toujours une partie importante de la population mondiale nous convainc à RCI que les ondes-courtes demeurent encore aujourd'hui un moyen vital pour rejoindre ces auditeurs et leur permettre d'avoir accès à de l'information de qualité, libre et diversifiée.

R. EUGENE PARTA
DIRECTOR, MEDIA AND OPINION RESEARCH
MICHAEL HANEY, ANALYST, MOR, RFE/RL
SUSAN GIGLI, SENIOR ANALIST, MOR, RFE/RL
RADIO FREE EUROPE/RADIO LIBERTY
RESEARCH INSTITUTE
MÜNICH - GERMANY (USA)

Using Quantitative and Qualitative Methods to Assess the Impact of International Radio Re-Broadcasts.

Rebroadcasting of international shortwave radio on local waves is a relatively new phenomenon that has spread rapidly in some of the countries of the former Soviet Union.

The reasons for this are clear: the electronic media environment of much of the former Soviet Union (which in the case of Russia means not just Moscow but provincial Russia as well) has become rich, complex and competitive. With the emergence of local commercial TV and radio companies, including those financed from abroad, it is becoming at once both internationalized (primarily through music, commercials and international news shows), and increasingly regionalized, or decentralized. In this newly competitive environment, rebroadcasting has been a bulwark of the international broadcasters' defense.

At the same time, the spread of rebroadcasting has been fueled by the widely held (and generally justified) perception that international SW audiences have been on the decrease for the last several years. Other assumptions closely interwoven with these first two are that rebroadcasting:

° contributes to audience expansion through "inheritance" from the local rebroadcast partner and also by recapturing lapsed SW listeners;

° improves reception;

° enhances the images of both the international broadcaster and the local station;

° can help save money by reducing high SW transmission costs.

In other words, rebroadcasting has been seen as a "win-win" situation, good for the international broadcaster and for the local station, too. However, even if the reasons which brought rebroadcasting into being are apparent, it should be stressed that to date little research has been conducted with the goal of establishing reliable rebroadcast audience measurements and verifying these working assumptions. In this paper, we will take a look at one approach to studying rebroadcasting and discuss the preliminary findings.

Although the results of this one approach may not be universally applicable to all rebroadcasting situations, in most cases, there will be some points of similarity and we hope that others will gain from and build on our experience.

Before discussing the research, a look at the different types of rebroadcasting arrangements is in order.

One possible classification of rebroadcast arrangements is simply financial: who pays whom? In some cases, the international broadcaster which wishes to rebroadcasts its product pays the local partner. In other cases, the local partner, happy to receive quality programming on a regular basis, agrees to transmit the broadcasts free of charge in the expectation that the programming will draw in an audience and/or add to the prestige of the local partner.

Particularly in the former Soviet Union, where "fair market" prices are still, at best, a rather relative and undeveloped concept, one finds both types of arrangements. There seem to be no hard rules which regulate the positions of the two negotiating sides. Much depends on the personalities and goals of those involved, particularly, it would seem, on that of the local partner, who may be strongly committed in purely ideological terms to helping build pluralism in post-Soviet society. Or, as happens often enough, the local partner might simply be out to make money and hold the position that the international radio station should pay for the opportunity to win more of the radio listening market.

While it is beyond the scope of this paper to explore in detail the range of financial agreements already in existence in rebroadcast arrangements, we will note some advantages and disadvantages of both. The disadvantage to paying for rebroadcasting is self-evident, particularly in the increasingly likely event of budgetary constraints. Obviously, the exact amount and other terms of the agreement are significant. Here it is worth noting that precisely the absence of established market prices that are ultimately based on something, and not just arbitrarily set by the local partner station, can make for difficulties in reaching an agreement.

However, when the international radio station does not pay for the rebroadcasting, demands on service and ultimately, the ensured continuation of the rebroadcasting arrangement are difficult to enforce. The local partner is more inclined to feel that he can pull any station off the air whenever he wants to, even in the case of a formal agreement, if there is no payment involved. The high inflation in the countries of the former Soviet Union might result in this problem even when payment is made by the international broadcaster.

Another possible classification of rebroadcast arrangements is by type of placement, and this is what has profound impact on the audience and overall effectiveness of the arrangement. The remainder of this paper will be devoted to a discussion of the different types of placement and their effects on audiences.

The simplest rebroadcast arrangement is the "independent frequency", with the partner being not another radio station but, most typically, the Ministry of Communications. This is not uncommon in the former Soviet Union where, outside of a few major capital cities, independent radio stations have been slow to develop. The airwaves have been guarded as a precious natural resource (sometimes the result of interagency squabbling over jurisdiction over them) and, compared to what could be the case, few new frequencies have been assigned or auctioned off in the years since the collapse of the Soviet Union. In the capitals of several former Soviet republics, there are, in fact, no independent radio stations at all.

In the "independent frequency" arrangement the broadcasts that are available on shortwave simply appear in "unadulterated" form on MW or FM. Often there are no other broadcasts before or after them. The advantage of being "unadulterated" and therefore safe from the danger of blurred identity with another station is offset by the disadvantage on being "somewhere out there", alone in the ether with no local station from which to inherit an audience or to expect advertising services. Add to this the relative lack of the habit of "experimenting" with the dial, at least in those locations which have never had a variety of local radio stations to choose from, and it becomes clear that an intensive and regular advertising campaign is necessary in order to successfully inaugurate an "independent frequency" rebroadcasting arrangement.

Another common rebroadcast arrangement is the "clean break", when the international station appears back-to-back with either the local partner, who goes off the air to make way for the international partner's, or after another rebroadcast international station. This type will be examined in detail in this paper.

A significant advantage of the "clean break" is the possibility of audience inheritance, those listeners to the local partner who automatically or by inertia continue to listen to the rebroadcast international partner. However, it should be stressed here that there are no absolute guarantees or ready formulas dictating the degree of inheritance which can be expected. Clearly, the complementarity of the identities of the two stations and the production elements governing the transition are two important factors to be kept in mind. Another advantage is that one can usually count on or require joint advertising to be the responsibility of the local partner.

The "clean break" arrangement, like the "independent frequency" has the advantage of keeping intact some block of the international broadcaster's product (typically one hour or two hours), which helps significantly to reduce the risk of blurred identities and false station recall on the part of listeners.

Finally, we have informally dubbed two other common rebroadcasting arrangements "mixed salad" and "peek-a-boo". An example of the "mixed salad" is graphically demonstrated in Figure 1, which shows an excerpt of the schedule of Radio Titan, Radio Liberty's rebroadcast partner in Ufa, Russia. In the space of just a few hours, Radio Titan plays half a dozen radio stations on a schedule that changes daily. Certain features of the schedule are preserved from day to day, and Titan frequently advertises its schedule in numerous local papers. Nonetheless, it should be obvious that the "mixed salad", which offers little bits of a lot in a small space, presents a greater risk of blurred identities and false station recall.

Also, it is almost certain in the case of such a "busy" schedule that there will be frequent changes to the schedule. For this reason, it is important to stipulate in the rebroadcast agreement at least a bare minimum of programming on a fixed schedule.

Figure 1. The "Mixed Salad". Radio Titan, Ufa. Sample of daily schedule.

7.00	Radio Liberty. News.
7.10	Radio Titan. Good morning, Russia.
8.06	VOA Europe. Music. News. Information. (in English)
8.50	Radio Canada.
9.00	VOA. Morning program.
10.10	VOA. Youth program.
11.00	Radio Liberty. News.
11.15	VOA. Everything About Business.
11.45	Radio Sweden.
12.00	Radio Titan. News.
12.20	VOA. Medicine and health care.
13.00	Radio Liberty. Live. News and Actualities
14.10	VOA. Country Music.

Nonetheless, even Titan's "mixed salad" offers, in most cases, an identifiable block of each partner station's broadcasting. Furthermore, in the given case, the local partner takes considerable pains to introduce and lead out each partner station, which helps orient listeners.

Another type of placement is the "peek-a-boo" arrangement, a version of the "mixed salad" in which the international partner's broadcasting is divided up in small segments of perhaps no more than 10 minutes, and played on an as-needed, "filler" basis. Examples of this might be a short piece about a certain aspect of life in a country, or a series of English lessons in which each lesson is a situation designed to run no more than a few minutes.

The "peek-a-boo" arrangement often results when the international partner makes large mailings of pre-recorded programming to dozens of locations throughout the world, seeking no compensation and offering no pay, only programming. As a rule, the international broadcaster is extremely hard pressed to keep track of the effect of these short segments of rebroadcasting, and often does not know exactly what part of its programming is aired, and when. Because of the short length of the segments and the sometimes irregular nature of the schedule by which they are aired, the "peek-a-boo" arrangement suffers from the highest degree of false recall or attribution on the listeners' part.

We observed a striking case of this in a survey conducted in Almaty, the capital of Kazakhstan in May, 1994. In that city, an international broadcaster (in this case Radio Canada International) has placements in Russian both once a week on the wired radio[1] at a popular morning time and throughout the weekend in a "peek-a-boo" arrangement on a popular commercial station. Even though the local commercial station has a daily audience of 25% and a weekly audience of 47%, reported weekly listening to the Western station in Russian was under 3%. One can only conclude that the listeners to the "peek-a-boo" segments are either not absorbing the information that the programming they hear is prepared by the international broadcaster, or they assume that the short rebroadcast pieces are simply longer reports from some of their own international correspondents.

Studying Rebroadcast Audiences.

A number of problems face the researcher who undertakes a study of rebroadcasting audiences. Part of the researcher's problem lies in the very nature of rebroadcasting: the task of measuring audiences is only made more difficult by the emergence of dozens of new "media scenes" on the local level. Even those international broadcasters most actively engaged in developing a rebroadcasting network could hardly be expected to keep track of the effect of their rebroadcasts in dozens of locations.*[1]

Another thorn in measuring rebroadcast audiences is the common low awareness on the listeners' part of wave bands of broadcast, which makes it difficult to assess the exact impact of rebroadcasting on audience sizes.

Finally, in Russia and the other republics of the former Soviet Union the researcher faces a unique and significant problem of terminology. If in English-speaking countries the terms "FM" and "shortwaves" signify to the average radio listener very different types of broadcasting, in Russia this distinction is blurred by the use of the term "UKV" for FM -- that is, "ultra shortwaves". The result is that some think that FM broadcasts, necessarily local in origin, are even more "foreign" than "shortwaves"; they are called "ultra", after all. Thus, a listener to Radio Liberty on FM who knows only that he makes no special effort to hear the broadcasts might say, "Goodness, no," when asked whether he listens to Liberty on "ultra shortwaves". Or, in the opposite case, a listener to Radio Liberty on shortwaves who knows that the broadcasts are coming from somewhere far away might incorrectly insist that she is listening to Liberty on "ultra shortwaves".

* Endnote [1]   See page 202

No single research approach would be sufficient adequately to cover the range of new questions posed by rebroadcasting. Over the period spanning the end of 1993 and the first months of 1994, the Media & Opinion Research Department of the RFE/RL Research Institute developed a two-tiered research strategy to study these questions. In Russia, a combination of city surveys and focus groups in two locations with differing rebroadcast arrangements has proven to be the most effective means of obtaining answers (which in some cases remain preliminary) to some of the many questions associated with rebroadcasting. These questions are outlined below.

Ufa, a large city in the Ural Mountains, and Nizhnii Novgorod, Russia's third largest city which is located on the Volga River to the east of Moscow, were selected as the research sites. Preference was given to these cities over Moscow and St. Petersburg for a variety of reasons. Russia's two capital cities have media markets which are unique and not typical of provincial Russia. They have been and will continue to be the focus of relatively refined audience research.

Furthermore, Radio Liberty's rebroadcast arrangements in Nizhnii Novgorod (a "clean break" with Radio Randevu) and Ufa (a "mixed salad" with Radio Titan) differ significantly and in this respect provide a unique opportunity for comparison and ultimately for developing recommendations for a rebroadcasting strategy.

The Research Strategy.

In both Nizhnii Novgorod and Ufa virtually identical research projects were carried out at about the same times. First, in December, 1993, focus groups were conducted in both cities by the same moderator, Masha Volkenstein of the Moscow-based research firm Validata/Yankelovich. The focus groups were designed to determine:

°   attitudes to and distinctions among different media.
°   awareness of and attitudes to international media appearing on domestic media.
°   awareness of and attitudes to different wave bands: FM vs. MW vs. SW. For example, are radio listeners usually aware of what wavelength they have tuned to? What associations do listeners have with stations on FM, medium wave and shortwave? What about the wired radio? Do listeners associate foreign radio with shortwave?

° the specific identities of local rebroadcast partner stations.

° the awareness, image and identity of RL rebroadcasts on the local station.

° ease of listening to the rebroadcasts: promotion, advertising, reception.

The recruitment for the focus groups was designed to get answers from the various types of listeners effected by rebroadcasting. With variations dictated by the differences in the rebroadcast arrangements, the following scheme was used in Ufa and Nizhnii Novgorod:

Group 1:   "traditional" listeners to Radio Liberty on shortwaves only.

Group 2:   deliberate listeners to Radio Liberty on the local station.

Group 3:   casual listeners to the local station who were not aware that the research was in any way connected with Radio Liberty.

City Surveys and Rebroadcasting.

The nuanced information gathered by the focus groups was used in the development of the questionnaires used in the city surveys. In Nizhnii Novgorod, the survey was conducted in February-March, 1994, and in Ufa, in April-May 1944.

City surveys in the two locations were used in order to determine:

° audience sizes of Radio Liberty and the local station;

° awareness of RL's presence on the local station;

° wave bands of listening to Radio Liberty;

° listening history and audience migration: how many traditionally SW listeners now listen to RL on FM/MW?

° audience inheritance: how many listeners to the rebroadcast partner now identify themselves as listeners to RL?

° preferred times of listening to Radio Liberty.

In an attempt to overcome the problem of the low level of waveband awareness, we developed a question which in each answer category provided respondents with both the generic name of the band and the name of the radio station (for example, "I listen to Radio Liberty exclusively on medium waves, that is, on Radio Titan.") A card containing all the possible answers was handed to all respondents answering the question and they were encouraged to select the answer which best reflected their situation.

Despite these measures, in Nizhnii Novgorod, where the city survey took place before the one in Ufa, as many as 43% of all respondents who had listened to Radio Liberty in the last 12 months could not identify the waveband on which they had listened.

In view of this experience, for the Ufa study, interviewers were specially instructed either to inspect the radio sets or to ask another family member judged by the respondent to be more knowledgeable in matters of wavebands (since the question came towards the end of the questionnaire, there was little concern that the other family member would then interfere in the interview). This innovation (perhaps together with a higher awareness of the local station than was the case in Nizhnii Novgorod) was successful in reducing the "Don't knows" to 15% of the 12-month audience.

Radio Liberty's local partners.

In order to render more meaningful to the reader the discussion of the research findings, a brief overview of each of Radio Liberty's rebroadcast partners will be given here.

In Nizhnii Novgorod, Radio Liberty has been appearing on the Eastern European FM frequency of Radio Randevu since July, 1993. In a "clean break" arrangement, Randevu goes off the air at 20:00 and is followed by Radio Liberty from 20:00-22:00. After Liberty's 2-hour block, there are no broadcasts on this frequency until Randevu resumes the following morning.

Most of Randevu's broadcast time is filled with light music which is generally popular Western rock but also includes Russian music. Other types of music are played but all of it could be called "soft". In the focus groups, many of its listeners referred to Randevu as "unobtrusive" and "pleasant", a "background" station. In addition to music, Randevu reports on weather and local commercial information throughout the day. In the hour before the break to Radio Liberty, Randevu generally airs a thematic music program devoted to a single artist or group, or plays listeners' requests.

In addition to broadcasting on its FM frequency, Radio Randevu is available on the wired radio for 40 minutes in the middle of the afternoon, and again for an hour at midnight. (While not of relevance to Liberty's rebroadcast arrangement in Nizhnii Novgorod, this information is included here for its general relevance to the topic of radio and rebroadcasting in Russia.)

The survey data show that half of Randevu's weekly audience listens *exclusively* to the 40-minute daytime slot on the wired radio system. This demonstrates the prevalence of the wired radio system. However, it should be noted that the wired radio brings in a different audience: the Randevu wired radio audience is 3/4 female and 60% of the regular listeners on the wired radio are over the age of 40.

In contrast, the Randevu FM audience is 60% male and 68% of its listeners are under the age 40. Although the different basic types of rebroadcast arrangements go a long way toward determining the success of the arrangement, it must be stressed that there are other important factors as well. Primary among these are announcements, bill boarding, listener orientation in general. Another is print advertising of the schedule. This has been a weakness in the case of Randevu, which, to date, has not provided regular and frequent announcements to their listeners that every day at a certain time another radio station (RL) appears on its waves.

This situation can be contrasted to Ufa, where Radio Liberty has been rebroadcasting its programs in a "mixed salad" arrangement on the medium wave frequency of Radio Titan, also since July, 1993. The terms of the agreement require the local partner to broadcast a minimum of three live, discrete hour blocks daily, but also allow the local partner to play any amount of broadcasting above and beyond that either live, or in the case of non-topical programming, in recording. The local partner makes frequent use of this prerogative, e, and often relays Liberty's news at the top of the hour and non-topical programming which is directly recorded from the satellite.

Radio Titan has an unusual profile in that it is on the air 24 hours-a-day and primarily exists to rebroadcast international radio. But the programming is by no means all "talk radio"; popular Western music shows occupy a prominent position in the station's weekly schedule, and in this sense it is not all that different from other young, independent radio stations in Russia. In Titan's case, the music is almost exclusively in English, as opposed to Radio Randevu in Nizhnii Novgorod, which plays "soft" Russian music, as well.

Radio Titan adheres to a strict policy of announcing the programs of every rebroadcasting partner both before and after the program ("And now for the next hour you will hear *Program A*, prepared by our colleagues at Radio *X*." "You have just been listening to *Program B*, prepared by our colleagues at Radio *Y*.")

Titan also constantly uses the standard phrase, "Radio Titan and Radio X work together," which, according to the station's general director, serves the dual purpose of increasing Titan's prestige and of preserving the identity of the original station. Titan further dispels the impression of being a local radio station by announcing only Moscow time, not Ufa time (which is two hours later than Moscow). Finally, Titan advertises its full schedule every week in the leading newspapers in Ufa.

The Results.

Space considerations and in some cases, the preliminary nature of the findings themselves, make it impossible to answer all of the questions posed in the beginning of this report. However, the most important findings and indications are given below. It is our hope that outside of their specific application to Radio Liberty, these findings will be of use to other international broadcasters engaged in rebroadcasting.

Audience Sizes and Expansion.

° In both cities, it appeared that rebroadcasting has had a positive effect on the size of Radio Liberty's audience.

In Nizhnii Novgorod, where we had also had the opportunity to take an audience measurement before the commencement of rebroadcasting, the indications were that, at 7%, the weekly audience had more than doubled by the time of the second survey.

In Ufa, although there was no measurement of the "before" audience, the very respectable weekly audience of 9% is an indication that rebroadcasting has made a positive contribution to the Liberty audience in that city.

More to the point, the data on wave band of listening and when respondents first heard a Radio Liberty broadcast support this positive assessment of rebroadcasting. Consider Table 2, which displays the results to the wave band of listening question as answered by the 12-month Radio Liberty audiences.

Table 2. On what wave bands do you (did you) listen to Radio Liberty? (in % of the 12-month RL audiences in both cities).

	Exclusively SW	Exclusively on rebroadcast	Both	Don't know
Nizhnii Novgorod	13	30	12	43
Ufa	19	44	22	15

In both cities, the rebroadcast audiences are larger than any other. In Ufa, where certain innovations in the interview process made it possible to reduce the "Don't know's" to 15%, the rebroadcast audience, at 66% (44+22) emerged as a significant portion of the overall audience.

Volatility In the Audience.

° Rebroadcasting brings volatility into audiences, at least in its initial period.

In both cities, those who reported listening to Radio Liberty in the last 12 months were asked when they first heard a Liberty broadcast. The results show a high level of volatility in the audience compared to the more stable SW audiences of several years ago. Also, a new phenomenon was in strong evidence in both 12-month audiences, that of the "returnees", those listeners who had stopped listening to shortwave broadcasts in the heyday of the *perestroika* years and are now returning to the audience.[*2]

Table 3. Entrants into the audience in the last 12 months (in % of the 12-month audiences in both cities).

	New listeners	Returnees	Total % of entrants in last 12-months
Nizhnii Novgorod	23	27	50
Ufa	26	55	81

Thus, in Nizhnii Novgorod, fully half of the 12-month audience consisted of those who had entered or re-entered the Radio Liberty audience in that period. In Ufa, the results are even more dramatic: 81% of the 12-month audience consisted of new entrants or re-entrants into the audience.

It is tempting to assume that the new listeners and returnees in the audience are there thanks to rebroadcasting. But while this is largely true, it is not the entire story. In Nizhnii Novgorod the patterns of listening to Radio Liberty on the various wavebands in this half of the audience are quite similar to those described in Table 2 above for the entire 12-month audience. That is, a sizable minority of the entrants and re-entrants listen to broadcasts on SW.

In Ufa, however, the case for rebroadcasting seems stronger in this regard: 72% of the new listeners listen to Liberty exclusively on rebroadcast. The same is true of only 37% of the returnees[2]. Here one should also keep in mind the significant numbers of returnees who, at least for the moment, listen to Radio Liberty on both short and medium waves. In Ufa, for example, they constitute 25% of all returnees. They may, in the future, eventually move over to exclusive medium wave listening. Or, particularly in the event of the loss of a favorite program due to a schedule change (initiated either by Liberty itself or the rebroadcast partner), some listeners to Liberty on both wave bands might, on the contrary, give up "local" listening and return to shortwaves.

Another question of critical importance is whether the new or renewed entrants to the audience will remain as listeners. At the time of the research, rebroadcasting of Liberty's programming had existed in

Nizhnii Novgorod and Ufa for less than a year. The 12 months in Russia prior to the research had seen both their fair share of dramatic political events (e.g., the storming of the White House in Moscow in October, 1993) and the emergence of new radio stations in both cities. Thus, one would expect a certain amount of "experimentation" with the radio dial in this past year, and it would seem reasonable to think that the high figure for new entrants might represent many who heard Liberty while experimenting with the dial. With time, such experimentation can be expected to taper off. Interest in programming and accessibility will play increasingly important roles in these competitive media environments.

The "two" Radio Liberty Audiences.

By making its broadcasts available on FM in Nizhnii Novgorod and MW in Ufa, Radio Liberty has given its real and potential listeners more choice. Just who has made what choice becomes clear upon examination of the demographic characteristics of the audiences on the different wave bands.

It is here that the choice of specific type of rebroadcast arrangement and the identity of the local partner or, rather, its local audience, make themselves felt.

In Nizhnii Novgorod, the demographic profiles of the FM-exclusive and the SW-exclusive audiences differ on a number of points, as was graphically demonstrated by the education levels of the two audiences. In the SW-only audience, 59% of the 12-month listeners have higher education; the comparable figure for the FM-only audience is 35%. Conversely, those with general secondary education or less comprise 41% of the FM-only audience, and only 12% of the SW-only audience. (Note here that the large category of those who could not identify the wave band of listening resembles in its educational profile more the FM-only audience than the SW-only audience).

Although both audiences are dominated by men, the FM-only audience pulls in more women (40%) than the SW-only audience (30%). Also, the SW-only audience is older than the FM-only audience . Seventy percent of the SW-only audience is aged over 40. In contrast, only 45% of the FM-only audience is over 40.

Further indications of differences between the two audiences emerge when profession is examined. Of particular note are the categories "workers", who comprise 30% of the FM-only audience and

12% of the SW-only audience, and "students, pupils", who make up 10% of the FM-only audience and in the sample are completely absent in the SW-only and even mixed wave bands audiences.

These are just general indications that could be used to forecast the future development of the RL audience, including the likelihood that new listeners will remain in the audience. Here it is important to keep in mind that part of the overall RL audience that listens on both wavebands and the particularly significant group of those who cannot name the wave band of listening. These groups are dominated by women and younger people, further indications that they are either now listening (or listened at least once in the last 12 months) to Liberty rebroadcasts on FM or, in the case of listeners on both wave bands, might eventually settle for FM-only listening. Or they might leave the audience altogether.

In Ufa, the disparity between the SW-only audience and the MW-only audiences is less pronounced. There was no differentiation by sex in any of the audiences, including those who listen on both wavebands; in all cases men accounted for 64-66% of the audience.

As in Nizhnii Novgorod, age was a discriminating factor in the audiences to Liberty on the different bands. The MW-only audience in Ufa is younger, with 78% of its members under the age of 40, as opposed to 66% for the SW-only audience.

Education proved to be the most discriminating factor here, but even then, the contrast between the two audiences is not as great as in Nizhnii Novgorod. Of the SW-only audience, 12% had general secondary education as opposed to 31% for the MW-only audience. Respondents with higher education accounted for 22% of the SW-only audience and 20% of the MW audience. Interestingly, the figure for higher education jumps to 32% for the audience to Liberty programs on combined SW and MW.

Radio Liberty and its Rebroadcast Partners: Images, Perceptions, Compatibility.

Of paramount importance in a rebroadcast arrangement involving a local partner station (as opposed to an independent frequency) is the relationship between the international broadcaster and the local station, the "compatibility" of the audiences to the two broadcasters, and specific advertising and on-air announcement services provided by the local rebroadcast partner. For the examination of these questions the focus groups and an analysis of the partner's programming in each city proved to be especially enlightening.

Beyond the basic consideration of type of placement, general listener orientation is extremely important in determining the success of the rebroadcast relationship. There is nothing that says, after all, that someone who listens to popular music cannot also be interested in talk radio; the listener simply has to be prepared for transitions and not subjected to unpleasant surprises.

In Nizhnii Novgorod, the various categories of listeners in the focus groups were generally united in questioning the appropriateness of rebroadcasting to both the local partner and Radio Liberty. (It should be kept in mind that under discussion are impressions from a few focus groups, and these impressions should not be taken to be representative of the views of the Liberty audiences or audiences to the rebroadcast partners in general. Obviously, in spite of the impressions under discussion here, there are clearly important rebroadcast audiences in both cities.)

In view of the abrupt transition from the pleasant, "easy listening" of Randevu to RL's international news and the fast pace of "Liberty Live", a program rich in current political information that comes on at 20:00, it is not surprising that, particularly, some in the group of evening listeners to Randevu expressed a negative attitude to the rebroadcasting of Radio Liberty. They spoke of their fatigue with politics and desire to use the radio to relax. These listeners felt the inappropriateness of RL's broadcasts on a radio station that is neither stylistically nor thematically consonant with Radio Liberty. For them, the contrast between the two stations is, at times, jarring, as illustrated by the comment of a Randevu evening listener (also a lapsed listener to Radio Liberty):

"To put Liberty on Randevu is the same as putting an ad for men's underwear on a cartoon for children." The element of humor aside, this comment should be understood in the context of Russia today, a conservative society coming to terms with the permissiveness of the advertising from the West that has assumed a highly visible place in Russia's television. In the given comparison, the issue is not, of course, the moral quality of Liberty's programming but rather, the appropriateness of its placement.

It is clear that these listeners are not being sufficiently prepared for the transition to Radio Liberty. Most people probably don't watch the clock when listening to popular music, or don't even pay much attention to that music; it is a "background". It is not surprising, then, that the transition at 20:00 is perceived as jarring by some. Specific production measures could probably greatly relieve the negative sensation of the interruption of something pleasant, the "invasion" of politics into the realm of relaxation.

At the same time, most of the regular listeners to Radio Liberty on SW in Nizhnii Novgorod had a negative reaction to the rebroadcasting of Liberty programming. For these long-time listeners to RL, shortwave is an inalienable feature of international broadcasting. Some even complained that Liberty on FM was "too easy" to receive or simply "too local".

More than that, these SW listeners, who were well acquainted with the wide range of Liberty broadcasting in Russian which is available 24 hours daily on SW, voiced the concern that but a small part of the programming was made available on local waves. New listeners on FM, they contended, simply would not be able to appreciate Liberty as they did. Furthermore, to the extent that FM broadcasts are necessarily local in origin, there was some concern on the part of these listeners that the choice of programming to be aired was in the hands of local officials who were not competent to make the selection or who were guided by political considerations in making their choice.

In this, one can see something of an "elite" complex among certain of the traditional SW listeners. Rebroadcasting, in making available to the wide public programming that was previously difficult to receive, of appeal to a small but significant part of society and, in fact, officially discouraged through jamming and media attacks, presents something of a threat to this group.

People Listen to Liberty on FM and Don't Even Understand What It Is. When you listen to the program from 10 in the morning to 1 at night you know all of the service members. But on FM somehow you become separated from them. Everything becomes no longer "ours"; it becomes alien, official.

To be sure, other events in the recent life of Russia, far more significant than the commencement of rebroadcasting, have contributed to this group's perception of loss of status. Nonetheless, for an international SW broadcaster engaged in rebroadcasting, it would seem a good policy to reassure its faithful SW listeners by stressing in its SW announcements and print advertising that rebroadcasting exists for the convenience of the listeners who continue to enjoy the full range of broadcasting only on SW.

For these listeners, it is particularly important to preserve the integrity of the rebroadcast programming. That is, it should not be interrupted even briefly by the local partner for a station identification or commercial.

In Ufa, the focus groups revealed some parallels and some distinct differences with the groups in Nizhnii Novgorod. The principle difference lies in the very nature of Radio Titan, Radio Liberty's rebroadcast partner in Ufa. As opposed to Randevu in Nizhnii Novgorod, Titan was generally perceived to exist precisely for the purpose of rebroadcasting Western international broadcasters. Thus, there is not the inherent conflict with the "home" audience that emerged in Nizhnii Novgorod.

A similarity was the attitude of Liberty's long-time listeners on SW. These, too, revealed a critical attitude towards the local station, distinguishing sharply between the experienced and professionals announcers and journalists of Liberty, and Titan's own announcers, most of whom are young and only beginning to learn the business of radio journalism. Nonetheless, this criticism did not stop these SW listeners from also listening on MW.

Clearly, Titan's strict adherence to its policy of listener orientation plays a positive and important role in attributing to the international broadcaster the responsibility for its product, which in addition to helping avoid a blurring of identities projects the image of a positive collaboration between the local and the international broadcaster.

In fact, as was noted by the focus group moderator in her report, almost all of the representatives of the various groups of the audience were of the opinion that they were the principal audience of Titan. This situation differs from the one in Nizhnii Novgorod, where the traditional listeners to Liberty categorically denied being part of the audience of Radio Randevu and the Randevu audience could be characterized distinctly by their own interests.

In Conclusion.

°Rebroadcasting helps to retain some former SW listeners who, sufficiently satisfied by the quantity and quality of information now available to them have given up shortwaves. New listeners can also be brought into the audience and, if certain conditions are observed, they can be kept there.

°However, rebroadcasting does not automatically guarantee only beneficial results. Arrangements vary, and have greatly differing impacts on the international broadcaster's ability to retain its essential identity and avoid becoming "lost in the crowd".

°The indications from the research are that the "peek-a-boo" type of placement is the least effective because listeners do not retain the source of the programming.

°Wired radio rebroadcasting represents the greatest danger of loss of identity and perception of editorial compromise because it is perceived as official, government radio. In the research examined in this paper, even those focus group participants who were most aware of the complex media situation in their town were confused about the nature of the relationship between BBC, which appears on the wired radio in Russia, and the governmental radio authority in Moscow.

°At least in the former Soviet Union, MW rebroadcasting is preferable to FM rebroadcasting both because the reception range is greater and FM remains relatively new and inaccessible to many radio listeners and potential listeners. The existence of Eastern and Western ranges of FM further confuses the matter.

°Close attention should be paid to the schedule of the rebroadcasts and the local station. The programming which precedes and follows the rebroadcast programming should be analyzed or, if possible, even stipulated in the contract. For example, news or analytical programs which precede the rebroadcast of Liberty's programs will, of course, diminish the listeners' "appetite" for the Liberty programming.

°Local rebroadcast partners should identify the international broadcaster as the source of the rebroadcasts both immediately before and immediately after the programs are aired.

°Even when the agreement between the international broadcaster and the local partner station grants the partner station the right to use as much of the international broadcaster's programming as desired, partners should inform the international broadcaster on a continual basis of all changes and additions to the partner station's schedule.

°If possible, partner stations should advertise both their station and the international rebroadcasts. At the same time, it would be desirable for the international broadcaster to arrange for its own advertising on a regular basis.

°Rebroadcast partners should not be allowed to interrupt live or taped rebroadcasts with advertisements or their own station identification.

VALENTINA ZLOBINA
HEAD, AUDIENCE RESERACH
RADIO MOSCOW INTERNATIONAL
MOSCOW - RUSSIA

**The effectiveness of audience research.
Its influence on broadcasting policy.**

Today we are facing one of the most important tasks - to understand whom and what information to address. As never before we are working in close contact with broadcasting services, their heads, journalists and announcers. The leadership of Radio Moscow International attaches great significance to the study of its audience. In his Christmas address to foreign listeners, the head of Radio Moscow International, Armen Oganessian, said that the effectiveness of information programmes would be increased, the format of broadcasting would be revised. All the changes would be introduced with taking into account the audience's opinions.

We understand that we should conduct our audience research to improve our broadcasting, to determine new directions of our programmmes in the new world information and political space.

The research planned for 1993-94 is designed to receive practically important information for broadcasting. We try to analyse the effectiveness of our research for our broadcasting policy. We intend to carry out a second analysis of information in various directions and a content analysis of those programmes which have the audience's opionions. To a certain extent our research have exercies influence on the decisons taken by the Board of Directors of Radio Moscow International.

There are some examples to illustrate the above points.

In December 1993 - January 1994 a fax survey of listeners of the information service in German was conducted. That was an experimental survey. It had never been conducted before by Russia's sociological services. The survey was designed to determine the attitude of the German-speaking audience to the coverage of Russia's election campaign and Russia's parliamentary elections on December 12, 1993. The respondents were the listeners who maintained regular correspondence with Radio Moscow's German Service by fax. Most of the respondents live in Germany's western provinces with a high living standard. Though their attitude to the coverage of Russia's election campaign is not representative for the German audience as a whole, it makes it possible to receive general information about the work of Radio Moscow in a difficult political situation.

Elections are an extremely difficult topic for foreign audiences. Unknown political realities, unknown names, a great number of political parties and candidates, difficulties of election campaign - all these create problems of understanding. The survey was designed to determine whether Radio Moscow's programmes met the requirements of the audience; whether the amount of information was enough and to what degree the information was accurate and intelligible.

The survey was conducted in two stages. At the first stage a questionnaire was sent to all the participants. The respondents were to answer how often they tuned in to Radio Moscow International during the election campaign in Russia, to express their opinion about the programmes of Radio Moscow of that period and about the special program about the election campaign WAHLKURIER, which had been prepared by Radio Moscow German Service.

At the second stage, the respondents selected by the researcher were to make their opinion more precise. Off all the respondents only one listener criticized Radio Moscow programmes during the election campaign, Bernhard Klink, 44, a highschool teacher. This listener was then asked

The listener to make his opinion more precise. He stated that there was not much background information; in his opinion such information must be accompanied by commentaries. The listener advised Radio Moscow to abandon its formal tone, banalities, lengthy discussions which have nothing to add to the analysis of events.

Practically every day from November 9, 1993 until the election on December 12, 1993 Radio Moscow German Service broadcast its program WAHLKURIER, the Herald of the election campaign. There were 33 editions of the program. At first it lasted for 5-6 minutes and consisted of press and news agencies reports, sound materials or Radio Moscow, reports by Radio Moscow correspondents, experts' opinions, voters' views and public opinion polls.

The listeners were unanimous in describing the program as good. So, why none of the respondents gave the excellent mark? The respondents were asked by fax to give a precise answer. Of the 14 pollees 8 responded to the request. The analysis of their opinions shows that the German audience is not inclined to give an excellent mark to political programmes.

The fax survey of German listeners was supplemented by a content-analysis of this special program. It helped to assess content components of the feature, the authors' approach to selecting information, the character of the sources used, the existence of appraisal elements, subjects of interviews etc.

The research was carried out at the request of the Board of Directors of Radio Moscow International and Radio Moscow Service. Its results were discussed by the staff of Radio Moscow German Service. It was decided that the results must be taken into consideration in covering other election campaigns.

The second example. At the request of the authors and hosts of the program "The Direct Link" which is on the air for Spanish speaking countries, the Audience Research Service carried out a poll among listeners who maintained regular correspondence with Radio Moscow. It was designed to find out the audience's attitude to the program. Six hundred questionnaires were sent to the audience in the Spanish-speaking countries. Ninety five questionnaires from 13 countries were returned.

The program was criticized within the Spanish Service of Radio Moscow for its subjective approach in presenting Russia's problems, forcing its ideas upon listeners, not always taking into account listeners' questions, views and opinions. There was talk about closing down the program. The research revealed that the audience rated the presenters very high and that the program itself was very popular with the listeners.

The result of the poll showed that the listeners tried not to miss any edition of the bi-weekly program. The researchers found out that the program was of great interest to the listeners of all ages who appreciated it for its high informative content and debating approaches.

The respondents underlined that the program made it possible for them to understand much better the situation in Russia. At the same time the research highlighted some shortcomings of the program: the listeners criticized it for being too politicized and for its excessively serious, edifying tone.

The research helped the programmers of the Spanish Service to review firmly their position. There was a special edition of the program on the air and thus the audience was informed about the results of its participation in the poll.

Radio Moscow conducts its regular audience opinions research quite often. Potential audience is studied rarely. One such research was conducted with a group of young Japanese (20 people), who studied at the Pushkin Institute of the Russian Language in Moscow. The participants of the study were asked to fill in a questionnaire. Later, a discussion took place about the program "The Youth's Wave". The program has been on the air for decades. Here are some of the results of the study.

In view of the sample audience listeners in Japan take interest in every day life of the Russian people, in Russian literature, art and culture, Russia's national customs and traditions. Such potential audience is also interested in Russian-Japanese relations and economic reforms which are now under way in Russia. This proves the right thematic direction of broadcasting.

The sample group named their national mass media and their teachers of Russian as the main sources of information about Russia. However, Japanese mass-media, in the respondents' view, do not give enough information about Russia. That is why all the members of the group would like to listen to radio and watch TV programs from Russia in Japanese, rebroadcast by Japan's networks.

During the discussion of the program "The Youth's Wave" it turned out that the program was interesting for those listeners who already had information about life in Russia. For the public at large, the program is too difficult in its contents and language, its style is completely unacceptable.

The participants in the discussion were unanimous that the program should be dynamic, simple and with modern music. Serious topics have no place in such a program for the Japanese youth. The study determined that the concept of the program needs to be urgently revised.

The above-mentioned research studies are part of the analytical program conducted by our Service. The program provides for the research of the audience's attitude to the programs of Radio Moscow International.

For the last two years the main direction of our activity has been to determine the role and mandate of Radio Moscow International in the new political situation. At the request of the Board of Directors of Radio Moscow, we conducted a survey using casual interviews. Members of Russia's leadership, officials of the Russian Foreign Ministry, psychologists, journalists, public figures, writers, and scholars are taking part in the research as experts. The team of experts includes Russian and foreign researchers. The first research was conducted in August of 1992.

Many recommendations from the first study have been acted upon. The most important change is that Radio Moscow International, according to the Russian President's decree, has acquired its new status as an independent broadcasting company, called the Voice of Russia. The question of its status was one of the main points in the research.

The formation of the CIS and the transformation of the former Soviet republics into independent countries in their own right has confronted RMI with the task of initiating broadcasts to the former republics of the USSR in their national languages. This, in the opinion of the experts, would enhance trust in RMI, would enable Russia to retain and strengthen its information presence in those countries, and would promote the flow of information between states. Thus, we do all we can to give new momentum to the work of our services and we try to provide them with new and more detailed information about the audience.

KIM A. ELLIOTT
AUDIENCE RESEARCH OFFICER
VOICE OF AMERICA
WASHINGTON. D.C. - USA

Voice of America and Audience Research.

Audience research has definitely made a difference in how the Voice of America is spending its money in these transitional times. A few years ago, we were looking at some audience data from Thailand showing consistently small audiences for our shortwave broadcasting in Thai. So the decision was made to curtail, to cut down our Thai service and eliminate all the shortwave broadcasts in Thai in favour of telephone feeds to domestic radio stations in Thailand. This is probably a successful effort because it gets on good stations at good times. We have to do some research to find out how successful that is.

We also saw some research from Germany, finding consistently small audiences for our service in German on shortwave and direct medium wave and also some surveys showing that German radio stations who are not independent radio stations are not all that interested in taking VOA German programming so the German service of VOA was eliminated about a year ago, even though it was a very talented service.

For Spanish and Portuguese, to Latin America, we have found consistent findings showing small audiences for shortwave in that part of the world because unlike other developing regions of the world, there's a very intense competitive pluralistic broadcasting system in Latin America and less incentive to listen to foreign shortwave broadcasting. As a result, VOA is no longer broadcasting in Spanish and Portuguese to Latin America on weekends on shortwave. In fact, it's looking like very soon, VOA will not be broadcasting in Spanish and Portuguese to Latin America at all on shortwave but there will be at least some token shortwave remaining but this is all in deference to satellite feeds to local radio stations in Latin America.

Also in Central Europe, Eastern Europe, the former communist countries, we've cut back quite a bit in our shortwave broadcasting in deference to rebroadcasting, especially on FM. Our evening Hungarian on shortwave is now history. That is in deference to an FM broadcast that's heard on the Kossuth Radio FM network. We've also cut back on the shortwave and are using more FM in the Baltic republics.

Our mainstay of research of course is sample surveys inside the countries but I'm also using a technique that was inspired by the BBC's "Can you hear me?" method which is asking questions on the air and we do that. We ask our listeners to tell us "what time are you hearing this announcement and on what frequency are you hearing this announcement". We did this recently in our Polish service and got 10,000 responses. We had a drawing for a small shortwave radio as an incentive. It showed that about 50% of our audience in Poland was listening via the Munich medium wave relay, 25% still on shortwave and about 25% listening on FM. We're only on FM in four cities in Poland representing about 4% of the population, getting 25% of our audience. It shows that FM is effective, if you can get it.

Here are some of the main findings that I've found after looking at the research data over the years. One is the importance of resources. To succeed in international broadcasting, you have to have a good signal, good programming and a convenient schedule. You need to concentrate those resources as much as possible. I think one of the reasons for the BBC's success is that it has been able to concentrate its resources into one international broadcasting organization and borrow from the resources of the domestic BBC. Whereas in the United States, we have two competing government financed international broadcasters not able to borrow to a large extent from the domestic resources.

Also, the importance of media deficient countries, and Graham Mytton's data base research has really shown, that in countries where there are government monopolies, this is where we seem to have the largest audiences for international radio. So we can't overlook countries like Bangladesh and Nigeria where there are some very big audiences even though they might not be at the top of the foreign policy agenda for the United States and for some of the other countries.

The importance of language. Sometimes, we Americans and other people in English speaking countries seem to think that if you speak English loud enough, people will understand. Audience research has shown that is really not the case. We've had very good success in our broadcasts in Hindi to India vis-à-vis our broadcasts in English, broadcasts in Bengali to Bangladesh vis-à-vis English, broadcasts in Hausa to Nigeria versus broadcasts in English for both BBC and VOA. One gets a great deal of economy out of using the local national language.

Finally, the audience listens to international radio, really, to seek reliable news - news that is more reliable than what they're getting from their own media at home, especially news about their own country. That is really the bread and butter of international broadcasting - providing news about a country to people in countries where that news is not available in the domestic media. The audience avoids propaganda, in fact it, uses international broadcasting as an antidote to propaganda. Using international broadcasting to sell a country or to promote a country, I don't think will really bear much fruit.

Finally, looking at the research over the last few years, I'm tempted always to build theory from it and I'd like to present one here, even though it may be completely bogus but it's a theory, nonetheless. We've been talking today about rebroadcasting. My view from looking at the media and the data and the research from international broadcasting is that there is rebroadcasting and there is rebroadcasting. One form I call "rebroadcasting" and the other I call "placement" which is really the VOA term for rebroadcasting. It comes out like this:

° Direct radio and TV is the traditional direct radio via shortwave, direct radio via medium wave, where you can get it, then soon to be direct radio and TV by way of satellite.

° Rebroadcasting is leasing or other acquisition of time on domestic or radio television stations in the target country. In other words, you get 30 minutes or 60 minutes or 3 hours. An example would be Radio Free Europe in the Czech Republic on medium wave. That's rebroadcasting because you have leased 12 hours a day, you've gone into competition with the Czech domestic radio.

° Whereas placement is where you integrate your programming with the programming of the domestic radio and TV service, usually short segments of programming, usually placed on an irregular basis. An example of that would be the BBC reports heard on "All Things Considered" which is a very influential public radio program in the United States. I think these same BBC reports are heard on "The World at 6" and Sunday mornings on some of the CBC programs here in Canada.

Looking at the difference between these two, direct radio and TV is of course direct whereas the other two involve a gate-keeper and that, of course, is the route. In fact, in the case of placement, it's a much more meddlesome gate-keeper than it is with just rebroadcasting where you might have a cable system that really doesn't care what you broadcast but if things get really bad, could pull the plug on you.

Also differentiating the three types of broadcasting, the direct radio usually involves long form programming: 30 minutes, 60 minutes, maybe 90 minutes or 2 hours. So does the rebroadcasting. Whereas the placement involves short form programming: 3-4-5 minutes reports mixed into the programming. This is a very different kind of international broadcasting.

I think the outcome for direct radio and for rebroadcasting is going to be smaller elite audiences for that kind of broadcasting. Maybe CNN on the cable systems is the ultimate form of rebroadcasting, and BBC World Service TV too. But I think the larger audiences are going to be by way of that placement because there is an adage "If you can't beat them, join them". It may be trite but I think it provides the foundation for a good theory for international broadcasting. Of course, you are subject to a gate-keeper and that's the price, I think, international broadcasters will have to pay for larger audiences.

So the two-prong theory I was referring to really comes down to this: Larger audiences for short segments of programming via placement. Small but elite audiences for long form programming via direct radio, TV, or via rebroadcasting. Put those two together and I think you could have a very interesting and useful and fruitful international broadcasting operation.

By the way, how small is small? When does your audience get so small that it's not worth the money? I think it's to the point where it's cheaper to fly out and visit your listeners and talk to them directly rather than broadcast. At that point, it's probably a good argument maybe to get out of the direct broadcasting business.

ROBERT S. FORTNER
DIRECTOR OF RESERACH
CALVIN COLLEGE AND INTERSEARCH
GRAND RAPIDS, MI - USA

The Changing Environment.

Most audiences for Christian missionary radio are so small that there is little apparent effect on existing audiences. The changing environment's principal impact is that it will become increasingly difficult to develop audiences, despite the efforts of the missionary broadcasting community - FEBA, FEBC, HCJB, SIM International, and TWR - to broadcast in every language of the world with more than 1 million native speakers by the year 2000. The changing environment makes it increasingly difficult to justify this effort. One example of this broadcasting community responding to the changing environment is the decision by TWR to abandon shortwave broadcasting into Latin America and to collaborate with HCJB to provide satellite feeds to Latin America domestic radio stations. By contrast, FEBC has been reluctant to give up the KGEI San Francisco shortwave operation aimed into Latin America despite audience research data indicating little awareness, or listening to it, outside its first hop coverage in Mexico. Existing staff and facilities unsuitable for other use conspire to keep KGEI in operation, although the expense of continuing the operation has now begun to erode commitment to it. I suspect it will leave the air sometime in 1994.

Audience Targets.

Audience research still has some way to go to begin to change management perceptions about targets and efficient means to reach them. Last week the board of Directors of FEBC agreed that audience reserch management summaries should have the widest possible distribution within the organization - to include the Board itself - and FEBC's CEO will begin to see the reports for the first time since they began to be produced two years ago. At TWR, the new Assistant to the President has asked for a training proposal that would begin the process of showing how audience research information can be integrated into strategic planning and program production decisions, and the consortium for audience research of several of the major Christian broadcasters has asked to make a seminar presentation to the CEO's of these organizations to demonstrate the value of audience research. At best, however, this community is barely underway in using research for strategic planning, audience targeting, and programming decisions.

Measuring Excellence.

The consortium will begin to measure listener perceptions of quality for the first time later this year, using focus groups conducted in target languages on-site.

Justifying Broadcasting Activity.

Justification within the Christian missionary radio community does not follow the model used within the "secular" community. It is different on two counts. First, this community does not seek on-going funds from the public purse to fund its activities. Money comes from individual donors who respond to fund appeals or who have on-going commitments to radio evangelism, from foundations likewise committed to those activities, from denominational general revenues, and from payments provided by program suppliers who pay for the air time provided from this third source. This funding mix both makes it difficult to change programs that are controlled by external suppliers and reduces the necessity to justify activities. Second, an increasing amount of Christian missionary programming is produced as part of a strategy that involves a variety of other media and non-media activities. TWR, for instance, promotes the use of solar cookers produced by other organizations in Kenya aimed at reducing deforestation. FEBA provides agricultural information in cooperation with the Christian relief organizations, World Vision, in southern Africa. FEBC cooperates with Christian literature organizations to train pastors in Asia. In such cases, broadcasting is not an end in itself and the goal is not maximum audience size. Justification comes in reaching a target audience, even if small, to get a specific end accomplished goal.

> FEBA = Far East Broadcasting Association
> FEBC = Far East Broadcasting Company
> HCJB = Heralding Christ Jesus' Blessings
> SIM = Sudanese Interior Mission

LYNN E. GUTSTADT
VICE-PRESIDENT, AUDIENCE RESERACH - CNN
ATLANTA, GA. - USA

CNN - A Global TV Network and Its Audience.

It seems particularly appropriate that I feel a little like a fish out of water today, both in my position representing a global TELEVISION network, as well as a commercial venture which is supported in most cases by both direct subscriber fees, as well as advertising revenues.

But, as has been referred to in many of the earlier sessions, given the dramatic changes that many of you are seeing in your industry, I hope my talk will be of interest to you.

First I'm going to describe CNN International, its history and current structure.

Second, I'd like to try and directly tackle the topic of this morning's panel, and explain how we at CNN address "Measuring Excellence and Efficiency" for a global TV network.

Third, I will touch very briefly on some of our future measurement plans.

Development: CNN International began broadcasting to Europe in 1985. The network is now available (unofficially) in over 210 countries and territories. When I say unofficially, this means all of the locations where we know we are received, not necessarily limited to those locations which are licensed to receive us.

Officially, we are seen in over 47.5 million homes and locations (outside North America) on a 24 hour basis, and an additional 26 million homes with partial day reception, and last but not least, in 580,000 hotel rooms.

Satellite distribution: The company has spent the past several years ensuring that, by the end of this year, CNNI will have the best possible satellite distribution available throughout the world.

This map, while fairly recent, is probably already out of date and, as mentioned earlier, CNNI will soon be seen from the Apstar satellite launching this summer.

Newsgathering: CNN International has available to it all of the newsgathering resources of CNN, including: 20 international bureaus, 9 domestic U.S. bureaus, 200 international TV affiliates which include a number of your organizations, and over 350 domestic U.S. affiliates.

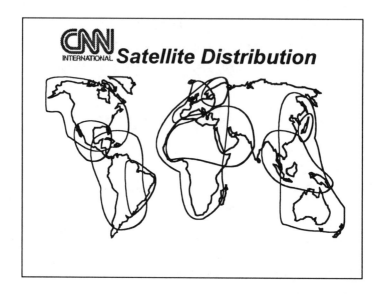

Programming: Although many of our international and domestic partners contribute material to the network, CNN International's programming is 100% original to the CNN organization, and broadcasts globally 24 hours-a-day, 7 days-a-week.

Three separate programming feeds, one to Europe, Africa and the Middle East, one to South and Central America, and one to Asia and the Pacific Rim, allow us to sell regional advertising and to customize programming for each region.

The programming on the three international feeds combines some CNN domestic programming with many programs developed exclusively for the international service.

International Programming: A sampling of the programs produced exclusively for CNN International includes: "World Business Today", "Business Asia", "World News Updates" throughout the day, "Diplomatic License" which is a new program about the United Nations, and "Noticieros CNN" which is a Spanish language news program exclusively produced for the South American feed.

"World Report", a program which many of you are familiar with, and indeed may contribute to, is not an exclusive international program but is aired by the domestic network as well.

Measuring excellence & efficiency: For CNNI research, "excellence" and "efficiency" really break down into the areas of "what we want to know" and "how we find it out".

To establish the "excellence" and value of our service to viewers, distributors and advertisers, we research the quality of our current audience, focusing on senior managers and business travellers, (in many ways rather more like a magazine or a regional newspaper than a traditional broadcaster), and the perceived quality of our programming so that we can continue to better target the programming on each of our regional feeds.

Typically, the term "efficiency" refers to the relationship between the audience and the financial support of the network, that is, finding the most efficient way to reach a target audience.

From my perspective, however, I wanted to take a slightly different approach and look at the efficiencies of how we use our limited research dollars to collect as much information about our audiences as possible. We use existing measurement services, we do collaborative projects with both colleagues within the industry as well as non media organizations, and we purchase syndicated data where it is available. However, because this information comes far from telling the whole story, we also rely heavily on custom research studies.

Quality audience: CNNI has been profiling the quality of our audience for many years. Since 1987, we have carried out a survey of viewers in hotels which receive CNNI. Given that CNNI is distributed heavily in three and four star hotels, this is indeed a quality audience, primarily business travellers.

We have also studied, through phone and mail surveys, random populations of senior managers in Europe and Asia, as well as used a mail follow-up to the International Air Travellers Survey to again focus on the upscale, business-oriented nature of the CNNI audience.

What I'm going to do is show you some examples, from a number of our studies, of the kind of information which we use to promote advertising and distribution sales. As you might expect, it will all be very positive!

Hotel viewing study: A concern of some of our advertisers is that CNNI is only viewed by U.S. business travellers abroad.

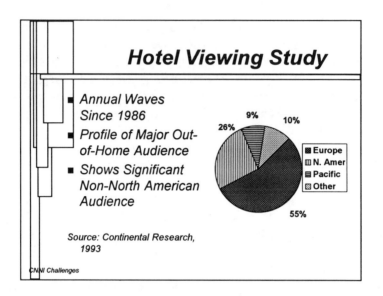

But as you can see from the graph from the most recent wave of the Hotel Viewing Study, CNNI's hotel audience is primarily European in origin, with only one-quarter consisting of North American viewers.

Seniour managers' viewing: The Senior Managers Viewing Study was conducted last year, in 17 European countries, and the results can be projected to a universe of 2.9 million Senior Managers.

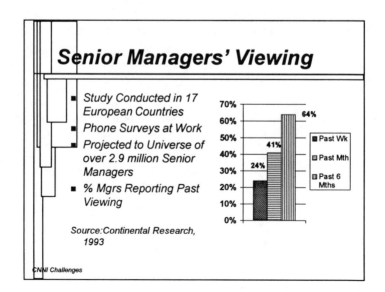

This chart shows that of all respondents, 24% reported viewing CNNI in the last week, 41% in the past month, and 64% in the last 6 months. As I mentioned before, this is a sample of data we use to position CNNI to advertisers and it does this more similarly to a print medium, focusing on our target audience and emphasizing the reach rather than average audience to the service.

Quality programming: To determine the perceived quality of our programming, we utilize attitudinal and comparative measures in quantitative studies, as well as carrying out qualitative studies with our target audience.

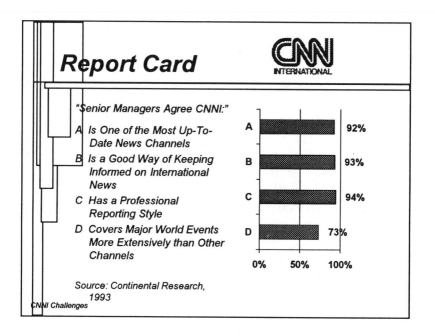

Report Card

CNN INTERNATIONAL

"Senior Managers Agree CNNI:"

A Is One of the Most Up-To-Date News Channels — A 92%

B Is a Good Way of Keeping Informed on International News — B 93%

C Has a Professional Reporting Style — C 94%

D Covers Major World Events More Extensively than Other Channels — D 73%

0% 50% 100%

Source: Continental Research, 1993

CNNI Challenges

For example, among European Senior Managers reporting any viewing to CNNI, well over 90% of them agree that CNNI is: "One of the most up-to-date news channels"; "A good way of keeping informed on international news"; and "Has a professional reporting style". And close to three-quarters of them feel that CNNI covers major world events more extensively than other channels.

And, since I couldn't resist needling my friend Graham here a little, I had to include a comparison of viewing to CNNI and BBC-WSTV by Senior Managers in Japan, Taiwan, Hong Kong and Singapore.

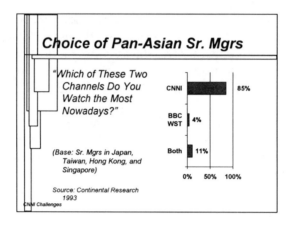

As you can see, the question was "Which of these two channels do you watch the most nowadays?" and CNN International does come out quite strongly at about 85%.

Targeted focus groups: Late last year, we carried out a series of focus groups with business men and women in eight European countries. Interestingly, the image that CNNI carries with it internationally is quite similar to how it is perceived domestically.

It is perceived to have a global perspective. It is perceived to be more objective than local news sources. It is strongly perceived as a first source for breaking news - we are constantly told how much people watched CNN during the Gulf War. They liked the fact they can always get a news update pretty much when they want it, which is more or less the case actually since there are some blocks of programming that aren't really news updates but again, the perception is you can get news anytime you want it. There was also a strong perception that CNN International, because it is available everywhere these people travel, and they do travel considerably, is "like a friend"; that they can find the same consistent information wherever they go.

Expanding reach: On the more quantitative side, to continue measuring CNNI's expanding reach, we rely on: existing TV measurement systems, "hitchhiking" questions onto very large international consumer research studies, and taking advantage of a number of ad hoc collaborative studies.

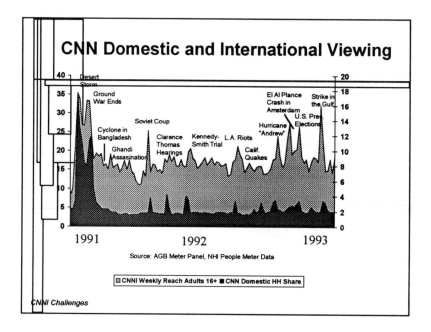

CNN Domestic and International Viewing

Source: AGB Meter Panel, NHI People Meter Data

CNNI Weekly Reach Adults 16+ ■ CNN Domestic HH Share

We use a few available sources of metered TV viewing date (from the Netherlands and Greece) to demonstrate that viewing to CNNI, directionally, generally parallels domestic viewing in the U.S. - that is, it rises and falls with the compelling international (and some domestic) events covered on the network. This kind of information indicates that the viewing to CNNI is probably not that different from a lot of the viewing in the U.S. We have a considerable amount of information domestically so we can try to extrapolate the domestic viewing to some degree to international viewing levels.

In some ways, this is an "apples to oranges" comparison in that the U.S. data represents a weekly SHARE or percentage of total viewing within the network's coverage area, while the data from the Netherlands represents the REACH of the network or the percentage of those within the universe who tune in to the network at least once per week.

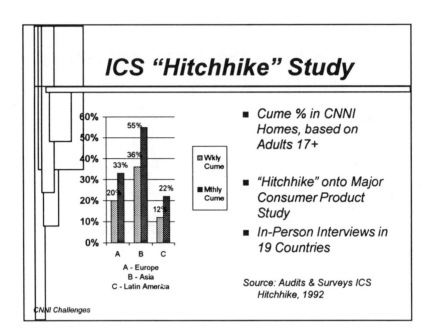

ICS "Hitchhike" Study

- Cume % in CNNI Homes, based on Adults 17+
- "Hitchhike" onto Major Consumer Product Study
- In-Person Interviews in 19 Countries

A - Europe
B - Asia
C - Latin America

Source: Audits & Surveys ICS Hitchhike, 1992

CNNI Challenges

For the last two years, we have been fortunate in having been allowed to "hitchhike" some television and CNNI viewing questions onto a major international consumer product survey. This chart show self-reported weekly and monthly reach viewing levels by adults 17+ in CNNI homes, in Europe, Asia and Latin America. This is total adults 17+ as opposed to the Senior Managers, again an attempt to get some degree of the broader audience beyond the upscale target audience.

And finally, we have used a combination of all these quantitative measures to estimate the global reach of the CNN services. We calculate, based on 1992 data, that some 45 million homes, on a weekly basis, or 33% of all those receiving the networks, tune in each week. Also, close to 70 million homes tune in each month, or slightly over 50% of receiving locations.

Future plans: In the future, plans to measure the excellence and efficiency of CNNI include:

(1) Continuing to develop custom research as needed for advertising and distribution purposes;

(2) Expanding our qualitative programming research, by region, to allow for further customization of our programming, and;

(3) Working with research vendors and our competitors and colleagues to develop REGIONAL SYNDICATED MEASUREMENT

SERVICES, a process that we have already underway with proposed projects in Asia and Latin America. What we are finding is that advertisers want to know, from a single source, what kind of viewing is going on within Asia or within Europe. There have been some attempts over the years, in Europe, to do a regional measurement service. It's difficult. We are going to try it again in Asia, first starting with the distribution study and eventually going to viewing that will allow us to compete on an equal basis among all of the new regional satellite services. It should be an interesting few years.

COMMENT:

Graham Mytton:

I'd just like to endorse and underline what Lynn said. You are all aware that in radio and television, in the developed world anyway, and increasingly in Eastern Europe and in parts of Africa and Asia, there are agreements between broadcasting stations about audience measurement, because there is nothing worse than different radio stations and television stations arguing with each other about the size and reach of their audiences. It's very important that CNNI and the BBC World Service Television and other international television broadcasters don't disagree with each other over the size and reach of audiences. So I'd like to say publicly that I agree with what Lynn just said about sharing the syndicated studies and trying to find some common agreement.

GRAHAM MYTTON
HEAD, AUDIENCE RESEARCH & CORRESPONDENCE
BBC WORLD SERVICE
LONDON - U.K.

I think what Lynn just said, perhaps, underlined the great difference between a lot of publicly funded broadcasting and commercial broadcasting. No self-respecting broadcaster would dream of broadcasting without doing a substantial amount of research. But often international radio broadcasting happens without any research at all.

And I'm going to be quite provocative now in the hope that I can stir this conference up into a certain amount of steam, if not outright anger!

There's an awful lot of international radio broadcasting which actually doesn't reach anybody, or reaches such a small number that it's not worth doing. It becomes a bit like a national airline or overseas embassy, a kind of badge of being a country. One is rarely asked to justify this activity, until now, that is. Most of it reaches almost nobody. Its justification is in existing at all. And in case anybody is thinking that I, from the BBC, am pointing at other stations here, may I say that there are one or two languages at the BBC of which this is true. When I say so, within the BBC I am not thanked for saying so. But some languages in the BBC... well, wild horses won't get out of me which ones those are today!

International public-funded broadcasting has had little reason up until now to justify itself. What I would argue is that this situation is changing. The reason we haven't had to justify ourselves is because we're not involved in advertising and not involved in sales. It seems to be a justification in itself just to continue the activity because it's there. Can this any longer be justified?

There is a thing happening within the public sector: greater demand for accountability and a greater demand for publicly funded bodies to justify what they do. So how do we justify what we do? I'm just going to make some suggestions about some of the things that are done and some of the ways in which we do it.

Most of us are being required to examine much more carefully what we do in order to provide value for money, to provide some kind of proof that we're doing what we set out to do. Obviously you have to have targets and priorities. What are they and how do you set them?

The first thing you need to decide is to work out what your objectives are. I'm going backwards here because it is, in a way, a process of going backwards when one is thinking about these things. For objectives, you need to have some kind of reason for existence in the first place. We talked about a mission statement or something of that kind.

Audience research has a pivotal position in this. Let's just think about it a bit further. Let's think about the way in which we operate in our organizations. Obviously some of the things we have to do is to challenge complacency - we've heard a lot about how organizations get stuck in a way of doing things for years and years and never actually ask questions about why they're doing it, on what basis they're doing it, and where they get their information from, to make those decisions about doing things.

Measuring Excellence and Efficiency

When I was first in audience research in the BBC, which I've been doing now for 11 years, the department existed really to justify what we did already. In other words, no matter what it was, my department existed to defend and protect all BBC services because it was taken as a priori, they were good. They were wonderful, they were meeting listeners' needs. We didn't need to find out; all audience research had to do was to prove that was so. Well I've changed that and I've started to challenge this complacency of the early days. I think it's very important that audience research does that.

The next point is to understand the audience. Not to put things from the organizational points of view but to put things from the audience point of view. To understand the audience and go from there to set realistic goals. There's no point in the BBC saying "We want to reach an audience on shortwave in Japan, in Japanese" because it's not possible. There's just not enough people any longer listening to shortwave in Japan to make it worthwhile, so we closed the service. This was the first example, by the way, in BBC history, of the BBC making a decision itself about closing a shortwave service because audience research showed that there were no longer any listeners and it's pointless broadcasting to Japan, in Japanese at this time. So we had a pivotal role in helping to make decisions like that.

We need to understand the market. I'm sorry to use this word but it is an important word to help us understand what we're doing. We are engaged in marketing a service, a broadcasting service. We need to understand that market. To do so, research is not a luxury, it is essential.

Also the research has to be recent. If you've got information that's three or four years old, it's almost certainly wrong. Especially if it's in the rapidly changing media circumstances of the Asian region, for example. Things move somewhat slower in the poorer areas of Africa, but even there things are moving surprisingly fast in some cases.

Audience research helps us to set realistic targets. I mentioned the case of Japan but there are many other examples you can give. We've been looking recently at opening an Uzbek service. We did some research just over a year ago in Uzbekistan which showed that there is very little shortwave there. In fact a lot of households do not have wireless radios. They have radio toczka, the wired radio. So the impact of any international broadcasting in Uzbekistan is liable to be somewhat limited. As long as you're prepared to accept that, then go ahead with an international service. BBC now needs to think very carefully whether it is worth broadcasting shortwave to Uzbekistan given the very limited audience that is there for shortwave broadcasting. Maybe there is some other way of reaching audiences there.

What can be achieved and where, but also what are audience needs? It's no good saying "We want to broadcast because we want people to know more about the Republic of Ruritania". It is a laughable concept that somehow or other a country like Britain should decide that we need to broadcast in order to promote Britain everywhere. I can just see people in different countries saying "I want to learn more about Britain and to think more highly of them, I'm going to go and buy a radio set so I can listen to them and think more highly of Britain as a result." I mean it is ridiculous. Things don't work like that. People don't listen to Radio Bulgaria, or Radio Albania, or Voice of America in order to think better of those countries. They listen to those radio stations only if they provide things that other stations do not, or add something to the medium.

Remember what I said earlier this morning about the situation in the Gulf War? The reason foreign stations like Radio France Internationale, BBC, Voice of America and other Arab stations were listened to is because they provided information that helped people work out what was going on. They didn't listen to the BBC to think better of Britain.

Yet, we are now under pressure in Britain, to increase the amount of content that we have about Britain, and there's quite a lot of discussion going on. People are now asking the BBC World Service: "How much are you reflecting British events? How much are you reflecting British science, British invention, British culture?" We have to say very patiently to them: "You may like us to do that, but we have to remind you that listeners don't come to us primarily for that purpose." They come to us to fill in the information gaps and so on. I could go on for hours on that one, but I won't...

Then we have the problem of why is so little research done? It's extraordinary how much international broadcasting goes on without research. At the BBC we are now spending 2.5 million pounds in the current financial year on research. There are still enormous gaps in our knowledge. Then, having done that research, why is there sometimes so little attention paid to what little research is done? That is also true in the BBC. There are still decisions made, I think, which are not sufficiently informed by research.

However, research can't do everything. As a former producer - I was a producer in the BBC for 10 years - I would have resented very much audience research people telling me how to make programs. There is no substitute for creativity, imagination and good program ideas. But research can help inform them and that's what it should be doing.

The message is you can't survive without relevant research information unless the people funding you are myopic or incompetent. That's a thought to review for a moment. I've got another one coming up.

You can't afford to do research and not use it. There's no point in doing research if you're not going to make use of it, especially if you're trying to work out what your impact is and how you can change and reform yourself in order to meet new challenges, to meet new audience needs, to look for new audience targets. You can't do without research, unless of course, your funder is incompetent and myopic, but also immortal. I don't know if it's a fortunate situation but when your funding just goes on and on, and nobody ever asks any questions, then I suppose you don't really need to do research. That is unless you really are involved in the business of broadcasting to really maximize your impact, to maximize the kind of value you put into the world. This surely should be the primary objective of all international broadcasting as a public service to the world in which we live.

Whether we're commercial broadcasters or publicly funded broadcasters, we're in the business of adding something of value to human life. At least that's why I went into broadcasting in the first place. It may sound a bit corny in these days when everything is measured in terms of value for money and bottom line money. It seems to me there's no point in radio or television broadcasting of any kind unless we're actually trying to improve the quality of life and the information and entertainment that people have.

I'm going to finish with one other thing because I wanted to kill stone dead a little thing that keeps flying around. Shortwave is not dying! The other point is about the inexorable growth of television. I want to show you a slide I did for a presentation I gave recently to the Christian station FEBA.

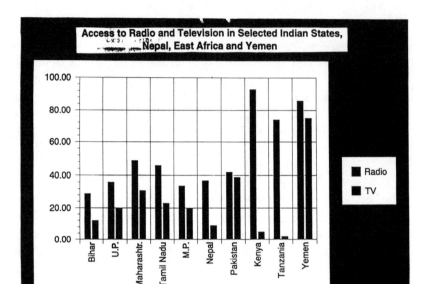

Access to Radio and Television in Selected Indian States, Nepal, East Africa and Yemen

I just put together some data from four states in India and in East Africa and Yemen. The first columns represent access by household, in these areas, to radio. The second column represents access to television. You'll see how in Yemen, this is largely as a result of the people who go to work in Saudi Arabia, bringing back money with them and being able to buy television sets and bring them back. There's a high point of penetration of television in Yemen. But look how low it is in Kenya and Tanzania. The interesting thing is that in India, radio is hardly changing. It's reaching a plateau at between 30% and 50% according to the wealth of the state, and it's not going up any higher. Television is rapidly reaching the same point. We have a situation in India where television is increasingly reaching the same people who have been reached by radio. Neither are meeting the needs of a large number of people, in some states the majority have no access to either.

Look at the contrast in Africa. We think of Africa as being even poorer but radio has a better penetration in Africa than in India. I will just give you that as an example of the kind of data that is so important for what you are all doing. These people here, by the way, all have shortwave, less in India. But in Africa, you can hardly see a radio set without shortwave because most African broadcasting still depends on shortwave.

QUESTIONS AND COMMENTS:

Discussion.

Derek White:

Please clarify the use of the figures for reach presented by Lynn, and also the ones we use as international broadcasters. One's domestic colleagues can get fairly sarcastic if you use a figure for reach that says "15 minutes a month" or "five minutes a year" or "one contact every six weeks". What are we referring to here as the standard measure of reach for international broadcasters? Is the one being used by Lynn the same, for television? What should it be if it's to have real effect?

Graham Mytton:

Among the radio broadcasters, we tend to use weekly reach or regular audience, which means more or less weekly audience. We do not expect listening to foreign radio to be of the same order as listening to domestic radio. It's not intended to be. It doesn't pitch itself in that way. It is intended to be a supplementary kind of activity. In television, Lynn made this point which is an absolutely valid one, you're measuring something which is less frequent than domestic. You have to remind people, when you're talking about all this research for international broadcasting, that you're using a different focus, a different currency, perfectly acceptable. It's done for magazines and newspapers which are specialists. We are specialist broadcasters.

Lynn Gutstadt:

One of the biggest problems right now in international audience measurement is there are no standards. You go through Europe and every country which has some form of audience measurement has a different set of values that they use. The issue, as it's generally referred to, of harmonization in terms of being able to compare one measurement to another, is the biggest mess you've ever seen. That's one of the things we're trying to get at in trying to develop some of these syndicated sources. Even when you're looking at reach, some measurements systems look at totally different qualifiers. There are no standards and that's one of the directions that the industry is having to move towards in trying to develop information that an advertiser, in trying to look at different options for regional purposes, can make some sense out of.

Graham Mytton:

In our weekly reach, it is done entirely on the basis of the person's own definition. I ask you the question: If I was the interviewer and you were the interviewee, and you were chosen as part of the random sample survey, I would ask you if you'd listened to any of the following international broadcasters ever, in the last year, in the last month, in the last week? Did you listen yesterday? So you're getting a focus on the frequency of listening. We also ask the question: " Normally, how often do you listen?" I'm not too happy about that question. The reason we're continuing to ask it is because we always have and it enables comparisons to be made. I think it's a soft measure and I think it doesn't measure actual behaviour; it measures what people say they do which isn't the same as if you ask people the blunt question: "Did you listen yesterday?" Usually people tell you the truth. The problem about length of time listening is you can only really measure that if you're using a diary, which we do from time to time incidentally, or a meter for television. There are no radio meters at the moment. They used to exist years ago and they'll come back.

Lynn Gutstadt:

Again in the course of that presentation you saw both report measures similar to Graham's where it was all done on a survey basis. "Have you watched in the past week or the past month?" In the line chart where we were comparing actual viewing data from the U.S. and the Netherlands, I believe the Netherlands data at that point was on the basis of a one minute qualifier. The domestic U.S. data is on the basis of a six minute qualifier.

Donald Browne:

At the last presentation, Graham, you made the point about who's going to use it once you've actually produced it? I would suggest first of all it would be a lovely topic for the panel two years hence, for audience researchers to talk about strategies to get other people to listen, how you develop cooperative relationships with producers to get the right kinds of questions to ask, how you get management interested in trying to get this stuff applied, and so forth. During Lynn's presentation, I couldn't help but think that almost all of this - and you're very upfront about it - was produced to help sell the service. But I also wonder whether there's been any use of it by CNN's management in changing program decisions?

Lynn Gutstadt:

Yes, as a matter of fact, it is used. Obviously what you saw was only a very small part of all of the data that is collected and I think it was, for purposes of contrast, to a large degree, specifically put together for this particular presentation. Yes, we do programming research. I can speak mostly domestically because that is actually where most of my responsibilities lie. We do programming research. We do intensive qualitative as well as quantitative analysis of specific programs. We work with producers in terms of refining content. Because we do produce all our own programming, we have a tremendous opportunity to be able to fine tune the programming we put on our air. It's also used in terms of scheduling, moving programs around, changing times, locations as well as content. So yes, it is used internally.

Details in terms of the reception and the interpretation by our audience are not something that we have the luxury of getting into. We have to spend so much of our time just looking at who's out there watching, how many are there of them and how can we get them to watch more, that the fine points of social and cultural interpretation we sort of have to leave to our friends in academia who do take that on from time to time.

Graham Mytton:

Absolutely and there's a Ph.D. topic for your students, Don. I'm being absolutely serious here. We, at the BBC, are very interested also in this question. What are the consequences of our activities in television and radio, and of other international broadcasters? How do people receive the same messages perceived in different ways? We are very interested in that. We can't afford to do the work ourselves but we are talking to some academic institutions about possibly funding some research projects.

Eugene Parta:

The question of how do you get management interested, programmers interested. It's very simple. You start by involving them in the process at the outset. You never launch a project without going to the Service Director, talking to people in the service, talking to the management, seeing what the problems are. This year, they'll probably be different from last year. Get them involved at the outset. Chances are they won't have thought about it. You have to help them in their thinking.

By helping them in their thinking, you get them interested in the project and they'll be waiting for the results and by that stage, the problem of getting them to pay attention to the results is pretty much solved. If you just go out and do a study and bring it in and say "Here are the numbers for this year", deaf ears. But you have to co-opt them at the outset.

Graham Mytton:

The other thing we must continually do is to remind the management of the costs of research. To carry out a full scale national audience survey representative of the target population, of the adult population of a country like Nigeria or Bangladesh, we can be talking about 30 or 40 thousand dollars or more. It can't be done for less. If it's going to be accurate, truly representative of the population as a whole, a sample of 2-3 thousand, costs a lot of money.

Ian MacFarland:

The ultimate gate-keeper is the listener. If our programming is no good, dull as ditch water, the listener, the gate-keeper will tune out, switch off, and we don't have an audience.

Graham Mytton:

I absolutely agree. Any comments on that? Can any of you think of examples whereby there's been a change in the size and the appreciation of an audience because programs have changed, perhaps as a result of audience research? We've actually improved things and there's been a change in audience behaviour?

Kim Elliott:

I might have half an answer. I can tell you that in the days when Radio Moscow reigned supreme in international broadcasting, it had the most powerful signal in most parts of the world, its audience was at most 10% of what the leading BBC or VOA international broadcaster would be. So even though it had a massive signal, its programming was just too predictable and not useful enough to audiences because of its lack of journalistic value, that for all the money it spent on international broadcasting, it never had that much of an impact.

Eugene Parta:

I think over the course of the past two years the restructuring has gone over a number of services but probably most dramatically in the RL Russian service which has been largely research driven, almost entirely research driven. I suppose over that time, I don't have the number off the top of my head but we probably conducted over 100 focus groups and held as many meetings. We literally went out and reviewed every part of the program with focus groups conducted in Moscow and in other areas, with other studies. The restructuring isn't complete, not because there isn't general agreement on the way it should go but it's a question of how you do it all with shrinking resources. There is a danger of the research getting beyond what the services are able to do. When I think we are just about reaching that point in our organization. We have a very good idea of who the audience is, what it is we need to do to reach them and the resources may not be there to carry it out.

Ben Slimane:

In our countries, in the South, the answer would be: only God knows, and now more and more, and probably CNN! But the following will help you to understand the answer. Three little Tunisian girls were talking about daddy and mommy. The first one said "When something happens in the city hall, a fire, a robbery in the bank, my father who is a journalist in the local radio will tell us all about it". The second one said "When something happens in the nation, problems with the parliament, my father who is a journalist with the national radio network, will tell us all about it". The third one said "My father

201

is a journalist too. He is a correspondent for an international radio network. Nothing interesting but listen, he still works before, during and after an earthquake". That's the international broadcaster.

Graham Mytton:

Our current data are from surveys in countries which have been surveyed for international broadcasting over the past few years, nearly all of them since 1989. I do not claim ownership of all those. Some of those are syndicated studies, for example many of the ones in francophone Africa we share with Radio France Internationale, Radio Netherlands and Deutsche Welle. Some of them are studies belonging to Gene Parta's office. Some are our own. Some of them are from Voice of America service. But we do try to get audience data as up-to-date as possible.

Endnotes:

[1]. A product of the Communist policy on the mass media, the "wired radio", which transmits sounds via electrical signals along cables to a loudspeaker in the home, reached the majority of the Soviet population in either their homes or places of work. It continues to be the favorite or most common form of radio listening for many in Russia. Generally one or three channels are available. As during the Soviet era, the wired radio in Russia plays mostly Moscow central state radio.

[2]. In both cities, SW-only listening is slightly stronger among the returnees, not surprising in view of their previous experience with listening to Radio Liberty.

CHAPTER SIX

GLOBALIZATION AND FRAGMENTATION: PUBLIC RADIO IN A NEW WORLD

Editors' Note:

International broadcasting and communications, in general, appears to be confronted by two conflicting and often paradoxical tendencies. On the one hand, the forces of globalization seem to be obvious. At the same time, there appears to be a process of fragmentation and particularization. These two tendencies often provoke heated debates and grave concerns.

Within the context of these two tendencies, international broadcasting must define a role and determine a strategy. In the chapter which follows, various aspects of these issues are explored.

ANDRÉ LARQUIÉ
PRÉSIDENT-DIRECTEUR GÉNÉRAL
RADIO FRANCE INTERNATIONALE
PARIS - FRANCE

Introduction.

Si on veut rentrer dans ce vaste sujet de la mondialisation et de la fragmentation et du rôle de nos radios publiques, nous, radiodiffuseurs internationaux qui sommes principalement des radios publiques en raison des moyens de financement qui sont les nôtres, que peut-on dire aujourd'hui pour situer justement ce rôle des radios publiques?

Conçue à l'origine pour animer un paysage radiophonique national ou pour porter dans le monde la voix d'un pays, la radio publique doit faire face aujourd'hui à une très profonde remise en cause en raison des frontières et des territoires, en raison des changements qui sont intervenus dans ces deux domaines.

La mondialisation des industries de la communication a déjà montré la voie de ce qu'on appelle vulgairement "le village planétaire". La chute du communisme a fait de deux blocs, tout au moins en l'apparence, un espace unique. La révolution numérique laisse présager une formidable accélération de la libre circulation des données. La diffusion directe qui en serait l'aboutissement, ou la concrétisation, abolirait les dernières frontières. Donc, globalisation, pourrions-nous dire.

Pourtant, dans ce monde en voie d'uniformisation, les identités nationales persistent. Les nationalismes résurgents morcellent l'espace planétaire. Dans nos pays, la diversité des attentes des auditeurs ou des comportements des consommateurs provoque une segmentation, une fragmentation des marchés. Nous avons donc simultanément à faire face à deux phénomènes en apparence contradictoires, deux globalisations et deux fragmentations.

Nous qui étions habitués à voir cohabiter nos démarches et nos traditions dans le cadre de chacun de nos pays, voyons l'ensemble des radios publiques plongées aujourd'hui dans un monde complexe dans lequel nous devons trouver notre chemin. Ce monde complexe, arrêtons-nous un instant dessus.

Chacun, bien sûr, a quelques idées simples sur ce monde. Le XXe siècle est venu à bout des derniers territoires inconnus de l'Occident. Le développement des moyens de transport qui a progressivement aboli les distances, a rapproché les continents. Par ailleurs, l'organisation économique planétaire mise en place après la seconde guerre mondiale, avec des institutions telles que la Banque Mondiale, le FMI, a provoqué une internationalisation des échanges, a mondialisé l'économie, homogénéisé les modes de vie.

La révolution des médias, cette révolution technologique que nous avons connu dans le domaine de la communication, peut se traduire par deux idées principales. D'une part l'instantanéité de l'information et l'accélération de la circulation des données qui diluent tous les repères et placent chacun au coeur des événements survenant dans le monde - dès que quelque chose se passe en quelque part, nous en sommes immédiatement informés.

D'autre part les industries de la culture: Nous l'avons souvent dit, le développement des industries de la communication fait de la culture et de l'information une marchandise comme une autre. Le citoyen voit donc son espace élargi et réduit cependant, sur l'écran de sa télévision.

Pourtant, jamais autant les comportements de chacun n'ont été aussi diversifiés. On l'a vu, les identités nationales et la vitalité de la création culturelle résistent vigoureusement. La montée du fondamentalisme islamique, le retour du nationalisme en Europe, les difficultés des transitions démocratiques en Afrique, offrent plutôt un regard éclaté et menaçant.

Enfin, la diversité des niveaux de développement et des modèles culturels donne naissance à des mondes parallèles entre lesquels des écarts de développement et des incompréhensions grandissent et ces écarts ne sont pas seulement à constater entre les pays mais on peut aussi les constater dans chacun de nos pays, et je dirais, y compris dans chacun de nos pays pourtant souvent, certains d'entre nous, les plus développés.

Dans ce monde, quels sont les espoirs que peuvent apporter les nouvelles technologies, en particulier la révolution dite numérique dont nous avons déjà parlé? S'agissant du numérique, je pense que trois changements importants interviendront. Tout d'abord, la compression numérique permettra une multiplication de l'offre de programmes en atténuant la pénurie des fréquences et en abaissant les coûts de diffusion.

Il en résultera un formidable défi dans l'évolution des logiques de programmation qui nécessitera une très forte croissance des capacités de production. Le numérique, plus de programmes, donc des capacités accrues de production si l'on veut faire face à cet extraordinaire élargissement de nos moyens de diffusion.

D'autre part, la combinaison des moyens de diffusion hertzien, câble et satellite, permettra d'obtenir, en tout point du globe, une qualité CD qui confrontera chaque radio à une double identité: globale correspondant à son projet, son format, et locale renvoyant au ressenti de proximité qui sera celui de l'auditeur.

Enfin, la perspective plus lointaine de la radiodiffusion directe par satellite risque de porter un coup définitif aux frontières et au contrôle public de la radiodiffusion.

Ces tendances de fond sont inéluctables. Il me semble pourtant que leur rythme sera ralenti par un certain nombre de contraintes. Il peut être ralenti par des contraintes techniques ou économiques. Les contraintes techniques, je n'y reviendrai pas. Nous les connaissons. Ce sont les contraintes liées à tout changement de technologie qui suppose un minimum de temps. Quant aux contraintes économiques, ce sont les contraintes liées aux coûts de ces nouvelles technologies et en particulier aux coûts de renouvellement des récepteurs que les auditeurs auront à supporter s'ils veulent pouvoir bénéficier de ces nouvelles technologies.

Toutes ces transformations technologiques prendront du temps et risquent, compte tenu des enjeux financiers qui les accompagnent, de renforcer une dualité des espaces radiophoniques si des continents entiers n'étaient pas en mesure d'accompagner les pays les plus riches dans ces mutations. Je crois que l'un des premiers problèmes que nous aurons à affronter, quand on regarde la diversification de nos moyens de diffusion et du rôle que nous avons à jouer dans le monde, c'est du fait de ces évolutions techniques, les risques qu'il y a à voir plusieurs mondes se créer avec des situations d'inégalités nouvelles qui risquent non pas de rapprocher mais au contraire, d'éloigner.

Une autre contrainte, mais je passe sur celle-ci parce qu'elle-même est relativement connue, c'est la contrainte politique. Dans la mesure où peu à peu, nous savons parfaitement bien que les règles qui s'imposent sur les paysages audio-visuels nationaux succomberont petit à petit à cette très grande liberté de circulation des signaux que ces nouvelles technologies nous apportent.

Les radios dites de service publique, dans ce monde nouveau, quelles peuvent être leurs missions? Vous me permettrez d'y réfléchir un instant. Un élément de réponse que nous pourrions apporter à cette question je crois nous a été donné récemment à l'occasion d'une conférence de l'Union européenne de la radio et télévision qui s'est tenue à Bruxelles en novembre 1993 et qui a essayé de rappeler les grandes lignes ou les fondements des radios de service public par rapport aux changements qui sont en voie d'intervenir dans le monde. Dans la déclaration adoptée à l'occasion de cette conférence, le rôle des radios de service public était ainsi précisé:

"D'abord des programmes pour tous. Des programmes fédérateurs prenant en compte la diversité des publics et accessibles à tous. Un service de base généraliste mais avec des prolongements thématiques. Des espaces pour un libre débat démocratique". Et là on insistait beaucoup sur l'indépendance et la rigueur de l'information, le pluralisme et l'exhaustivité de l'information. "Un libre accès du public à tout ce qui fait l'événement une référence en matière de qualité, un esprit innovateur, une production originale abondante, une vitrine culturelle, une contribution au renforcement de l'identité européenne et de ses valeurs sociales et culturelles."

Vous voyez donc que l'ensemble de ces éléments situe le service public de la radio dans une logique d'exigence et de rigueur clairement en rupture avec la pure logique du marché. Face à ce que l'on pourrait appeler la "dictature de la demande", le service public doit donc continuer à développer une logique d'offre de qualité qui évite la ringardise ou l'obsolescence en collant aux évolutions de son temps.

Vous voyez donc à travers cette déclaration, les missions du service public sont très clairement affirmées par rapport aux rôles que peuvent jouer d'autres médias, notamment les médias qui obéissent à la logique du marché privé.

Mais si nous souhaitons aussi que cette conception du service public puisse s'épanouir et permette aux radios publiques d'affirmer cette identité que je viens rapidement de rappeler face aux transformations du monde, un choix doit s'imposer en faveur de la coopération internationale et de moyens importants à cette coopération si l'on veut éviter ces ruptures entre différentes radios de service public à l'échelle internationale dont je vous parlais tout à l'heure, compte tenu des enjeux financiers et économiques.

Vous me direz que ce que je viens de dire sur la radio de service public, cela vaut dans nos espaces nationaux, cela vaut-il à l'échelle internationale? Je crois que cette même thématique que nous venons de développer dans un espace national, et si je parlais de mon pays, pour une radio comme Radio France en particulier, est-ce qu'une thématique du même type pourrait être développée par une radio de service public internationale telle que celle que je représente ou telle que celle que nombre d'entre vous représente?

Si nous voulions aussi définir le rôle des radios internationales de service public, je pourrais dire qu'il leur revient d'assurer la diffusion en tout point du globe d'une information fiable et indépendante. Il leur revient également d'illustrer l'universalité des valeurs démocratiques et d'assurer leur promotion. Elles doivent témoigner des cultures nationales et des espaces culturelles issues d'une communauté linguistique mais en contribuant au dialogue entre les cultures. Elles doivent parler du monde au monde et assurer ainsi un équilibre des flux d'information entre le nord et le sud, dans un espace mondial où le nord a le monopole des moyens et souvent de l'information. Bref, elles doivent assurer les communications entre les territoires en vue de renforcer la tolérance et de favoriser ce que j'appellerais le passage à la modernité.

Voici donc quelques réflexions peut-être un peu trop générales que je souhaitais vous présenter au début de cet échange de vues. En brodant sur ce thème nouveau pour nous, enfin nouveau - récent depuis peut-être dix ou quinze ans - dont nous ne mesurons pas encore la totalité des conséquences et qui doit nous amener à continuer à remplir un rôle dont on sait qu'il se joue de plus en plus au niveau de la planète mais dont on sait aussi qu'il doit de plus en plus prendre en compte une multiplicité de besoins, ce qui est probablement pour les radios internationales un élément tout à fait nouveau puisque, du fait des moyens permettant aux signaux de traverser l'espace planétaire aujourd'hui, il nous faudra de plus en plus tenir compte des besoins respectifs des auditoires auxquels nous nous adressons.

PIERRE JUNEAU - PROFESSEUR
UNIVERSITÉ DE MONTRÉAL
ANCIEN PRÉSIDENT
CONSEIL DE LA RADIODIFFUSION & DES
TÉLÉCOMMUNICATIONS CANADIENNES
ANCIEN PRÉSIDENT
SOCIÉTÉ RADIO - CANADA
MONTRÉAL, QUÉBEC - CANADA

Conseil Mondial pour la Radio et Télévision.

Le paysage audiovisuel a changé et va continuer de changer. Le nombre de télévisions s'est multiplié et continue d'augmenter. Les gouvernements et les organismes régulateurs dans les pays démocratiques n'ont pas été entièrement libres dans leurs choix. Ils demeureront forcés de tenir compte des multiples pressions socio-économiques qui militent en faveur d'un nombre accru de chaînes: exigence des populations, concurrence avec les pays voisins, pression des entreprises, des milieux publicitaires et des professionnels de l'audiovisuel eux-mêmes.

Cette multiplication des chaînes de télévision est encouragée par le développement des techniques électroniques: ondes hertziennes, cablodistribution, satellites, numérisation, compression des signaux, etc. Elle entraîne et entraînera une concurrence croissante pour retenir l'attention des spectateurs. Des millions sinon des milliards de dollars sont en jeu. Dans un système concurrentiel strictement commercial il devient donc inévitable de faire appel aux recettes du divertissement qui ont déja fait la preuve de leur capacité à capter l'attention des consommateurs. L'ampleur des enjeux économiques, le primat donné à la rentabilité ont conduit dans un grand nombre de pays au recul de la notion de service public pourtant inhérente à la mise en oeuvre de médias de masse de cette nature. Un réveil de la conscience civique et politique à cet egard est essentiel. Il est urgent de faire revivre dans le monde l'idée que ces instruments extraordinaires de communication que sont la radio et la télévision sont aussi indispensables au progrès de l'humanité que les systèmes d'éducation. Si cette mission de service concerne <u>au premier chef</u> les radios et télévisions publiques, elle s'applique également aux organismes privés qui ne sauraient en faire totalement l'abstraction.

Les données de ce problème doivent être analysées avec rigueur. Il faut ainsi se garder de confondre le phénomène général de commercialisation de la radio-télévision avec l'emprise de la culture américaine dénoncée par certains. La télévision commerciale à sa propre logique et dans la mise en oeuvre de cette logique, les chaînes américaines ont pris une grande avance.

Cette logique entraîne l'absence presque totale des grandes oeuvres culturelles dans les domaines du théâtre, du roman, de la musique, de la danse, de l'architecture et cela vaut pour les oeuvres américaines comme pour les autres. Ce sont les richesses culturelles de tous les pays, y compris celles des Etat-Unis, que la télévision pourrait, devrait, faire partager aux citoyens du monde. C'est pourtant le contraire qui risque de se produire. Et ce d'autant plus que les télévisions publiques sont souvent entraînées elles aussi dans la spirale du mercantilisme. Elle se sentent en concurrence avec les télévisions commerciales, elles doivent toucher elles aussi de vastes auditoires ne serait-ce que pour justifier leur existence auprès des responsables politiques et des hauts fonctionnaires. Comment y parvenir sans recourir aux recettes des concurrents privés et sans renoncer ainsi à la différence et à leur vocation propre? La difficulté est aggravée lorsqu'une télévision publique doit recourir à la publicité commerciale pour une part de ses budgets comme c'est le cas au Canada et en Europe de l'Ouest, sauf en Angleterre.

Le problème est mondial. Si l'on assiste dans les pays developpés à un affaiblissement de la notion de service public en radio et en télévision, il y a lieu de craindre aussi que l'impact d'une telle régression se fasse sentir dans les pays de l'Europe de l'Est, de l'Asie centrale et dans tous les pays du Tiers monde. L'absence d'une tradition médiatique pluraliste et démocratique dans un grand nombre de ces pays plaide en faveur d'une action internationale en vue de renfermer la notion d'institutions de service public, notion essentielle au progrès démocratique qu'il s'agisse de la radio et la télévision ou des services d'éducation. Il ne s'agit pas pour autant de transformer la radio et la télévision en outils d'enseignement et encore moins en instruments de propagande politique. Ces médias peuvent être certes utilisés à des fins éducatives. Mais ils doivent d'abord et surtout être ou devenir des entreprises libres, indépendantes, vouées à la démocratisation de la culture et de l'information, y compris les aspects les plus populaires de la culture qui permettent à toute une population de se reconnaître dans un média de masse, de renforcer ainsi son identité tout en étant ouverte sur le monde. Une telle démarche passe par un nécessaire renforcement des institutions du secteur public.

Partant des ces considérations, un groupe de personnes à décidé de mettre sur pied le Conseil Mondial pour la Radio et la Télévision (CMRTV) consacré à la promotion de la radio et de la télévision comme services publics. Il s'agit principalement de personnes et non d'institutions ayant une connaissance et une expérience personnelle de ces médias ou d'autre part, une conscience aiguë de leur rôle essentiel. Cette démarche à reçu le soutien de l'UNESCO.

NICOLAS D. LOMBARD
DEPUTY DIRECTOR
SWISS RADIO INTERNATIONAL
BERNE - SWITZERLAND

Swiss Radio International: Justifying Our Existence.

Graham Mytton, this morning, intrigued me with his statements and questions. I thought: given the choice today, would the Swiss parliament vote for Swiss Radio International knowing exactly what we cost? I'm not so sure. Why is that? It might be because Swiss parliamentarians don't really know enough about what we're doing. Or, it might also be the fact that maybe we are not quite doing the right thing.

If I look at the title: "Globalization and fragmentation: Public radio in a new world" it leaves me a little perplexed because that is exactly the situation in which we find ourselves as international broadcasters around the world. What do we do under these circumstances?

Another question I ask myself is: How, under the circumstances, can we justify our existence? Perhaps by the mandate we have? Certainly towards our fellow countrymen inside the country who are financing us, we can say "Yes. We have a mandate which says we've got to do this, that and the other. That's what we do." Is that listener friendly or is it just an excuse for our existence?

Our audience research man keeps telling us we should gear the product to the market. It sounds terrible but of course, it's true. And I'm sure Graham Mytton would agree with this man who says "Make the program in such a way that it would be heard by those you want to listen to it." Here is the most difficult problem we are all facing. If we look at the technical situation: first we have the satellite. Many people think that the satellite is not really the instrument of today but certainly the instrument of tomorrow. But if you want to introduce the instrument of tomorrow, I think we better start soon and get onto the wagon while it is in slow motion. It's very difficult to jump on a train when it is in full speed.

This is one of the reasons why, at our little organization, Swiss Radio, we have thought: "How do we find our way out of the dilemma?" We have an incredible amount of potential audience. We have one audience that is safe and sound, that's the Swiss abroad. Juhani Niniistö said this morning this was the major "raison d'être" of many international radio organizations. It's true. However it is just one important aspect, and an easy one. We can count on the roughly 500,000 Swiss living abroad. That is part of our mandate.

The second part is the reflection of Switzerland. Here it becomes very difficult. Graham Mytton made fun of those who try to broadcast in order to reflect their country. I tend to agree with him. But then, what else is there left for us to do? Should we all not be as big and as strong as the BBC? Should we all try to come up with a sort of copy of what the BBC does much better? This is a constant discussion we have in our newsroom, in our program department. Why should we do this since the BBC does it much better? In other words, are there niches that we have to try and detect?

I happen to think that is probably the fate of the smaller and medium sized radio organizations. Because to go out and say "Here we are. We know the world is waiting for us. Everybody waits to listen to Swiss Radio International." I think this would be just a little exaggerated!

What do we do? Rebroadcasting - another wonderful word. What does it mean? Does it mean we have a specific program for a station in Nigeria? That we have a special program for someone in Columbia? And another one for the station in Australia? Does that mean we would have to multiply by hundreds the program output in order to satisfy all the needs of all the people we try to serve by rebroadcasting? This is another question that is incredibly difficult if you are, like me, a program director: How are you going to handle this?

We are on stations in France with our French program - slots of 45 seconds. What the hell is that? Would that be very useful to testify to our identity as a broadcasting organization? I don't think so. So is it really worthwhile to gear a whole structural part of an organization onto the production of that kind of program? Doubtful. But then the rebroadcaster will only take you if you give the goods he and his public wants. He knows his public better than you do. That is another dilemma. The dilemma we are finding ourselves in program terms is not going to get any easier from the technical point of view. I think it's getting much more difficult.

Just one more thought. I believe that in order to be successful, we would have to be imaginative, innovative, use an enormous amount of energy and come up with not yet produced program ideas. As a matter of fact, it's quite a task for a poor programmer to try and reinvent radio since the instrument has been invented for quite some time and many very intelligent, highly imaginative and creative people have already tried to do better. So we are in competition. With the digital explosion of possibilities, not only should we be definitely more imaginative but what's worse, much more prolific. We should come up with tens and hundreds of wonderful programs because the technical means would allow for their distribution.

ROMAN CZEJAREK
VICE - PRESIDENT
POLSKIE RADIO
WARSAW - POLAND

Polish Radio - From Monopoly to Fragmentation.

I'd like to say something about my experience from my part of Europe. I think the situation in radio stations of Eastern Europe is quite different than that in radio stations of Western Europe.

Eastern European broadcasting is now at a very interesting stage. The former communist countries, as you know, are undergoing fundamental changes. Economic and social problems, unemployment, political instability and new commercial radio stations, all have weakened public broadcasting in Poland and in the other Eastern European countries as well. I think the situation in Poland is a very good example of the transformation in broadcasting and other media.

In my opinion, thinking about globalization in a new radio world, in Eastern Europe, we must consider two issues. The first: Global radio stations as international radio networks. The second: Globalization as a phenomenon reported on in individual radio programs in our countries and covering with such global topics as terrorism, pollution, mass culture, etc.

About global stations: I know only one global station in my part of Europe. Unfortunately, this is a TV station. I am thinking of the Russian television from Ostankino, which is still available in different parts of Poland, including Warsaw. TV Ostankino is now transmitting in Poland via old transmitters installed by the Russian army in my country many years ago.

Some years ago, Poland had only three neighbours. New countries became independant in Eastern Europe and Poland now has borders with seven countries.

During communist times, Polish Radio and many national radios in the USSR, East Germany and Czechoslovakia had many special programs about each other. Political will gave us the possibility to prepare joint radio programs. Of course the slot of Radio Moscow on Polish Radio was one of the most boring programs on the air, but it had to be there, there was no choice. Polish people had to listen to Russian music and critics, they had to learn about Russian heroes, cosmonauts, scientists and communist politicians. The same was on the air in Russia, about Poland.

After 1989, all this ended. Polish listeners started to demand that western radio stations be allowed to transmit from Poland. After this, the BBC and Radio Free Europe started transmitting, using Polish radio transmitters. Radio Free Europe is still part of this fall program for Polish Radio. It transmits about four hours a day. The BBC is on the air in Poland on different regional stations.

These subjects are popular in Poland and I think it is the same situation as in the other former communist countries. But to tell you the truth, we have no programs about our neighbours and no programs prepared together with broadcasters from Russia, Ukraine, Slovakia or Germany, for instance.

The Polish broadcasting system has been transformed. Polish Radio was created many years ago as a monopoly. From January 1st 1994, Polish Radio is a system of one central and 17 local independent regional radio stations. Each of these stations has its own programming. There are about 200 commercial radio stations. All of them are rather small. Only three received a licence for nation-wide broadcasting. It is still proving too difficult for them to produce such a service and to organize a good, national transmitting system.

Polish listeners prefer easy listening with pop music and radio competitions; they prefer programs which inform about traffic jams in the center of town rather than about new legislation passed by parliament or terrorism by the IRA in London, or problems in the former Soviet republics. When it comes to global topics: What do listeners in Eastern Europe want to hear? Can we find common topics covered in various radio programs? Poland is a very good example of the fragmentation of public radio.

As the Vice-President of Polish Radio, I am aware that our radio has some public obligations. We should provide the national audience with a complete set of local, national and international information, broadcast artistic and educational programs, create an image of the country, etc. The problem is how to find the golden middle between fragmentation and globalization in our times. Only public radio will be able to present a new image of global radio in Eastern Europe. I can't say now how long we will have to wait for it but I am sure it will happen. We must find proper ways to present global problems in our radio programs. What is the role of the State in this process? What methods will the State use to affect these changes? How much regulation and deregulation will be done? Finally, and this mainly concerns the public sector, what is information and what role should it play?

I think the future of public radio is both globalization and fragmentation. In which proportions? I can't say now. In Poland and in former communist countries, we have only fragmentation of public radio now. We must create change. I hope that maybe CHALLENGES will help us to do it.

The question is: How long will it take?

COMMENTAIRE:

André Larquié:

M. Czejarek nous fait la démonstration que chaque fois qu'il y a un débat, nous nous posons de fausses questions. Quand en particulier nous voulons poser deux termes tels que celui de mondialisation ou de fragmentation, nous savons parfaitement et il nous l'a très bien rappelé, que le choix n'est pas entre l'un ou l'autre mais que bien sur l'avenir sera fait d'un savant dosage entre ces deux vocations ou entre ces deux tendances des évolutions que nous ressentons dans le monde de la radio comme dans celui de la télévision, comme nous le disait tout à l'heure le professeur Juneau.

GAETAN TREMBLAY
PROFESSEUR
UNIVERSITÉ DU QUÉBEC A MONTRÉAL
MONTRÉAL, QUÉBEC - CANADA

Quatre facteurs influant sur la radiodiffusion internationale.

A la deuxième rencontre des radios internationales, à Québec en 1992, on sentait l'inquiétude, voire l'angoisse, omniprésentes. L'échec récent du communisme avait conduit au démantèlement de l'URSS et mis fin à quarante ans de guerre froide. Certaines radios internationales, dont la création avait été largement motivée par cette guerre froide -- pour diffuser dans les pays communistes une information libre du contrôle gouvernemental --, s'interrogeaient sur leur avenir. Avaient-elles encore une raison d'être, maintenant que la plupart des anciens pays de l'Europe de l'Est accédaient à des régimes politiques plus libéraux ? Les médias nationaux émergents n'allaient-ils pas prendre la relève efficacement ? Les gouvernements occidentaux continueraient-ils de subventionner à coups de millions des radios dont le rôle stratégique avait beaucoup diminué ?

D'autres radios publiques, quant à elles, étaient confrontées aux rigueurs budgétaires consécutives aux difficultés financières de leurs gouvernements. Des coupes sombres dans les budgets rendaient les responsables nerveux et inquiets sur l'avenir de leur radio. On ne trouvait guère que Radio France Internationale qui, loin d'être affectée par des compressions connaissait un accroissement de son budget, pour afficher un réel optimisme.

Deux ans plus tard, je ne sens pas, ici à Vancouver, cette même morosité. La plupart des discours que j'ai entendus jusqu'à présent se font rassurants sur la mission des radios internationales et sur l'avenir de la diffusion par ondes courtes. Malgré la libéralisation politique des pays d'Europe de l'Est, des artisans des radios nationales sont venus témoigner à cette tribune du rôle encore très positif, voire nécessaire, joué par les radios internationales. Malgré la suppression de la censure et du contrôle politique direct, la production et la diffusion d'une information libre et objective rencontre encore dans ces pays de grandes difficultés, d'ordre administratif et économique.

D'autres sont venus rappeler, chiffres à l'appui, que de larges portions du globe, surtout dans les pays du Sud, n'avaient encore accès qu'à peu de sources d'information et que les radios internationales en étaient souvent la seule. Des millions de personnes sont en cause.

En ce qui concerne la technologie, on a évalué que la radio à ondes courtes constituait toujours, et sans doute pour encore plusieurs années, le moyen de communication le plus économique et le plus répandu dans les pays les moins économiquement développés. La diffusion par ondes courtes a encore plusieurs belles années devant elle.

Si l'atmosphère est plus sereine, les difficultés ne se sont pas pour autant évanouies et les radios internationales restent confrontées à des défis de taille, que cet atelier évoque largement sous le titre de la fragmentation et de la mondialisation. M. Larquié a bien évoqué, dans sa communication, ces multiples problèmes de nature technologique, politique, culturelle et économique. Je me contenterai donc de quelques remarques complémentaires.

1) Changement technologique et demande de programmes:

Les plus récentes innovations technologiques -- dont la transmission par satellites, la compression numérique, etc. -- posent de redoutables défis aux radios internationales. Il faudra sans doute, à moyen terme, envisager d'autres modes de diffusion que les ondes courtes et assumer les coûts associés de la modernisation.

Mais le développement technologique offre également de nouvelles possibilités dont les radios internationales se doivent de profiter. La multiplication des canaux de diffusion, l'une des principales conséquences du progrès technologique, entraîne un besoin considérable de programmes. Ce n'est pas pour rien qu'on assiste, depuis quelques années, aux États-Unis mais également ailleurs en Europe de l'Ouest et en Amérique du Nord, à des opérations d'achat, à des fusions et à des alliances qui visent à assurer aux grands groupes internationaux de diffusion et de distribution un accès à des réserves importantes de programmes.

Les radios internationales sont productrices de programmes et de contenu. Dans ce contexte de forte demande, il y a là pour elles une opportunité dont elles se doivent de profiter.

2) Contribution a la diversité de l'offre:

Des insistances et des silences m'ont frappé dans ce colloque. On y parle beaucoup des pays d'Europe de l'Est et de l'Asie, beaucoup moins de l'Amérique latine et de l'Afrique, et pas du tout des pays occidentaux.

On pourrait penser que les radios internationales ne se définissent qu'en fonction des pays du Sud (les références moins fréquentes à l'Amérique du Sud et à l'Afrique s'expliquant par leur absence de représentants). Les participants proviennent pourtant majoritairement des pays occidentaux.

A certains égards, il faut s'en réjouir. Je fréquente beaucoup de colloques où, trop souvent, on a l'impression que le monde se limite à ces mêmes pays occidentaux. Il y a quelque chose de rafraîchissant ici, dans ce renversement de tendance.

Mais d'un autre point de vue, ce silence étonne et pose question. Signifie-t-il que les radios internationales considèrent que la diversité de l'information, dans les pays occidentaux, est largement et adéquatement assumée par les médias nationaux ? Faut-il y voir la conception sous-jacente implicite d'un monde divisé en deux, l'un adéquatement informé et l'autre dont il faut à tout prix s'occuper pour y assurer le minimum ?

Mon propos ne vise certes pas à minimiser le rôle fondamental que jouent les radios internationales dans la diffusion d'une information libre et la plus objective possible dans les régions du monde qui en sont le plus dépourvues. Je ne voudrais pas non plus mettre sur un pied d'égalité les pays du Sud et ceux du Nord eu égard à la richesse d'information auxquels ils ont accès. Mais ces précisions faites, il reste surprenant que les représentants des radios internationales s'interrogent si peu à propos de leur rôle dans les pays occidentaux. Car il faut bien l'avouer, malgré l'existence reconnue de la liberté d'expression et d'information, la diversité de l'information, surtout celle qualifiée d'internationale, laisse grandement à désirer y compris dans les pays occidentaux.

Au Canada, par exemple, pays reconnu pour ses libertés démocratiques, sa tolérance et son ouverture, il existe des centaines de stations radiophoniques. Eh bien, il faut admettre qu'à part Radio-Canada, les stations AM de ce pays ont un "son" qui se ressemble beaucoup de l'une à l'autre. Les nouvelles qu'on y transmet sont sensiblement les mêmes, à part quelques informations d'intérêt purement local. Et la part réservée aux informations internationales y est fort réduite. Toutes les études effectuées sur le sujet le constatent et le déplorent.

Les radios internationales ont un rôle à jouer à cet égard. Elles doivent contribuer à la diversité de l'offre, y compris dans les pays occidentaux.

J'applaudis à une initiative comme celle de World Radio Network qui offre, depuis l'automne 1993, une programmation de nouvelles en anglais en provenance des radios publiques nationales et internationales de plus d'une dizaine de pays. Un bouquet de radio journaux présentant, à travers différentes lorgnettes, une information plus complète et plus variée sur les principaux événements du monde! On nous promet pour bientôt une version en langue allemande. A quand la version française d'un tel réseau ?

Voilà une initiative intéressante qui permet aux radios internationales de faire face aux nouveaux défis technologiques tout en jouant mieux leur rôle à l'échelle de la planète. Une telle réalisation n'a été possible que grâce à la coopération de plusieurs stations de radio à travers le monde. M. Larquié a appelé à une plus grande collaboration des radios internationales. Je ne peux que renchérir sur l'invitation et en répéter la nécessité.

3) Augmentation de la demande:

On peut prévoir que la demande d'informations et de contenu étrangers ira croissante au fur et à mesure des progrès de l'internationalisation, tels qu'ils se manifestent par exemple par l'adoption de traités de libre échange. De même, la composition démographique des pays occidentaux, qui ont connu ces dernières années une autre vague importante d'immigration, accentue cette demande de contenus internationaux.

Il y a là un autre défi et une autre possibilité intéressante de développement pour les radios internationales. La mission de la plupart d'entre elles comporte non seulement un objectif d'information mais aussi de contribution à la compréhension entre les peuples et les cultures. En répondant à cette demande croissante d'informations et de programmes d'origines diverses, même si elle n'est encore le fait que de secteurs minoritaires de la société, les radios internationales peuvent se développer tout en remplissant encore mieux leur mission fondamentale.

4) Reprendre les discussions sur le nouvel ordre mondial de l'information et de la communication:

Je termine ces quelques remarques par une réflexion d'ordre plus général mais qui concerne au premier chef, il me semble, des organismes actifs sur la scène internationale de l'information et de la culture comme les radios internationales.

Si la culture est participation à la vie d'une nation, elle est également communion à des valeurs de civilisation tout autant qu'enracinement dans une communauté régionale et locale. Les multiples niveaux d'appartenance à une culture ne sont pas toujours faciles à harmoniser; ils ne sauraient être dressés les uns contre les autres. La négation des aspirations légitimes des peuples à leur affirmation nationale conduit aux mêmes aberrations que leur expression exacerbée et intolérante. L'histoire ancienne comme contemporaine montre éloquemment à quelles atrocités peuvent conduire l'une et l'autre voie.

L'accélération des échanges est non seulement une tendance qu'il faut constater. Elle constitue probablement une dynamique d'enrichissement culturel qu'il faut encourager. Il incombe aux États nationaux d'assurer tout à la fois les ressources adéquates à l'expression créative de leurs talents nationaux, l'existence d'une véritable diversité dans la circulation des produits culturels et l'accès le plus large possible de tous les citoyens aux diverses formes d'expression culturelle.

La sauvegarde et la promotion de la diversité culturelle, richesse du patrimoine universel, passent d'abord par l'adoption de politiques nationales adéquates. Le Canada, État fédéral confronté tout à la fois à l'invasion de produits culturels étrangers et à la volonté d'une diversité d'expressions culturelles internes, constitue à cet égard un cas dont l'analyse peut se révéler fort instructive. La nouvelle politique culturelle du gouvernement québécois constitue, à n'en pas douter, une étape importante dans cette direction. Elle couvre l'ensemble des aspects de l'activité culturelle (de la création à la réception), donne cohérence aux interventions gouvernementales et définit un cadre de concertation des différents acteurs dans le domaine. Elle donne avec raison priorité à la création et à l'éducation.

Il reste peut-être à arrimer davantage politique de communication et politique culturelle. Les deux peuvent de moins en moins être séparées à l'ère de la convergence technologique qui fait du domicile le principal lieu de consommation culturelle. Cette harmonisation, le Québec ne peut la réaliser seul dans le cadre constitutionnel actuel, la plupart des pouvoirs en matière de communication se trouvant à Ottawa. Sans entrer dans les méandres du débat constitutionnel, il faut souligner l'urgence d'établir une ligne de conduite pour assurer une véritable diversité des productions culturelles qui seront distribuées, par le satellite ou par le câble, sur les 200 ou 300 canaux qu'on nous promet pour bientôt.

La production nationale ne pourra suffire seule à la tâche. Une véritable diversité de l'offre culturelle implique qu'on présente autre chose que des produits américains, comme risque de nous y conduire la seule logique commerciale. Il est plus que temps qu'on définisse les règles et qu'on adopte les mesures qui puissent faire servir les immenses capacités de distribution à une large circulation des meilleures productions culturelles en provenance de partout dans le monde. Un organisme international de promotion de la traduction, par exemple, ne pourrait-il pas y contribuer?

Plusieurs gouvernements occidentaux, au rang desquels les gouvernements québécois et canadien, encouragent l'exportation et la coproduction pour faire face à la concurrence internationale. Cela ne suffira peut-être pas. Le problème de la diversification de l'offre culturelle ne pourra être résolu par chaque nation isolément. Maintenant que la Guerre froide est chose du passé, ne serait-il pas temps de remettre à l'ordre du jour la discussion sur le nouvel ordre mondial de l'information proposé, sans succès, par le rapport MacBride en 1980? Le droit à la communication n'implique-t-il pas plus qu'une circulation à sens unique des productions culturelles comme de l'information?

La France a eu raison de proposer l'exclusion de la culture des accords du GATT. Mais après une entente générale sur le commerce et les tarifs, ne serait-il pas temps d'enclencher des discussions à l'échelle mondiale sur la circulation des productions culturelles? Les radios internationales ne pourraient-elles pas se faire l'écho d'une telle proposition auprès des instances internationales concernées? Bien sûr, il ne sera pas facile d'y rallier les États-Unis, qui ont jadis quitté l'UNESCO en grande partie pour protester contre sa position en matière d'information et de communication. Il faudra une forte coalition pour y parvenir

Pour faire face aux défis que posent la globalisation des échanges, l'intégration des immigrants et le développement technologique, des politiques culturelles nationales comme celle adoptée par le Québec en 1992 s'avèrent nécessaires. Une concertation internationale s'impose avec la même urgence.

COMMENTAIRES ET QUESTIONS:

Discussion.

André Larquié:

Permettez-moi de rebondir sur un des termes qui vient d'être utilisé par le professeur Tremblay qui nous parlait du problème de la coopération entre les pays dits "du Nord" et les pays "du Sud", pour simplifier. Ce faisant, il faisait référence aux débats qui ont eu lieu à une certaine époque à l'UNESCO sur le nouvel ordre de l'information. Pour être moi-même en France résident de la Commission française de l'UNESCO qui suit les problèmes d'information et de communication, je suis très attentif à ces questions. Je crois que nous pourrions à nouveau, dans les instances de l'UNESCO et cela fait référence aussi à l'organisation non gouvernementale dont nous a parlé M. Juneau, reprendre ce débat qui à l'époque avait été enterré du fait des réactions pour le moins réservées que ces problèmes avaient suscitées auprès de certains pays dans un contexte international où la logique de la confrontation entre les blocs continuait à dominer. Aujourd'hui que cette logique de confrontation a disparu, peut-être est-il désormais possible de poser en termes plus objectifs cette relation entre pays du Nord et pays du Sud, ce problème du libre accès de l'information quel que soit le pays auquel on appartient et quels que soit les moyens dont on dispose. Ce qui signifie qu'il faut mettre de nouveau à l'ordre du jour ces problèmes de coopération entre Nord et Sud sinon nous verrons se recréer, ou plutôt continuer à s'aggraver les fossés considérables qui existent au niveau de l'information et de la communication entre les pays développés et ceux qui le sont moins. Je crois que nous qui sommes attentifs au rôle que le service national ou international peut jouer aujourd'hui dans le monde de l'information, nous devons être parmi les premiers à combattre, sur tous les terrains que nous connaissons et en particulier à l'UNESCO, pour éviter que ne se créent, du point de vue de l'information et de la communication, de nouveaux risques d'affrontements parce que les uns auront des moyens et d'autres ne les auront pas. Nous ne pouvons pas laisser plus de la moitié de l'humanité en dehors des grandes évolutions que nous connaissons.

Kim Elliott:

Mr. Lombard was worried about the role of Swiss Radio International and some of the other mid-sized international broadcasters. If there is a role for these stations to broadcast programming about their own countries in international broadcasting, or what would be the role for doing that.

In January, I visited Radio Netherlands, to a large extent, because I wanted to see the results of a study done by Diana Janssen and her colleagues. They did a massive study of their English audience around the world. They asked people in various parts of the world what mix of news they want. The listeners in South Asia said they want mostly news about South Asia. The listeners in Africa said they want news mainly about Africa. The listeners in Africa said they want news about the Netherlands. That makes sense if you think about it and if you think about the mass media, and the news, and the journalism available in those regions of the world. So there are parts of the world, mostly the media rich parts of the world, where listeners want to hear from Swiss Radio International news and information and features about Switzerland and from Radio Netherlands, news and information about them, and from Radio France Internationale, news and information about France. So there certainly is an important niche for that kind of broadcasting. I think you'll find a very enthusiastic audience for that kind of content.

André Larquié:

C'est vrai que nous sommes dans un monde où il y a plusieurs strates de domination possibles. Vous venez d'en rappeler une nouvelle qui s'ajoute à celles qui étaient connues. Chaque fois que des systèmes se désagrègent, ce qui a été le cas évidemment en Europe centrale et en Europe de l'Est, une désagrégation qui a été extrêmement rapide. Elle était attendue mais elle n'était pas prévisible. Là aussi on risque en effet de créer des divergences de développement parce que nous arrivons avec des schémas et modèles qui ne sont peut-être pas encore ceux qui sont souhaités par les opinions publiques ou par les auditoires dans ces pays. On a vu, au plan politique en tout cas, des retournements de tendances assez inouïes et que nous avons du mal à comprendre compte tenu des critères à partir desquels en général nous analysons les faits. Ce que vous venez de dire est particulièrement juste sur les problèmes culturels. Une chose est d'analyser un tremblement de terre, une chose est d'analyser un coup d'État, une chose est d'analyser les résultats d'une élection dans tel ou tel pays, autre chose est d'arriver à comprendre les phénomènes sociaux et culturels à partir desquels des sociétés entières évoluent ou, à défaut des sociétés, des hommes sont en mesure de comprendre les événements. De ce point de vue, les radios internationales peuvent jouer un certain rôle dans la mesure où, ayant été ou ayant supposé être à l'écoute des autres, elles devraient être plus que d'autres capables de rendre compte de ces évolutions et de savoir tenir compte du temps, de la notion du temps.

Je crois que si tout à l'heure le professeur Tremblay a fait allusion à l'angoisse qui étreignait un certain nombre des participants au colloque de Québec, c'est qu'en effet nombre de radiodiffuseurs dans un monde qui changeait, se demandaient ce qui allait leur arriver. D'ailleurs il s'est passé des choses. Certains d'entre nous ont eu à subir des restrictions budgétaires car les pouvoirs publics n'ont pas toujours compris que ce n'est pas parce que en moins de deux ou trois ans certains changements étaient intervenus, qu'il ne fallait pas néanmoins maintenir un certain nombre de radios qui véhiculaient dans le monde des valeurs diverses, principalement les valeurs de droits de l'homme, du pluralisme et de la démocratie. Parce qu'on a pu croire à un certain moment que les choses iraient très vite et nous nous rendons compte que nous sommes en ce moment, je dirais dans une période un peu de régression par rapport à l'euphorie qui nous a saisi il y a quelques années. Voilà une bonne raison pour maintenir les radios internationales de service public mais ça je pense que nous ici, nous en sommes convaincus.

Graham Mytton:

It's really a comment on what Mr. Lombard said and also something that Kim said. It goes back to what I was saying this morning. What are you actually trying to do? Are you trying to achieve a sense of public service internationally, to provide people who have a need for information, a need for services, to provide for that need? Or is it a matter of being a publicist for the country from which you come? I'm speaking here quite personally at the moment. I have to tell you that the BBC at the moment is looking very hard at some of the things it's doing internationally. One of the things we're looking at, Mr. Larquié, is whether we should continue to broadcast in French to Africa considering the fact that Radio France Internationale is the most successful international broadcaster in French and it's providing a public service to francophone Africa, an area of great information need. Is there any point in the BBC trying to compete. We are both European countries. We give free and independant information. So is it worth it for the BBC, and Radio Netherlands, and Deutsche Welle, and Radio France Internationale, and Swiss Radio International, and Radio Portugal, and Radio Spain, to provide all a service in French to Africa? There are other things that we could do. I'm speaking here quite personally, not as a BBC person. If my bosses back home heard me say this, they'd probably be a little annoyed with me.

A few years ago, in 1988, before the fall of communism in the Soviet Union, Radio France Internationale, Deutsche Welle, the BBC and Radio Nederlands shared in a syndicated study in Mali. The most successful broadcaster in Mali at that time was none of us, it was Radio Moscow. Radio Moscow achieved the largest audiences it's ever achieved in any country anywhere, at any time. Why? Because it was broadcasting in Bambara. After the fall of communism in the Soviet Union, Radio Moscow reevaluated its choice of language and it closed its "exotic languages." By so doing, it closed down its most successful service, Bambara, and one or two others too. I don't want to make fun of Radio Moscow in this sense. I understand why they did it but there's a point to be made here about need.

There are many languages in Africa and in Asia which none of us broadcast in. There are 20 languages in the world spoken by many people which are broadcast by no country in this room. We are trying to compete with each other in the same languages. Perhaps we should diversify a little bit.

There are many languages in India and Africa which none of us broadcast in, which would provide a service to those people who have information shortages at the moment. I do think it is something that we, as Europeans, within the EC, within the EBU, should be actively discussing in the months to come.

André Larquié:

Je ne peux qu'aller dans le sens que vous venez d'indiquer. Je crois que ce sont des propos iconoclastes que vous prononcez mais j'avoue que je serais prêt moi-même à me lancer dans une telle réflexion qui, dans un cadre européen en tout cas, devrait pouvoir trouver sa place. Nous pourrions peut-être commencer par en parler informellement et voir si, nos conversations progressant, nous pourrions en parler plus formellement avec nos autorités respectives.

CHAPTER SEVEN

TECHNOLOGY: REALITY AND VISION THE IDEAL RECEIVER FOR INTERNATIONAL RADIO: SHORTWAVE AND SATELLITE

Editors' Note:

No discussion of international broadcasting would be complete in any way without addressing the issue of technology and technological change. This CHALLENGES conference put the following question: "What would be the ideal shortwave radio?" If international broadcasting is to have a future, the mechanism whereby the broadcaster meets up with the audience, real and potential, must be of ongoing concern.

This chapter starts off with a rather simple question , but what emerges is an endless set of inter-related concerns, issues, problems, ranging from technology to regulation, from past history to futuristic visions.

KIM A. ELLIOTT
AUDIENCE RESEARCH - VOICE OF AMERICA
WASHINGTON, DC - USA

Introduction.

This is the session on the design of the ideal radio, shortwave or international radio. But I think what we are going to be talking about today is really what is the ideal radio reception technology for international broadcasting in the 1990s and as we move into the new decade. I'm very glad that the organisers of CHALLENGES picked this as a subject. It's very important. It's the interface with your audience.

International radio is important not because stations are transmitting but because people are listening. All of this is very much similar to the terrible philosophical question that is: If a tree falls in the forest, nobody is there to hear it, is there a sound? Similarly, if international broadcasters are transmitting but there are no listeners listening, is there international broadcasting? Maybe not. Philosophically, one could look at it that way.

Among the issues are:

The importance of receivers and how people receive them. How people pick up your broadcasts. The cost of these devices. The availability of these devices. The convenience of them. The type of audio quality you get out of them. This is all very important.

I want to start by saying that I've been a shortwave listener since 1965. I'm still a shortwave listener. I tune in almost every day to some international broadcast to get the news or to hear music from places that I can't get music from in the United States. So I'm an avid shortwave listener. I'm sentimentally attached to shortwave but I realize that the medium has problems.

Some of the problems are having to do with propagation, which is a physical problem. For instance, in the United States we now have a proliferation of privately owned shortwave stations, from U.S. soil, but they're being beamed to Europe nominally. But because of propagation, they don't quite make it to Europe. They are heard in North America.

Meanwhile I'm not able to hear certain stations from Europe because of interference from the stations in the United States that are not actually reaching Europe. So we have a situation now where shortwave broadcasters may be strangling shortwave by transmitting on frequencies and in certain ways in which they don't reach their target area but they do succeed in causing interference short of their target area.

I want to play a quick tape. Last night, I stayed around the hotel room because I wanted to listen to shortwave beamed to western North America.

This was prime time for western North America, 7:30 p.m., when a lot of international broadcasters are beaming into western North America. I was also earlier playing a good signal from Deutsche Welle's relay in Antigua.

Looking in the World Radio/TV Handbook, I also tried to tune to a lot of the other stations that are supposedly beaming to western North America. I was not able to hear Radio Budapest, nor Radio Prague, BBC only with great difficulty, Radio Japan even via Canada, I was not able to. So, many of the stations which nominally broadcast to us, North America, I was not able to hear.

It's true I'm in western North America and I was in a hotel but even back in Washington where we're closer to the broadcasters and where I'm in a better listening situation, there are still quite a few international radio stations that, on the books, broadcast to North America but I can't hear them because of certain flaws with shortwave technology.

For that reason, I think it is time for us to start looking to new means of transmitting and new means of receiving international broadcasting. This is not a negative comment on Sangean because while we still are broadcasting on shortwaves, Sangean radios will give the listeners the best fighting chance to hear those signals and also, if a new technology comes along, I'm sure Sangean will be one of the first to jump onto that technology and provide receivers to the listeners.

There are new technologies, not just soon but now available for international radio broadcasting. There are certain DBS television systems through which one can broadcast audio. This of course is what World Radio Network is doing via Astra. Soon in North America, we're going to have a high powered DBS system called Direct TV which will be continent wide. It will also allow audio to be broadcast through its facility to the entire North American continent.

The media economics of that are very interesting. A cable system with 30,000 subscribers might not be so interested in the 1% of its subscribers who are interested in the international or ethnic radio because that's 300 people. But a direct TV which can cover all of North America can perhaps pull in a million or a million and a half people interested in international or ethnic broadcasting. That becomes economically feasible. Radio via DBS systems could be a very interesting proposition.

The satellite service Inmar-Sat, which is aimed mainly for ships at sea or maritime users, is interested in getting involved in the international radio broadcasting business conveying international radio through its resources. They are going to be doing some tests with digital radio, with their new generation of satellites coming on later this decade. But the really interesting thing about Inmar-Sat is that right now they downlink on about 1.5 GHz. There is international radio available to put up on those transponders. There are a number of receivers built by ICOM, the R-100, the R-7000, the R-7100, a few other fancy scanner receivers owned by tens of thousands of people, mainly in North America, West Europe and Japan.

The receivers are there. The programming is there. The satellite transponder is there. We could have an international radio satellite service in place next week if we wanted to. It would be an interim experimental international radio service but maybe enough to prime the pump and get things moving very quickly.

Internet is the worldwide computer network that many of us use to send text messages back and forth. Internet is capable also of transmitting audio files and in fact CBC is using Internet to transmit some of its programming. The problem is that it takes about six minutes to download one minute of audio so if you want to hear a half-hour program, it will take you three hours. Only for the most avid enthusiasts but if we get to the point where people will have fiber optic cables coming into their homes, or in other words everyone will have a "driveway to the information superhighway", to use an awful analogy, that could provide a very interesting means, a very viable means, to convey international radio.

Finally there is the European proposal for a full-fledged BSS sound broadcast satellite service sound using digital audio techniques which would be the Rolls-Royce of this system. It would offer a universal approach that the whole world would adopt.

Some of us are concerned that it may take so long for the legal framework for this to get into place and will there be the band width for CD quality or very good quality audio if, given the fact that about 100 countries are originating some form of international radio?

I think the future will probably be that most people in the media rich countries will continue to buy radios to hear their domestic radio stations. Right now we buy AM-FM radios but in the future that will be digital audio broadcasting, probably terrestrial, maybe satellite. A few of us internationally interested people buy world band radios. Right now that means shortwave but in the future that will probably be a satellite radio system of some sort, probably digital, maybe even analogue.

The new technologies that I'm talking about now will probably be most feasible in the wealthy countries: North America, West Europe, Japan, Australia, New Zealand. While these new technologies become available - and this new type of receiver is probably initially going to cost a lot of money - eventually the price will start to come down as more and more people start using these receivers. Eventually it may become possible to use this new reception technology in the developing world as well. In the meantime, in the developing countries where most of the international radio listening goes on, shortwave will have to remain the means to hear international radio.

This is a radio I bought last summer while visiting Shanghai. It cost maybe about a month's salary in China but it is affordable for someone who is truly interested in listening to international radio. It's expensive for people living in those parts of the world. This is actually a high-end radio for people living in Africa or India. With shortwave radios now being barely affordable, it will be a while before the new technologies become affordable.

I see at least about 20 years of a co-existence of the new satellite radio technology and the old shortwave technology and we will be putting our programs out through both of those media for a while at least.

KEVIN WANG
PRESIDENT - SANGEAN AMERICA INC.
SOUTH EL MONTE, CALIFORNIA - USA

Sangean Electronics.

Sangean America which is located in Los Angeles, California, is the branch sales office for Sangean Electronics which is based in Taiwan. The service and the sales area for Sangean America covers North America, including Canada and the United States and Mexico.

Sangean Electronics - some of you have probably heard about or own some of our equipment, and some of you probably don't - are shortwave set manufacturers. As a matter of fact, Sangean is probably the largest shortwave equipment manufacturer - I'm talking about private labels - around the world. Our major customers, to name a few, include Radio Shack, Siemens, Philips and Hitachi.

We have been in business now for 20 years. We have sold millions and millions of shortwave radios over these 20 years. We sell to more than 80 countries around the world. Our radio output is about half a million radio sets a year, as of 1993.

Our main factories are located in Taipei, Taiwan. We just started a new factory in China to produce quality and low price radios. To produce quality radios at a more affordable price is always our target. Through the years, we always come out with several new models of new radios to keep up to date with technology.

We just started a new market a few years ago in Eastern Europe and we find now, in that particular market place, we have a very steady growth rate. Our major market is Western Europe and North America but the market declined after the Gulf War in 1991.

We have found that one of our strong market areas is in religious broadcasting through shortwave. The market had a very good growth rate for the past couple of years.

During the Gulf War in 1991, we had a very strong demand for shortwave radios and since then, the market has declined somewhat but we still believe there is a large population interested in listening to international shortwave broadcasts.

The ideal shortwave receiver of the future, in my own opinion, is a good quality, easy to operate, good sensitivity, and, most important, priced more affordablly. As you all know, at present date, a good shortwave radio can easily cost more than $200 U.S., which is quite expensive.

Our goal with today's technology is to manufacture a quality radio at a more affordable price to the general public so the populations of shortwave listeners can grow.

Our sales data show that more and more shortwave listeners prefer the digital receiver over the analogue receiver. The sales ratio of the digital radio to the analogue radio is about five to one. Easier and accurate tuning for the digital receiver is the main reasons.

Some of our new lines of radios will also include a digital radar system, RBS have this receiving capability. Also, as we predict, the next generation of radio listeners will be receiving their signal from a satellite so, we will be one of the first to manufacture this kind of radio in the world. Our R&D staff in power is already geared for this direction.

Finally, Sangean Electronics was selected by WRPH of Netherlands as the most innovative receiver manufacturer of the year for 1993. It is quite an honour for us.

ARNO SELDERS
HEAD, TECHNICAL DIRECTOR'S OFFICE
DEUTSCHE WELLE
KÖLN - GERMANY

Current and Future Trends in Technologies.

The subject of this session is of great importance to all international broadcasters because the best program is useless reliable way. But this is our main aim and our constant challenge, that as many people as possible all over the world receive our programs-in countries without democracy and without access to free and objective information, in developing countries as well as in developed democratic countries.

To achieve this, international broadcasters have to select for each region the most suitable technique for their program distribution such as shortwave, medium wave, FM, cable and satellite networks, or a combination of them.

Another challenge comes from the fact that listeners are becoming more and more quality minded as regards program contents and signal quality because they are offered daily more and new programs.

This requires us to analyze regularly the kind of technology that is used for a specific area and adopt, if necessary, additional or different techniques and invest in future technologies in order to optimize the standard of signal quality. Only in this way will we be able to compete in the worldwide market of media and keep or increase the number of listeners in these times of increasing budget pressure.

We all know that for large parts of the world, especially for developing countries, shortwave is still the only means to cover large areas over long distances with radio programs, and this on the basis of a uniform worldwide standard of technology and an established frequency spectrum.

According to our information, the 66 biggest international broadcasters are operating together 1,200 shortwave transmitters with a total output power of 360,000 kW, and 100 additional transmitters with a total output power of 47,000 kW are planned to be installed in the next few years

This is a very large distribution network placed all over the world, transmitting daily 2,500 hours of programs, in up to 47 different languages, for worldwide 600 million shortwave receivers on the market. Such receivers with digital displays are mass products of high technical standards and can be bought for $150 U.S. and more.

But the disadvantage of shortwave broadcasting is well known: Low signal quality due to limited audio band width and overcrowded shortwave bands and interference.

Even the additional allocation of 790 kH frequency spectrum by the World Administrative Radio Conference in 1992 in Spain will not change the situation because the use is not possible before the year 2007 and only for single-side-band transmissions. In order to benefit from this additional frequency spectrum, most of the transmitter operators would have to invest heavily and most listeners would have to buy a new receiver.

I have doubts that by that time, in the year 2007, broadcasters and listeners are willing to invest any money when there is a substitute technology for shortwave in sight.

The only innovation that could make shortwave broadcasting more attractive is called AMDS - Amplitude Modulated Radio Data

System. This system is being tested currently by Deutsche Welle for shortwave transmissions and allows to transmit, besides the normal audio signal, additional data informations such as:
- name of station the receiver is tuned to (a maximum 6 letters of numbers can be displayed);
- alternative frequencies for the received program (up to 31 frequencies can be displayed);
- additional information such as name of program, schedule information, target area, transmitter location, etc. (up to 80 letters or numbers can be displayed);
- last but not least, in-house information such as information for network operators could be made available.

If the tests are completed successfully, AMDS could be introduced in a few months time as an additional service for our listeners. With such a system, they could be guided better through the programs and helped with the selection of the most suitable frequencies. This innovation requires investments on the transmitter side of approximately $5,000 U.S. for each transmitter, and also the listener has to buy a new receiver that can display AMDS. Such a receiver will be more expensive than a normal one - about $200 U.S. at the beginning but with increasing quantities, this difference will go down.

This short summary about the current and future situation concerning shortwave broadcasting may not sound very exciting to you, but this is the reality until an alternative technology is introduced.

Concerning developed and industrialized areas with established modern telecommunication infrastructures, the situation is different. For these areas, international broadcasters are using more and more satellite audio subcarriers to transmit their programs, to attract new listeners that would have never listened to shortwave or to keep old listeners that change for quality reasons from shortwave to satellite reception. But also in developing countries, these systems are introduced more and more to supply rebroadcasters.

In all, there are currently 750 subcarriers worldwide in use to transmit radio programs from national and international broadcasters, mainly in analogue, but some, as well, in digital technique. Such transmissions can be received onlywith stationary receivers and fixed antennas that have to be pointed to the satellite, and these antennas need dimensions between 30 and 300 cm, depending on the powerflux. The price for such receiving equipment is about $250 U.S.

Through digital compression techniques, the antenna dimensions will go down further and the number of channels will increase by the factor 4 to 8, depending on the required signal quality. Some systems have been introduced already and others will be introduced soon, such as: Astra Digital Radio (ADR), European Digital Radio (EDR), Digital Satellite Radio (ESR), and Direct TV with a digital radio service.

But for developing countries where most of our listeners are - and I would like to mention that two-thirds of the 510,000 letters we received from our listeners in 1993 came from developing countries - for these countries, such systems with stationary receivers and fixed antennas are not applicable because of the high price, the complexity of handling and the required power supply. I believe we will soon have to find a replacement for shortwave with its poor signal quality if we do not want to lose too many listeners.

This brings me now to the second part of this short report: The Vision - the future that is in sight for international broadcasting. In the following, I will refer to Satellite Digital Audio Broadcasting as satellite DAB.

This technology will be the biggest innovation for international broadcasters for the next decades because it will improve the quality and reliability of our broadcasts substantially. With satellite DAB it will be possible to bring the obtainable CD studio quality down to the listener, although it is likely that international broadcasters require at the beginning only something equivalent to mono FM quality.

This is a very important economical aspect because the price for a satellite channel is about proportional to the required bandwidth and therefore, the rate has a great affect on the price. For example, a mono FM channel costs about one-fifth that of a CD channel.

In order to introduce and operate satellite DAB successfully as a substitute for shortwave, in my view, three basic requirements have to be fulfilled:

1. The definition of a worldwide uniform technical standard.

For this, ISO/MPEG Layer 2 is proposed, but unfortunately has not yet been implemented.

2. The worldwide allocation of a frequency spectrum.

The World Administrative Radio Conference of 1992 in Spain made available radio spectrum for satellite DAB in the 1.5, 2.3 and 2.6 Ghz range, so that this requirement is fulfilled.

The allocation is on primary basis but only from the year 2007. Until then, the use is based on a secondary and non-interference basis in order to protect the current services in this frequency bands. A planning conference is scheduled for 1998, at the latest. Until then, only the upper 25 MHz of the allocated spectrum can be used on an experimental coordinated basis.

3. The third basic requirement which is the most vital one in my view, is the worldwide availability of inexpensive table-top or car-mounted DAB receivers on the market.

This is a key factor and very vital for the success of such a new system, because international broadcasters are limited to using only such transmission systems for which the intended audience has a receiver. Since it will take a long time to replace 600 million shortwave receivers, it will be necessary to place multiband receivers on the market and to operate in simulcast during a transition period of 10 to 15 years from the start of satellite DAB, in order not to lose established listeners.

Taking these conditions into consideration, the ideal receiver of the future should have the following specifications:

-    inexpensive, which means $200 U.S. or less;
-    easy handling table-top or car-mounted type with solar power supply;
-    multiband configuration for MW, SW, FM, L-S-Band.

VOA, NASA Research Center and Jet Propulsion Laboratories (JPL) announced in June 1993 the successful tests of digital audio broadcasts from a geostationary satellite in the S-Bands in CD quality.

The audio signal was coded at the source digitally compressed to 128 kbits/sec. for a stereo signal. This could be received with a table-top or car-mounted receiver with an omnidirectional antenna that did not need direct line of sight to the satellite. According to our information, VOA has ordered the development of a prototype DAB receiver for consumers' use. Perhaps our colleague from VOA can give us some information on this subject later on.

As well, Afri-Star an organisation based in the USA that intends to operate from 1996 the first satellite DAB system in the L-band to cover Africa and the Middle East, has ordered the development of a table-top receiver. Unfortunately, according to our information, the receiver will work with a new digital compression technique that is not compatible to the ISO/MPEG Layer 2 and that would make it a closed-shop system. The receiver will be designed in a multiband configuration to cover AM, FM and the L-Band.

Another organisation called Indo-Star, based in Indonesia, intends to operate a satellite DAB system in the L-Band to cover Indonesia from 1995 or 1996. According to our information, the development of a table-top receiver using digital compression based on European MUSIC AM systems is in progress.

These two examples show that for some parts of the world, satellite DAB could become a reality very soon and international broadcasters have to follow the development very closely in order "not to miss the bus".

I believe that the possibility for instant coverage of relatively large areas by satellite DAB is attractive to national broadcasters in developing countries and to international broadcasters. Therefore, it is advisable that these organisations cooperate in order to bring this advanced satellite technology to developing countries. We international broadcasters, even taking budget pressure into consideration, are more able to contribute funds for such a new technology and we could make cost and satellite-channel sharing arrangements with national broadcasters to establish this very effective broadcasting system. Such an approach would have the big advantage of stimulating a more rapid introduction of the required new receiver base, a key essentiality for the success of satellite DAB.

Before I come to the end of my short report, I want to recapitulate the essential points, in my view:

-    Shortwave broadcasting will remain, for large parts of the world, the only economical way to cover large areas with programs for the next years. (I am purposely not giving any figures).

-    The only valid alternative to shortwave will be satellite digital audio broadcasting which is very economical and which will improve the signal quality and reliability substantially.

-    To introduce this vital innovation successfully in the near future, the following actions should take place in the shortest possible time: First, the definition of a worldwide technical standard. Second, the development of an inexpensive small multiband receiver.

In January of this year, the BBC-WS organised a symposium on DAB for international broadcasters and two working groups were set up -one to concentrate on policy issues and one to concentrate on technical issues. I believe that it is very important that as many international broadcasters as possible join these groups and use all their influence towards governments, industries and any other organisations that could help in order to implement this new technology in the shortest possible time.

COMMENTS:

Kim Elliott:

That's going to be the big debate in the next few years: What will the standard be? Will this European standard find its universal acceptance or will upstart entrepreneurs come along and find a standard for us in the meantime, and perhaps not give us universality? Remember we had three color TV systems in the world and somehow we survived but it would have been better if we just had one.

JEFFERY COHEN
DIRECTOR OF DEVELOPMENT
WORLD RADIO NETWORK
LONDON - UNITED KINGDOM

Shortwave and Satellite in International Radio.

I believe there is place for both shortwave and satellite in the delivery of international radio. There's no ideal method. Each has its strengths and its weaknesses. Of far more importance is knowing what delivery method is best suited for transmitting to a particular locality because the pattern of broadcasting varies greatly, even between apparently similar neighbouring countries.

When I speak of satellite, I'm referring to both the primary distribution from the satellite and the secondary methods that follow on such as cable and rebroadcasts. All that I'm going to speak of now is existing technology, not the future technology that we've heard of.

So what are the issues of concern in the delivery of international radio? These I believe are the issues of concern to broadcasters. First of all, what is your audience size going to be? Globally, the shortwave audience is far larger than satellite. There are significant changes going on. These began in the western world and are now set to become the pattern elsewhere, as we heard earlier, the pattern for instance in India is changing very greatly at the moment.

The driver for the development of international broadcasting is television. There isn't a huge wave of people buying shortwave radios in the way that people are paying out good money to get satellite and cable television. So a successful radio strategy would be to piggy-back on TV's development. But what is the audience size you're going to get? For satellite and cable, the potential audience is high but we must be realistic about what we can actually achieve. It's a specialist area, as we heard earlier. It's like a specialist publication. People have to be persuaded to tune in to the radio stations, even if they've got the technology in their homes.

Increases of a few percent in the audience of international broadcasting are significant. What are the relative audience sizes? A persuasive example for satellite delivery is in Western Europe. Shortwave ownership is estimated at about 2%. Satellite and cable ownership is at about 15% of whom about one-third use it for radio or at least know how to use it for radio. But the cable audience is growing very rapidly and shortwave isn't. There is the audience composition.

Why do people listen to shortwave? What characterizes the audience is their great enthusiasm for the medium. Perhaps there are three motivations: One is a special link with a country. People are perhaps an expatriate or they have a special ethnic link with the country. In many cases it's because people have limited sources of local news. Thirdly, it's an enthusiasm for shortwave and picking up the stations is an end in itself. It's that magic of that little radio. You're listening to a program that's come to that radio from the other side of the world. It's a very personal thing, listening to shortwave. Shortwave listeners feel very close to the stations they listen to. They write to them a lot. That's a traditional activity.

The shortwave cable and rebroadcast audience is very difficult to characterize accurately although there is some overlap with the shortwave audience. It's very general in its make-up. It's much less of a specialized audience than the shortwave audience. The audiences are different in that the cable satellite audience doesn't have to know about the technology, the frequencies, UTC and summertime schedule changes. That means some of the aspects of your scheduling may need to be looked at differently when you're broadcasting to the cable and satellite audience than when you're broadcasting to the shortwave audience.

Then come transmission costs. Shortwave is an expensive activity, especially if it's done effectively with relay sites. If you want to be reliable, you've got to have several frequencies per service, per region. Satellite is much less expensive but on the other hand, you have a lot of work involved in obtaining the extensive cable and rebroadcast distribution which is necessary in many places, and also to publicize the service and get people to actually tune in to it.

Satellite is greatly expanding in its capability. With compressions, we heard, there'll be 500 channels soon on the Astra system in Europe, which is an enormous extension to what it is at the moment and costs will tumble when far more channels become available due to technical innovation.

The cost of reception is very important. How much do listeners have to pay to get your service? As I mentioned, the satellite and cable strategy is largely on the back of TV. You're not actually asking people to go out and buy equipment for radio at the moment. The cost of satellite TV equipment is not very great. In fact, in the U.K., in the post-Christmas sales, satellite TV equipment was on the market for $150.

Reception quality is another important issue. We all know that shortwave quality is not very good by today's FM standards that listeners demand. Cable and satellite reception can be very good quality. This is crucial if you desire to have local rebroadcasts of your service.

Then there's reception reliability and the ease of reception. As a rough guide, shortwave achieved something in the region of 60% reliability over long distances, 80% for medium distances and 90% for short range reception, with some exceptions such as the problem of the evening reception of European stations that are our neighbouring countries.

To get this reliability, you have to assume that you have skilled listeners who know how to get the best out of their shortwave receivers with all the frequency changes, seasonal and daytime changes. They also have to have a reasonably good receiver.

Satellite and cable is totally reliable once it is set up. But it has drawbacks. It's not portable. Car reception is out. The ease of reception is something that does need to be worked on and we're looking at.

Home satellite and cable equipment will easily produce a radio program coming out of the TV set. But this isn't very satisfactory. What we've done is to develop a small kit which costs less than $100 U.S. It allows simultaneous reception of any TV channel and any radio channel. The radio doesn't come out of the TV set. The radio comes out of any conventional radio placed near the receiver. It's probably got enough range for you to be listening on your radio in the kitchen from the satellite receiver that's in your living room.

There are other benefits, as well, that satellite gives you. At the moment you can get teletext pages which produce a lot of information. It's a European system. It's not available in North America but teletext will allow you to augment your audio with pages of information about programs.

Finally, there's the issue of security and gate-keeping. Every broadcaster desires a transmission system which is totally under their control. But these days, to be effective, you need collaboration. Most large broadcasters are involved in collaborative ventures and relay arrangements. There the security of your signal has to be compromised. The actual potential for interfering with the program content is not very great. It's quite unlikely that people are going to take you off the air unless you find yourself at war with another country.

Satellite is subject to legal restrictions because of television. Television, because it's such an important slice of medium, suffers legal restrictions and those legal restrictions also get passed on to satellite radio. At the moment, shortwave doesn't have any of those restrictions, largely because no one has ever challenged the fact that programs are relayed in one country from another.

In conclusion, there's a lot of change going on in broadcasting and it's being driven by TV. I think that instead of fearing this competition, you should exploit it. You should use the equipment that people are paying good money to buy television reception. Direct satellite radio, DAB and the other developments, will eventually come but it's another matter whether the public will pay out good money in order to get new forms of international radio. There's also the global information superhighway which is bound to be used for the conveyance of international audio.

International radio needs both shortwave and satellite at this moment. Above all, it's not just the technicalities of DAB or DTH, it needs to be effectively marketed to the public. That's where I hope we are leading the way.

MARK FRASER
DIRECTOR OF BUSINESS DEVELOPMENT
NATIONAL WIRELESS COMMUNICATIONS
RESEARCH FOUNDATION
VANCOUVER - CANADA

The subject of Internet has come up today and two quick anecdotes: Anecdote number one was listening to the BBC interviewing someone from the Oxford English Dictionary talking about "technobabble" (that's my word, not theirs) and that if you had any words to add to the lexicon, please contact the Oxford English Dictionary via their Internet address.

The second one was that Internet has a shortwave news group which I read quite regularly. I had not seen anything on this conference in that news group so I posted a quick message saying that this conference was taking place and guess what? I got a couple of replies back. One from an academic, I believe in Texas. But the other one was quite notable in that it came from somebody who is very interested from HCJB. So the Internet is here, ladies and gentlemen, and it's quite a valid medium. I think that's a natural for a digital or other subcarrier on whatever broadcasting medium we come to.

By the way, I listen to Australia in the morning, coming to work. It's quite refreshing. I'm the only person I know who has a shortwave receiver in the car!

Over the last few decades, I've watched technology make quite a lot of progress from AM broadcasting through FM broadcasting and shortwave broadcasting. The audiences are changing, demanding things other than middle-of-the-road rock-n-roll, going to NPR, public radio.

In Canada, and probably more specifically in the U.K. and even more specifically in Eastern Europe, culture control has been the issue and as the airwaves become more liberated, there is more demand for, let's call it "niche listening". I listen because I like the news neutrally presented. And even if it's not done so neutrally, I like to be able to interpret the propaganda myself and there's not nearly enough of that around as there used to be although some of the commercial broadcasters we find on this continent are reintroducing their own brand of that!

My concerns are that there are treaties governing international broadcasting. There may not be treaties governing satellite rebroadcasting or broadcasting. These treaties keep things more or less under control, except for these aforementioned North American purveyors. You have dollars in pursuit of more dollars and anything that has to do with the spectrum is a medium through which those dollars can be extracted, if it's advertising revenue. Advertising revenue, I guess, is more important in a capitalist environment than cultural dissemination is, or has been, in almost any kind of environment. So that concerns me.

Jamming used to be the method by which cultural dissemination was controlled. Jamming is still possible. It's not as popular as it used to be.

Ownership of the medium is the one that probably concerns me more than any of the others. There are lots of things that balance that. We can only hope that there are some treaties that govern control of the frequencies that are used for satellite broadcasting.

Of course, we've heard that HF radio, direct broadcast, satellite, various subcarrier methods, various encoding schemes, things like Inmar-Sat, the Canadian-American Im-Sat vehicles may also carry some kinds of broadcasting. We've also watched the evolution of devices. The old crystal set that I first saw coupled with the radio that almost electrocuted me at age 10, multiple conversion receivers, synchronous detectors, all of which have made quite a difference to what you can pick up and how good it sounds, and how much interference you can avoid. Signal processing has come a long way. I look at complex modulation schemes that are being used to carry data. You used to be able to pick out the teletape over radio and the weather fax stuff by ear. Well there's a lot more variety of things that you can listen to on HF radio, and some of that is going to start carrying programming to the, let's say, "accessible audience". For example, I very easily envision a service that would let me see weather maps as well as listen to my favourite program material.

There have been fits of interest in different technologies for shortwave radio. I think everybody remembers the pain of the stereo shortwave broadcasting and the financial pain to the investors in it and the talk about some of the digital technologies. Quite frankly, I don't see that taking off as quickly as we would all like it to. I use the example of the digital audio tape recorder. It's not technology that got in the way of wide adoption, the ubiquitous presence of the DAT. It's the royalty battle and control of the media, and control of that revenue that had enough stroke to stall it, keep the price high, and the DAT is not an issue. I don't see that digital broadcasting is going to have a very much easier time than that if the program material cuts into the royalty stream. It disturbs me but I think that's going to be a factor.

Look at some of the other things that have happened with technology. Ten years ago, I listened to a lecture on global positioning systems. I was told that around 1995, I'd be able to wear a wristwatch that would allow me to receive radio pages and to read and find out where I was, how fast I was going, in what direction and at what elevation. I thought: "This ain't going to happen." By the way, this was going to cost less than $200. I want you to know that it ain't that small yet but this is my computer. I no longer carry a lap-top. I have on order a GPS receiver which is going to cost me $150 U.S. That'll tell me not only those other parameters but what time it is with considerable accuracy and resolution, a microsecond, I think.

I look at the L-Band technologies. Well, GPS is an L-Band technology. You don't need a very large antenna to make that work. L-Band technologies for M-Sat, for Inmar-Sat. In 1999, a prototype M-Sat receiver was projected to cost a consumer something in the order of $10,000 U.S. Today that's projected to be, at launch, probably $2,000 U.S. or less. That's a very sophisticated box.

Single processing, as I mentioned, has come along to the point where you're getting extremely complex forms of modulation and information carriage that's very robust, will go through the electronic curtain, electronic warfare - that's what generated a whole lot of the technology that's now finding its way into consumer products.

For $100 I bought myself, from Texas Instruments, a little module that has a jack in, a jack out, for audio and it has an RS232 data connector on it. I can write and program my own digital signal processing algorithms. This is something I would only have dreamed of five years ago.

For $150, according to the magazine QEX which is published by the Ham Radio Organisation in the U.S., I can build myself a direct digital receiver. It begins processing signals at frequencies as high as 26 MHz apart from a little bit of filtering or tuning, there's no what we know of as "RF" involved in that. This is in this month's issue.

In the March issue of *Elector Magazine*, there's an item on, I think, Digital Copy Bit Removal so that digital audio tape recorder, that digital broadcast signal, will allow the experimenter maybe for a few more months or years yet, to remove that copy protection bit, take that direct broadcast digital signal, put it onto his digital audio tape recorder and not be prohibited from doing so.

What have we got? Program material, receiver technology, transmitter technology, carriage media-the battles are going to be partly in technology. You can fit a lot of stuff into a very small box now that's not going to cost very much. By the way, they're buying these for - and it's a full MS-Dos computer - $399 U.S. Next month it's going to have my radio data receiver on it and Gee Whiz... maybe I'll be able to pick up my Radio Australia news in the morning on my way to work!

Kim Elliott:

I want to make a few points. You mentioned the problem of regulation of international broadcasting. It's interesting to note that among the most successful international radio broadcasting is on medium wave. BBC for medium wave from Cyprus was very successful in the Middle East, Voice of America on medium wave, from Munich was very successful in Central Europe. There still is no provision for international broadcasting on medium wave. It's basically a flouting of international law to do that.

Let's also take as an example the world's most successful international radio broadcaster which of course, Graham, is MTV! As I mentioned before, MTV is probably consumed in more homes than any other international broadcaster, is a completely extra-legal international broadcasting operation. Astra is not really a legal DBS broadcasting operation. It's a fixed system, supposedly going to cable systems but, of course, people can receive it on 60 cm dishes so it has "de facto" become a DBS TV system. It is also very popular on Asia-Sat which is not a direct-to-home system to a great extent. Most people get their Star TV, which includes MTV, through cable systems which receive Asia-Sat but that too is not a legal broadcasting system. It's a fixed system.

So, entirely outside of the framework of international broadcasting regulation, a very viable broadcasting medium has come along. I predict that it won't be bureaucrats in Geneva who will determine the future technologies of international broadcasting. It will be entrepreneurs like Jeffrey Cohen and Karl Miosga and others, maybe our friend of Afro-Space, will simply push the envelope and not wait for government officials to make their decisions.

Also, I want to talk a little bit more about Internet. The interesting thing about Internet is that it would solve not only the problem of reception quality but the other vexing problem of international radio which is schedule convenience. With Internet, you don't have to be at your home at 8:00 in the evening to hear Dateline on Swiss Radio International. You can download it whenever it's convenient for you to do so. So two of the big problems of international radio would be solved by Internet.

The other interesting thing is that Internet is used mainly for text. Now why did international broadcasting use the radio medium? Because radio is the most effective means to convey information? No. Because radio is the only feasible way to get information across national boundaries and across national long distances. Now, with Internet and other computer systems going across national boundaries with impunity, you can do your international broadcasting through text.

If you're going to do a 20-minute long documentary about wildlife in central Canada, maybe it would be better to use text because that will give the consumer of this information a chance to read it at his or her own speed and also to re-read passages if necessary. And it's much more economical from a bandwidth point of view, to send text through electronic means than to send audio which involves great huge megablocs of information.

So I think we maybe ought to look at text. And also look at what's the role of international radio in a television age. Probably one of the best defences of international radio in a television age is that it's economical to do radio whereas it's not economical to do long-form international television. So the small but elite, internationally interested audience, if they want to get a variety of countries and a variety of viewpoints, will have to listen to radio rather than watch TV to get a lot of cultural and political viewpoints from many countries, because that just won't be possible with the economics of television.

Finally, some points on the human behaviour of international radio listening which is something I look at as an international broadcasting researcher. In countries like Bangladesh and Nigeria, the human behaviour of listening to international radio is very similar to domestic radio listening because people listen to it as a substitute for domestic broadcasting. But as countries have freer media and more diverse media and VCRs, the human behaviour of listening to international radio is very different than just listening to domestic radio.

Domestic radio in a media rich society is a matter of jumping in your car, going down to the store and listening to the radio while you're doing that. Listening to international radio is much more purposeful, something you make an effort to do because you are interested in international affairs. When your broadcast comes on may not be the time you happen to jump into your car and go to the store. That means that most international listening is probably going to be done in the home. This means we can have antennas in fixed locations rather than in the car, which means the economical feasibility of international radio listening is easier than maybe we think. A solution for satellite radio may be closer than we think because of the human behaviour of international radio as opposed to the human behaviour of domestic radio listening. We have to differentiate the two. They are very different types of activities.

QUESTIONS & COMMENTS:

Discussion.

Derek White:

For somebody whose technical knowledge stopped with the manual typewriter, I am now more confused than I was when I left London after the recent conference. If I understood correctly, Kevin Wang was saying that his company is already working on the development of a direct satellite receiver which would match up with the development and work being undertaken by Motorola for the Afro-Space system and by a Sony subsidiary for the Indo-Star system. If I heard Arno Selders correctly, he's taking both of those developments, perhaps more seriously than anyone was at the London conference, that they now may seem a reality. Is that the feeling of both Kevin and Arno? And if that's the case, doesn't the discussion about future legislation and so forth go out the door? Just from a personal viewpoint, if Indo-Star came into Indonesia, it would potentially cut some 3,000 regular listeners from Radio Australia's audience in a stroke. I'm assuming the reception from the satellite, if there was a cheap receiver, would be such that no one would choose shortwave over the quality signal.

Kevin Wang:

We will start manufacturing the receiver, the RID for Siemens starting in May. With that capability, we are ready for the next generation of radio. As far as the question Derek asked, I'm not really a technical person but I can get the information from my factory.

Technology: Reality And Vision

Arno Selders:

Definitely we are taking the possibilities that - and I must say we have only very limited information concerning Afri-Star and Indo-Star - and we are taking it very seriously because if they prove to be right, that they are able to start such a system even with a zero receiver base, it could develop a snowball effect and it could become more than competition to us international broadcasters. It could become very dangerous because we would lose the listenership which we have built up over the last 40 years in a very short time, for these areas. Definitely anyone who would have to decide to buy a new receiver, would definitely opt for the new technology and not for the conventional shortwave receiver.

This will take time and I have doubts wether the industries are capable of supplying so fast for instance, the one million receivers Afro-Star or Afro-Space wants to place on the market in the next 24 months. First of all, to our great surprise, and we were very interested although we did not sign a letter of intent for Afro-Star, we were very interested as long as we could be sure that a technical standard would be used that is compatible to MPEG Layer or to MUSICAM.

But a few months ago we heard, through the international press, two informations that are very important for us. The first was that Motorola had been ordered by Afro-Star to develop a chip, a processor, which is the basic requirement for such a receiver. Anything else is comparable to conventional receiver. Anyway I mentioned already, a new receiver has to be a modern configuration. After that, if I got the information correctly, Voice of America signed a letter of intent as well, for Afro-Space. These two informations surprise us because it seems that they don't bother about the uniform worldwide standard which the ITU is working on with all international broadcasters. It could happen that this system would dictate the standard later. This is what we are worried about.

One has to take this very seriously because much has been said about direct satellite broadcasting in the last five years and no real action was taken. That's why I was very pleased to hear that two working groups had been formed. But I hope that these groups will work very effectively and not "miss the bus" as I said before, so that we finally can take over what others have introduced already. That I think could be a very big disadvantage because definitely, I think that Afro-Star is clever enough not to introduce something that would remain a closed-shop, although a very big continent, just for Africa and the Middle-East. So they have some thoughts behind that. Definitely a closed-shop system would have no real chance as a full substitute for shortwave because that would imply that only in such an area with a specific receiver, the signal could be received. Unless a substitute for shortwave has been introduced that is for universal use, like in our days a shortwave receiver, we don't give such a system a big chance. But, one has to take the development very seriously.

In the publications that we have concerning Indo-Star, there is a clear indication that they want to take a great proportion of the market over. They see this as a test case for the new technology in the developing world. One cannot take this seriously enough. I come back to my question concerning the test that Voice of America is conducting or has conducted with JPL and with the NASA Research Center. Perhaps you tell us something about this because it seems that the results were quite promising. Although, unfortunately, in the S-Band. I am an engineer and I can tell you, if you have to cover already AM, FM and the L-Band, and additionally the S-Band because the United States insisted in 1992, in Spain, on the 2.3 GHz range, that will make it more difficult and more expensive.

Kim Elliott:

I'm not an engineer at VOA so I'm not really intimate with those tests except to know they were done, they were successful. VOA is keeping its options open about technologies. I think that's the reason for the letter of intent which is not that much of a binding agreement.

It is a letter of intent and we can get out of it if we absolutely have to. Also the S-Band that he refers to is up around 2.3 GHz, 2300 MHz, and the L-Band is 1600 MHz, and the S-Band seems will probably be adopted by India and some of the other countries in that region.

Arno Selders:

Just as an additional allocation. Worldwide 1.5 GHz, except for the United States of America, was allocated. Additional, just for the United States, 2.3 GHz. And, for some countries, an additional allocation of 2.6 GHz.

Kim Elliott:

So in other words, it looks like it boils down to two different allocations which would boil down to two different types of receivers, which is not perfect but it's not the absolute complete disaster either. I agree it would be nice to have that global standard and Arno just made a very good point and that is if a satellite broadcasting conveyor like Afro-Space gets the monopoly on conveying international radio but it has limited channels, then that will become the mother of all gate-keepers and will be very dangerous to the future of international radio.

Graham Mytton:

There are so many issues raised by Arno, we could be here all evening. But one point to make about Noel Samara is that he's going on 1.5 GHz and that is obviously the best in terms of portable radios and table-top radios. The problem with Samara-and he's a great visionary and a great guy and I wish him success-is I think he's using the wrong technology. It's not just the question of the 1.5, it's a question of the system which he uses which we think is an inferior system. It may not be usable inside a building. It may not be usable inside a moving vehicle. There may be many difficulties. And the critical issue about any digital audio broadcasting system and the first question is: Is it going to be used by a domestic broadcaster? If the answer is no then forget it. Shortwave has succeeded not because it is an international broadcasting system; it has succeeded because it was primarily a domestic broadcasting medium. Who were the great pioneers of shortwave? The Soviet Union. The Soviet Union developed shortwave in the 1920s as a means of delivering radio programs to that vast country. India and most of the African countries, all still use shortwave to get full national radio coverage. Brazil, China, all these countries depend on shortwave for national broadcasting. This is why radio sets in all those countries have shortwave on them. Let me just show you a chart.

This is what people have. Again it's the same countries as I said before. If you had a radio, it's virtually certain you have shortwave. In Kenya and Tanzania, almost all radios have shortwave. In Yemen, it's much less likely although the data may be unreliable. We're not absolutely sure whether that is correct because the difference seems a bit too large to us. Generally speaking, in the south, if you have a radio, it's probably got shortwave on it. The reason is that domestic broadcasters use shortwave. The reason why we have to keep our eyes on Samara is if he gets domestic broadcasters interested... When I saw him last month in Washington, I asked him: "How many domestic broadcasters have you got?" He hummed and hawed and he didn't answer me. I pressed him on this and eventually he said that eight were interested. Well there are 53 African countries in his domestic reception area. I'd say to all of us here: Much as I admire Samara, much as I wish him every success, I don't think it's going to fly, I don't think it's going to run and I don't think there's any point in it until he's got domestic broadcasters interested, committed and involved.

Digital audio broadcasting is the answer for domestic broadcasting in a country like Nigeria, Zaire, Zimbabwe, with the enormous problems of running series of FM and AM relays, with all the problems of security, electricity supply, transport, people steal the cable, steal the antenna and all sorts of things in remote areas. It's a real problem running a national FM or AM network. Satellite, the bird in the sky, right above you, of course you're in the tropics, it's right overhead. It's a dream come true for African engineers making broadcasting available. Of course, if it happens it will become an international transmission system too. But I think the domestic thing has to come.

CHAPTER EIGHT

REALITY AND VISION IN INTERNATIONAL COMMUNICATIONS: INTEGRATION OF MEDIA/ CROSS-BORDER BROADCASTING

Editors' Note:

If the present is upon us, can the future be far behind? And, what will that future be? There appears to be some trends which are rapidly emerging which indicate that the future may be considerably different from the past. The integration of the media poses some astonishing possibilities and also some perplexing realities for all people involved with communications and international broadcasting.

This chapter attempts to provoke some consideration of the various issues, possibilities, complexities associated with the "next wave" of development in international communications.

HOWARD ASTER
PROFESSOR
MCMASTER UNIVERSITY
HAMILTON, ONTARIO - CANADA

Introduction.

There is an ominous sense shared by many people in the communications industries and those people who are involved in programme production that we are quickly entering a new era. To this point in time, we have witnessed the maturing of various media in their own particular manner. However, what is unique about the present moment and the immanent future is that as various media mature, they are also becoming fused, interconnected, integrated. This fusion is being propelled by technological innovations but it is also being compelled by a recognition that the inter-connections between television, computers and telecommunications is creating colossally large business and industrial opportunities. The worlds of leisure, entertainent, information and education are all poised to be transformed by the new integration of the media.

We have a number of individuals who will provide us with some unique insights into these emergeing developments. Mark Starowicz has spent most of his professional life as an innovator in radio and then in television. He was the individual who defined for the CBC the "As It Happens" public affairs radio program. He then went on to define the special quality of the CBC evening public affairs documentary program, The Journal. He is now the Executive Producer of the documentaries unit for the CBC.

Professor Donald Browne of the University of Minnesota has been one of the most astute analysts of international broadcasting. He has contributed widely to the academic literature on international radio broadcasting and he will raise some vital questions for the future directions of international radio.

Howard Aster is a political scientist whose concerns have centered on the inter-relationship between national culture and international communications. He will attempt to assess some of the emerging trends in the integration of the media and to raise some issues relating to our assumptions in understanding these developments.

Catherine Murray, a professor at the Simon Fraser University School of Communications, will express some healthy skepticism with regard to the developments of the "information highway". She reminds us that communications developments must be lodged in some considerations of democracy in order for those developments to serve the public interest.

Finally, The Niagara Institute present for us some broad considerations of the factors and influences which ought to guide us as we consider change into the 21st century. It may not be possible to know the future. But we can certainly equip ourselves with some ideas which will make the analysis and anticipation of the future more sensible.

MARK STAROWICZ
CBC TELEVISION
TORONTO, ONTARIO - CANADA

The Gutenberg revolution of Television
Speculations on the Impact of New Technologies

(This paper expresses the personal opinions of
the author, not the views of the CBC.)

Preface.

In Lyons, France, the Lumière family owned a large film plate manufacturing plant. In 1895, Louis and Auguste Lumière had devised the world's first portable film camera. They called it the cinematograph.

Edison had invented moving pictures a couple of years earlier, but not a portable camera or a means to project the image. His camera was a huge room into which you stepped to be photographed. And his film could only be viewed by peering into a box.

The Lumière camera was half the size of a briefcase, and doubled as a projector by reversing the lens. But the Lumières weren't quite sure what to do with it. They shot some factory scenes and a sequence of a train arriving at Lyons station.

Perhaps this instrument might have some application in medical photography, they speculated. Perhaps it might have industrial applications. They planned to manufacture two hundred and to market this apparatus for its presumably limited applications.

On December 28, 1895, the two brothers went to Paris to hold a modest public screening at a small theatre they had rented off the Champs Elysées: Le Salon Indien. It was the first public projection of moving pictures in the history of civilization. People were amused, but when the scene of the train arriving at Lyons station came on - a low angle of the locomotive coming towards the camera - spectators reacted in fright, because it seemed the train was coming at them.

Later in Lyons, the sons reported this to their father, Antoine Lumière, who instantly ordered all the cinematographs to be locked up. *None*, absolutely none were ever to be sold. Instead, factory workers were to be recruited to travel around Europe recording images. But they must guard their cinematographs with their lives, sleep with them, and never let anyone examine one.

The sons, perplexed at this order to shroud the camera in secrecy, protested: "Why?"

"Don't you see the point?" Lumière said. "The product is not the *camera*. It' the *film*."

That moment in Lyons, in 1895, less that one hundred years ago, was the dawn of a medium that would shape our century.

Visual Factories and Monasteries.

Although the camera invented one hundred years ago was small, the industry which grew around it was cumbersome, and required large institutions to create the product. Massive newsreel companies arose. When television came, the institutions became even larger - networks, powerful television stations and news agencies.

The visual equivalent of the book had been invented, but it was still being produced by modern monasteries. A newsreel or a television program was still terribly expensive. The crews were large and cumbersome. The editing, distribution and transmission required millions of dollars of equipment.

So for most of the last hundred years we've had large monasteries, and also a priesthood of administrators, editors and a select corps of journalists with rules and codes and myths as intricate as the Old Testament. In fact, you became a journalist the way you became a priest - you started at the bottom, apprenticed, helped out at the altar, and eventually were admitted to the sacrament. (Can you imagine this in publishing? Do we tell Paul Theroux that before he can write a book he's got to work his way up from the mail room?)

Now, one hundred years after the invention of the camera, many of the monasteries are about to fall, and much of the priesthood will disperse. We are at the threshold of the Gutenberg Revolution in Television and Film. The effect will profoundly transform politics, commerce, and art. The result will be both liberating and terrifying.

But before we consider the results, let's look at what is causing the revolution.

There are three stages to the television process - recording, processing and transmission. All of them are extraordinarily expensive, so you couldn't play in this game without assembling enormous capital and infrastructure. Monasteries. Visual factories.

Now three revolutions have sequentially fallen into place.

The Recording Breakthrough.

The first and most profoundly revolutionary instrument made a very innocent appearance under our Christmas trees ten years ago. The Handycam. In those ten years it has developed in sophistication to the extent that an entire 24-hour all news channel in New York City functions with these. Make no mistake: This is the most profoundly subversive instrument of communication since the Lumière cinematograph. This, even more than satellites, destroys borders - who can stop someone from recording in China or in Iran? This places the power of recording within the hands of average people.

And I don't mean for tornadoes and *America's Funniest Home Videos*. This camera, and most particularly its more expensive brother the three-chip Hi-8, is *broadcast quality*. You can buy it on your credit card. The monopoly of the priesthood is broken. A talented young producer or journalist has the means of production within his grasp.

The Processing Breakthrough.

But even if you can record very cheaply, and cross frontiers easily, there is still the next barrier. Editing and processing everything you have recorded required a $250,000 edit suite, and an expensive editing infrastructure.

The next instrument of revolution, which destroys this barrier, has been on our desks for most of a decade too. The computer, which has already revolutionized every newspaper and magazine and publishing house on the planet, is taking us from desktop publishing, to desktop video. The instrument which replaces a half-million dollar edit suite at a TV network is a desktop computer. Enter your field tapes into the computer memory though a videocassette machine, the machine digitally stores all the moving images, and you then edit your entire story or documentary with a mouse. Right now you can buy a top of the line system for $100,000, and do in your rec room virtually anything a television station can do. This means that thousands of small companies can proliferate, literally in rec rooms, editing and assembling productions. A pair of talented people with a second mortgage on a house can enter the television game - you no longer have to be part of a visual factory, a monastery. This is a massive devolution of the power to create from large institutions, to cottage industries.

The Distribution Breakthrough.

The final barrier is transmission. You had to negotiate with someone who had one of those scarce franchises-a spot on the dial or on the converter. These were the gate-keepers to the system.

Over the next five years, the gates will disappear. Through fibre-optic cable and direct broadcast satellite, the number of channels doubles, triples, quadruples until they become virtually infinite.

In fact, the idea of a channel is really an old style of thinking. We will be summoning up whatever program we want at any time we want from the data storage systems which are in evolution today. We will come home and summon up the local news at our convenience - it may have gone out over the air at six, but if we got home at seven thirty simply summon it up from a central data bank. Television will become completely a la carte. I might want the local news, followed by tonight's *MacNeil/Lehrer* followed by *Dinosaurs* which I missed last night, followed by a video on sibling rivalry because my kids are fighting, followed by the series on The Civil War, which I never did get around to see two years ago, followed by tonight's *Arsenio Hall*.

The television set is an appliance which accesses a gigantic magazine stand, which is being constantly replenished. A magazine stand which not only contains this week's releases, but remembers every magazine that ever appeared on that newsstand before. Another way of thinking of the TV set is as a terminal which accesses a gigantic central library. The programs are the books, periodicals and newspapers in the library.

The Revolution.

The conjunction of these three breakthroughs - recording, production and distribution - is the Gutenberg Revolution of television, which I define as the moment at which the means of production becomes democratically accessible. The importance of this Revolution parallels the invention of the offset press and the computer for the liberation of information flow.

It's potent not only because it will cause thousands of new enterprises and voices to arise in an explosion of pluralism, but because it destroys the tyranny of linear time. Remember when college kids used to come to your door asking you to subscribe to the *Reader's Digest* or *Cosmopolitan*?

What do you think the circulation of the *Reader's Digest* would be if the terms of the contract were this: I will come to your door every Thursday evening at 8 pm, hand you a copy of the *Reader's Digest*, and regardless of whether or not you're sick, or you're having a fight with your spouse, I will come back and collect it at 9? Yet I've just described the distribution of ABC's *20/20*. It's primitive, linear, and probably reaches ten per cent of the people who might otherwise have considered watching it.

The VCR has not solved this conundrum; surveys show 85 % of VCR owners have no idea how to program them to time shift.

Just as the telephone answering machine is being replaced by voice-mail message banks, so the VCR will be replaced by the digital program bank. You will watch *20/20* at any time you choose, and if your tap is leaking, you'll request a video on basic plumbing.

We are witnessing one of the fundamental re-organizations of the world's distribution and storage of knowledge: The hybridization of the computer, the satellite, the visual archive and broadcasting. Its scale parallels the great information revolutions of the millennium.

We can take many paths in examining the future. I want to take only two tonight: One, the impact on our social and political lives. Two, how countries will become winners or losers in this fundamental shift of information distribution.

The "Atomization" of Television.

First, let's begin to imagine the effect of this infinite channel universe.

We've already gone through the *fragmentation* of the television audience in the late eighties through the spread of cable and the birth of satellite services. Network shares have plunged to the 50 to 60 percent mark. This is nothing compared to the *atomization* of the audience which will be brought on by the advent of current technologies.

The 1,000 channel universe, whether it comes through cable or satellite, will destroy regulation. The moral basis for regulating broadcasting throughout the 20th century has been the limited spectrum. There were only so many channels possible on the radio or television dial. Not everyone could have a spot on the dial, so a mechanism of licensing these scarce spots was required. Therefore the state appropriated it as a public space, and devised a system of allocation and a regulatory agency to administer it.

The moment one can have an <u>infinite</u> number of spaces, television becomes like newsprint -- there is no apparent justification to regulate the allocation of this resource in a democracy. Regulation will collapse, and the unrestrained marketplace will shape television and radio.

The consequences of this are extraordinary. We are embarking on an age which will parallel all the great newspaper wars of the 1920's - press barons, mergers and acquisitions, the emergence of new collectivities and interest groups, and considerable political impact will flow from this.

In this world, nothing restrains a community of interest, or taste, or political conviction from establishing a channel or service, any more than they're restrained now from starting a magazine or a newspaper or publishing a book. There will be a national gay channel within a short space of time, several channels serving women's interests, regional interest services will spring up, there will be a second explosion of evangelical services, ethnic services...the list is infinite. (I use the word "channel" for convenience; I don't mean they would all be full 24-hour channels; they may be daily two or four hour services, something between a channel and a program. The data storage systems of the future make the word "channel" somewhat antiquated.)

In fact, the future is visible in the present by staring at a large newsstand. Channels will parallel the magazine covers. Natural history channels, book channels, left wing and right wing channels, a variety sex channels, a battery of sports channels, channels that address taste constituencies (in effect a Rolling Stone constituency channel, a Vanity Fair constituency channel, a home repair channel, a spectrum of children's channels, and a vast array of shopping channels, which I'll return to later.)

If there are enough people to sustain a reasonable national circulation for a magazine today, these people will be serviced by a channel within a decade. A hundred thousand people will soon be a commercially viable community for a service. Just stare at the largest periodical newsstand you can find and you see the future.

Social and religious constituencies, who already have organized followings, will flourish. Nothing restrains a Jehovah's Witness Channel, nothing restrains a channel by the Rev. Sung Myung Moon, any more than anything restrained his purchase of the *Washington Times*. The Televangelism phenomenon of the Seventies and Eighties will appear tame compared to the explosion that is imminent. Television is approaching accessibility to virtually any medium-sized cult. Elizabeth Prophet will recruit and maintain her flock through a specialty channel.

It's wise to remind ourselves that at the dawn of radio, fundamentalist religion was almost the dominant force in the early days of the medium, and entire stations arose around individual orators, with considerable political impact. Father Coughlin's violently anti-New Deal and anti-semitic broadcasts out of Detroit were a considerable irritant for the Roosevelt administration.

That era also suggests to us that demagoguery will appear not only in evangelical but in political form. Senator Huey Long was a potent national force with his "Every-Man-A-King" movement which had membership in the millions. Channels will emerge around political and social demagogues. Pat Robertson, and his translation of a religious following into a political one, is the smallest hint of the inevitably emerging television landscape. The political landscape will be more vulnerable to demagogic and charismatic leaders.

David Halberstam, in his book *The Powers That Be*, chronicled the fundamental change in 20th century politics as television created the single mass audience, helped destroy the party apparatus, and allowed the executive branch to communicate directly with the popular base without intervening local party bosses. The reverse trend is in the ascendancy now, as the majority fragments, and one can extrapolate the ascendancy of special interest groups.

These special interest groups, already powerful within our democracies, are effective users of the print form today, and will increasingly assemble their constituencies through the television form. A National Rifle Association Channel? Why not? What one sees now only at election time in commercial spots from political action committees will become constant services, with consequences we can only speculate on. The re-ordering of the televisual world will re-order the political world. Any revolution in communications has always changed the political power equations.

The Commercial Impact.

The revolution will also radically change the commercial world. Once again, let's turn to the birth of radio. In the Twenties and Thirties, there were stations owned by commercial enterprises and entirely devoted towards distributing and advertising that enterprise's products. The most extreme example was one station in New Orleans which was devoted entirely to selling a patent medicine based on extract from goat's glands. It did very well. Radio very quickly became a strange amalgam of patent medicine peddling and bible-thumping evangelism.

There is a national horoscope infomercial I saw last month: A charismatic woman has a team of twenty numerologists, spiritual advisers, fortune tellers who operate on 1-800 numbers. The infomercial was repeated three times during the night and it was clear that this woman had tapped a huge market where we can easily extrapolate entire horoscope channels that almost resemble the Home Shopping Channel.

The apparent conversion of late night television into hours upon hours of infomercials is not just amusing, but very indicative of a commercial revolution. I don't know if you've viewed the latest generation of infomercials, some of which last an hour, but their growth is geometric, and it's not hard to extrapolate that what's an hour now will become an entire channel within a decade -- a channel for each product line. The new television age will see a re-ordering of the marketplace, because the very nature of commercial distribution will change. What is a cosmetic franchise informercial today, repeated endlessly on late night, will become a much vaster enterprise which is organized through a combination of television sales and pyramid distribution. Mary Kay Cosmetics is a distribution phenomenon of the Fifties and Sixties and Seventies. The new mass distribution enterprise of the year 2,000 will be much larger, with wider product lines, plugged into a human sales force working from home, and which will dwarf the marketing phenomena of the past. That means the emergence of new corporations, and totally new methods of product distribution, which will have an unimagined restructuring effect on the consumer market-place. An amalgam of the old franchise phenomenon, computer networking and television marketing. Corporate franchise channels.

A fascinating article in a recent *New Yorker* chronicles Barry Diller's speculations into the future. After building the Fox Network for Rupert Murdoch, he struck out on his own and considered what to invest in, where the future lay. He passed on buying the NBC network, and finally shocked everyone by embracing the Home Shopping Network. The moment of epiphany is instructive. He was in the studio during one fashion clothing sales session:

"Diller made one more visit to QVC, at 9 a.m. on Saturday, November 7th, for Diane Von Furstenberg's first sale. Surrounded by her silk clothing, she sat beside the host on a smell stage in a large brick cavern. Diller stood behind one of the eighty telephone operators there and watched the toll free calls pour in. Diller was awed... In less than two hours, the computer showed, Von Furstenberg had sold twenty nine thousand items to nineteen thousand customers, for a total of a million two hundred thousand dollars." [*New Yorker Magazine*, Feb.22, 1993 p.60]

In another session, soap opera star Susan Lucci sold almost half a million dollar's worth of a hair care product carrying her name - in just one hour.

The QVC shopping channel made a net profit of nearly twenty million dollars in 1991; in the first nine months of 1992, it already showed a profit of thirty-six million dollars.

Liberty Cable Television in New York wants to create separate Bergdorf Goodman and F.A.O. Schwartz channels, and incidentally is on the verge of announcing agreements with Lincoln Centre to offer a live concert, plays and operas service.

Once again, we can see from this the possible scale of the change in the future marketplace. So far we've been conditioned to think that the future will make it possible for us to book a flight from our touch-tone keypad, or pay a telephone bill by phone or computer, or check our bank balance. The temptation to buy cubic zirconia jewellery or Elvis busts on the Shopping Channel did not seem like the stuff of revolutions any more than the drive-in teller had been. This is pretty tepid stuff, and if that's the impact of the television and computer revolution, we can take the interactivity revolution in stride.

But what we haven't been seeing is the complete re-ordering of the consumer marketplace, the transformation of retailing and distribution as we know it, and the consequent emergence of entirely new retailing and marketing corporations dependent on the television - a sort of televisual mall. The television distribution revolution will transform the nature and structure of world retailing.

In fact, we may see a blend of general service and commercial interest. Take any industrial lobby which already produces a considerable amount of public propaganda - the nuclear industry, for example. It has an interest in advocacy advertising. It produces documentaries and magazines and educational material. Why would it not find common interest with other like-minded industrial interests and see merit in joint ownership of a technology/science/environment channel which is not overt advocacy or advertising, but which is a visually rich general interest channel which nevertheless commissions programs and works more fitting with its technological perspective - a sort of "technology is good" channel?

Now stand back from this televisual newsstand, stand back from the Technology channel owned by such a consortium of high tech companies, imagine the Green channel funded by Greenpeace and the World Wildlife Fund, imagine the ten or twelve Shopping channels divided into high fashion, home repair, automotive, and cosmetics, stand back and see the horoscope spiritual readers channel, the ultra conservative channel, the local and national gay service, the multiple women's channels, the Jehovah's Witness, the Moonie channel, the channels built around regional interests and a dozen different Ross Perots, the political action committee channels and even political party channels, the Catholic Church channel, the channels built around literary interests, the vast array of music channels which will replace MTV, the health and medical channel, the personal fitness channels, the computer buff channel. The variety of all news-channels catering to ter buff channel. The variety of all news-channels catering to specific interests.... stand back, look at the news and magazine stand of today, and you see the future.

In it you see both excitement in the multiplication of voices, pluralism, the acceleration of debate, the film and book channels, and you also see the re-ordering of commerce.

But most of all you see the scale of the revolution.

And also, we see a new information order, not all of it comforting.

The Disappearance of Public Space.

The Israeli scholar Elihu Katz points out that a radio was once a force for national integration, then, with the advent of television, it become a medium of segmentation and individualization, with stations tailored to micro taste constituencies. Television became the medium of national integration . But now television is becoming a medium of segmentation, but as Katz puts it " there's nothing there to replace television as a medium of integration."

This leads to what he and a number of scholars have called "the disappearance of public space."

As I alluded earlier, this appears to be the single greatest impact of this Gutenberg age of television - not the *emergence* of a majority, a body politic, a public arena which eventually followed the invention of the printing press, but ironically, the reverse, the *disappearance* of the majority, or at least its atomization into regional interests, commercial, cultural and demographic clusters.

The so-called majority, which you could imagine watching the major newscasts and making informed civic judgements on the basis of that, was never that large, really. The combined evening viewing of the three US network newscasts has hovered around 45 million, and CNN is consumed by a very small percentage of US households except in times of major events.

In fact, as Les Brown observed, historically, US newscasts have been scheduled where they will do the least possible damage to commercial revenue, not where they will reach the most people; it's always been interesting that the program which has been arguably the most influential forum of policy debate, ABC's *Nightline*, has always had to be banished to the periphery of the schedule.

But even this fragile assembly of a civic prime time majority seems to be doomed, and we learn from a recent article by Ken Auletta [*New Yorker Magazine*, March 15/93] that NBC Nightly News might well disappear if GE sells the profitable parts of NBC off, and we also know that American TV News services are evacuating many of their world bureaux. Television News in general, it appears, is destined to be another segmented specialty service. There may be two or three national all-news services like CNN, just as there will undoubtedly be three or four cartoon channels and even more shopping channels. The atomization of TV News will accelerate the segmentation of the body politic.

Just as the large movie theatres fell to the Cineplex cubicle theatres, so the public television space is being "cineplexed".

Not only is public space being cineplexed, it is being segregated into economic layers. A lot of what we get for "free" now, through commercial sponsorship, will have a value attached to it. Just as we pay five dollars a month for *Time* or fifty cents for a newspaper, so most of the times we access the central television data bank or library, we'll be spending money. We have been accustomed to this in the electronic print form by toll changes to access a database. Television will surely go down the same road.

There will be rich neighbourhoods and poor neighbourhoods. There will be high value specialty services, where your child can access a rich televisual blend of programming and CD-ROM information on a subject. And off-air, or basic cable commercial television will survive, but on a very low grade. The high-value product will have been stripped out, and off-air TV might, supported by commercials, becomes more of a poor man's medium.

Thus, not only is public space being segmented - "cineplexed" - but effectively being auctioned off into neighbourhoods, and televisual slums - which is the ultimate pernicious segmentation of public consciousness.

The gradual replacing of the collective experience by the individual or cluster experience extends far beyond news into comedy, drama and all forms of televised entertainment.

And if the 1000-channel universe combined with the production revolution accelerate this disappearance of the majority, we are witnessing a social and political sea change of fundamental proportions.

Elihu Katz, in an essay entitled "Individualization, Segmentation and Globalization", observes two simultaneous trends in the technology: Segmentation and transnational globalization, and observes that these apparently contradictory trends have one common effect: neither addresses the nation-state. "If the medium is the message then media theory foresees that these new technologies mean the effective end of the nation state" . [Translated from the French text].

He writes:"Why are governments contributing to this erosion of nation states and national cultures? Why don't they see that more leads to less - to insignificance...to endless distraction, to the atomization and evacuation of public space? Why don't they see that national identity and citizen participation are compromised? Why don't they realize that they're contributing directly to the erosion of the enormous potential which television has to enlighten and unite populations into the fold of national cultures?" [Chapter 13 of *Le défi des Télévisions Nationales à l'Ere de la Mondialisation,*les Presses de l'Université de Montréal, 1992]

He speculates that governments of the past decade, particularly in Europe, have been more interested in economic than in social well-being, are happy to unload public broadcasting systems, and are more attracted by the potential benefits of globalization.

Whatever the motives, the trend is inescapable. Domestic space is being segmented. And transnational space is emerging, but in private hands, and outside the control of the nation state.

The Transnational Mega-Channels.

The 1000 channel universe is not only allowing micro-channels, but *macro* channels. Again, as in the 1910's and 20's, we are seeing the emergence of press empires, the new Hearsts and Pulitzers and Beaverbrooks. The difference this time is that the clusterings will be transnational.

We are seeing the emergence of transnational Media Barons in Murdoch, and Turner and Berlusconi; the empires are not as local and personal, and maybe because of that not so political, although that remains to be seen.

If we've underestimated the political and social effects of atomization, we should not underestimate the scale of globalization's effects either.

Let's go back a few years to when Time-Life was contemplating its merger with Warner communications. Time-Life, one of the ten largest communications conglomerates on the *planet*, stared at the future and decided that this communications giant was *too small a corporate unit to compete on a world scale.* Consequently, we see the re-organization of international communications into ever-larger vertically integrated corporations like Bertelsman and Hachette and Time Warner, at the same time that we are seeing services atomize.

For many years there's been a corporate vision of "global marketing" which has paralleled the financial community's vision of "global banking". The collapse of Communism has now opened up the Eastern European market; satellites have allowed such forces as Hong Kong's "Star" channel to have a satellite footprint which extends from Indonesia to Dubai, and which has tapped into India's burgeoning middle class in a way that has frightened the New Delhi government. China, which manufactures 60 million television sets a year, can't keep up with basic demand. The vision of global channels and global marketing to emerging middle classes hitherto inaccessible through terrestrial channels has been a communications and advertising Holy Grail which has transfixed many of the world's communications giants.

This has raised many spectres - cultural homogenization, transnational media barons, the Coca-colonization of the planet - which are not for us to explore here, and which are, at any rate, quite familiar scenarios by now.

National Strategies in the Television Revolution.

What I want to address now is some idea of strategies for survival in this televisual revolution which is shattering into atoms one the one hand, and clustering into transnational conglomerates on the other. What are the policy consequences?

Policies of exclusion or controlled access to domestic markets have been suffering erosion throughout the world, though Katz is right that the principal reason so far has not been technological so much as the national government's enthusiasm allowing such services in.

Britain, which has most successfully limited the fragmentation of its own market, has proven to be farsighted. It has incubated and nurtured one of the two most powerful television industries in the world - the other being the United States' - and consequently is well poised to take the next step, enter the world arena with a sophisticated television production apparatus. The BBC, despite the depradations of the Thatcher era, survives now as the centrepiece of Britain's industry, and the most efficient exporter of televisual products in the world. The BBC Television World Service is growing throughout the planet.

The United States, as the largest single market in the English world, has never had to worry about protecting itself, and rather is more interested in world electronic barriers coming down.

However, the so called "disappearance of public space" will probably have its most profound effect *in the US*, where cost of fragmentation of the body politic will probably exact its greatest price. The price may not be cultural, because the US is such a powerful generator of its own popular culture, but it may be political, in the sense that special interests and regional concerns will predominate at the expense of national consensus.

To the US, I suspect, the key is the significant enlargement of public broadcasting, as the decline of networks diminishes public space. The American idea of public broadcasting has been unlike the British - for the British it was the main stage, for the Americans, public broadcasting was seen as a mechanism for minorities, classes and interests disenfranchised by the commercial networks.

The impending segmentation of public space into premium neighbourhoods and commercial slums will, I think, create a moral imperative for the United States to assure that free basic television, television which serves the public agenda, is preserved and enlarged in in the face of the electronic segregation of knowledge and information.

The US will need the national stage, the arena for public policy, national news, national events, and needs public broadcasting in the national arena sense, the collective experience, and one hopes it will see fit to invest heavily in public television for the health of the democratic process. The home for national news, aside from CNN, may well become PBS. I suspect the public broadcasting era in the U.S. is just beginning.

For smaller markets, such as Canada and most European countries, the prospects are indeed difficult. The 1,000 channel universe, once the satellite cracks the regulatory borders, will become a fierce challenge to the nation state's capacity to define its agenda. Regulatory exclusion will at best retard the inevitable.

In the television revolution, a nation will be either an aggressive player, or a cultural victim. Governments will eventually realize that television production is like steel or aeronautics. You're either in the game or you're not, you're just an importer. Unless you have a significant domestic television production industry, you will not only increasingly lose control of your market, but you will not be able to participate in one of the emerging mega-industries of the 21st century.

The only formula for televisual survival in the global era is to *produce* television, not merely to *exclude*.

In a world where Time-Life feared that being the sixth largest in the world was too small to be a player in the field, the smart policy is not to dismember or fragment whatever television industries or corporations a country has. It is smarter to double their size and assure that you have global class industrial units. Had the British fragmented the BBC, and flooded their own market (which they seemed tempted to do under Prime Minister Thatcher), it would have been the equivalent of dismembering an aircraft industry at the threshold of the jet travel era. Now they will reap the benefits of nurturing their public sector investment.

Just as Japan targeted automobile production and the computer industry and focused a national industrial strategy based on an assessment of the future, so national governments have to develop an industrial strategy for the television age which is upon us. This means not only rebuilding the public sector, as an investment, but also developing a very strong private sector.

But governments have been slow to apprehend what is coming, and even slower to realize that television production is one of the most powerful growth industries on the planet. And the battle will not be over technology, but product.

The 1000 channel universe will create an unimagined market for programs. Distribution, in effect, is massively outstripping production. We have satellite footprints encompassing Indonesia to the Red Sea, we have the coming on stream of the East European markets, the addition of viewers in the millions annually from India and China - but where are the programs coming from? Right now, the most precious resource in the industry is not a satellite in the sky but a vault of films and series. But those vaults, which reside largely in Britain and the US, will feed only a minuscule proportion of the appetite shaping in the global market.

Here, intermediate countries can find hope in a future that otherwise looks like an obliterating tidal wave.

The playing field is relatively level. Except for the head start of Britain and the US, the world television does not inherently belong to anyone yet. Youth and children do not yet belong exclusively to Disney. Animation is not a Japanese monopoly - yet. Britain does not have a monopoly on the classics.

Astute national governments will read current trends and see the equivalent of the automotive age or the computer age and will develop an industrial strategy to assure a significant national television industry. They will not only renew and refocus their public sector, but assure the emergence of a globally competitive private sector. They will invest in craft training and development programs in their educational streams. They will also identify their niches in the global market, as the British have capitalized on their news tradition.

The traditional idea of export will change too - not by sending a sales team to a program convention, but by launching international satellite services. A country without two or three international satellite channels will be the technological equivalent of a third world country in the emerging global competition. Unless you are home to a proportion of the channels in the 1,000 channel universe, you will lose the coming competition. In the global village, you're going to need an address.

In the era of the televisual central library, an industrial strategy must assure that you put your cultural and information product on the shelf.

An exhilarating and terrifying re-ordering of the world information order is under way. It presents colossal opportunities for countries able to lead the way in the production of the visual form, and cultural perils for those countries which misread the awesome scale of the world industry that is dawning.

So far, most governments have been obsessed by the technology - the fibre optics, the satellites, high definition, the computer networks. The revolution is *occasioned* by technology. But the most dramatic competition, and the greatest rewards, will not be in the technology. They will be in the *software*, the programs and the services.

Remember what Antoine Lumière said when his sons reported the impact of their first public film exhibition at the Salon Indien in Paris. He held his invention, the cinematograph, in his hands and said: *"Don't you see the point? The product is not the camera. It's the film!"*

DONALD BROWNE
PROFESSOR
UNIVERSITY OF MINNESOTA
DEPARTMENT OF SPEECH-COMMUNICATION
MINNEAPOLIS, MN - USA

Toward 2001 and Beyond: International Radio in a Multimedia World

Introduction.

To note that we live in a rapidly changing world is to state the obvious. Or is it? We see and hear so much that is amazing, that we may be losing our capacity to be amazed and to note what those amazing things are doing to our own lives, and to our livelihoods. Where international radio is concerned, we now have a world of one super-power, represented by several official and unofficial international radio and television services; several major economic and/or political powers, each with one or more international radio services and some with international television; an emerging (if with difficulty) European Community, with a regional television news service; and more sovereign nations than ever, especially in the former Soviet Union, where the new nations have retained their once-Soviet-administered international radio services, if they had one, while some of those which did not have created them.

There remains a great deal of strife and rapid change, which certainly provides radio with plenty to cover. But this also is a world of rapidly changing technology, which holds out to international radio listeners and practitioners the promise of relatively interference-free reception over most portions of the globe. In short, despite the end of the so-called Cold War, times seem quite good for international broadcasting, and technological change holds promise of making them even better.

Whether most listeners, and, for that matter, most stations, will be able to afford that technology is another question. If we presume that they will, there will be a far tougher question to answer: will they want to? The technological advances that someday (sooner rather than later, I think) will make international digital audio broadcasting from satellites far more common, and receivers for it far more economical, is part of the same technological progress that is bringing BBC World

Service Television, CNN, and a host of other program services delivered by satellite, cable, and VCR, from near and far, into almost unimaginable places: the slums and villages of India, the Amazon jungles, the heart of Africa.

Measured in absolute terms, the audiences in those locales are not numerous. It may be decades, if ever, before they become so. But there are audiences within audiences, and increasing we see the longstanding "target" audiences for international radio - government officials, businesspeople, teachers and students, perhaps religious authorities and military officers - gaining access to TV sets, videocassette recorders, satellite dishes, FAX communication links, etc. It should not be difficult to foresee a world in which more and more of international radio's best customers have an alternative source of international communication at their disposal. After all, many of them are in a good position to be able to afford it, and have the curiosity to want it.

I am very familiar with the many aspects of television in particular which make it less than suitable for international communication, even to the sort of target audience I've described. Can a given visual image mean one and the same thing to diverse cultures? Don't visuals quite often distract from, or contradict, the aural message? Isn't it much easier for the authorities to detect someone watching a "forbidden" program than it is for them to detect someone in the act of listening? And then there are the various issues of cost: of program-making, of transmission, of reception, of repair, etc.

I grant all of that. But I also argue that international television, whether its originators <u>mean</u> for it to communicate internationally or not, is communicating both entertainment <u>and</u> information even now (and many viewers - perhaps even more for international audiences than for audiences in the country of program origin - may not distinguish between the two). Those audiences are increasing, and very likely will continue to do so, thanks to changing technology.

Is international radio ready to face that challenge? My almost four decades of listening, and of meeting with international broadcasters, lead me to a range of answers, from a qualified yes to a resounding no. I shall not name names. Rather, I shall ask a series of questions, which aren't terribly original, and which certainly aren't all that complex. But I feel that they will become increasingly vital as the next millennium nears, and as more of the world becomes a more multichannel environment. I invite international radio broadcasters to measure their programming in this light.

1. Who might want to hear the programming on offer?
2. Why would broadcasters and their paymasters want them to have it?
3. Where else might they get the material it provides? And how effective is such programming likely to be in comparison with similar material from other generally available sources, especially other media?
4. How will they know what the broadcaster is offering, where to find it, and when?
5. How will broadcasters know that audiences are getting what the broadcasters want them to get - not so much to receive clearly and reliably, although that is crucial, but to understand what broadcasters want them to understand. (Whether they agree with broadcasters' points of view is another matter, of course. But if they don't understand, there's very little prospect for agreement).

Who Might Want the Programs? Most international broadcasters have some sense of the nature of the audience, or at least of the audience they'd most hope to reach. The advent of world television is quite likely to fractionate audiences even more, both in terms of amounts of time and of specific day parts available for international radio listening. I feel that it will become increasingly important for international radio stations to carry more repeat broadcasts, and more varied times of day and week, and with greater amounts of publicity regarding their nature and availability. Furthermore, both the program-making and the publicity that promotes it should be increasingly thought of in terms of precise interest groups.

Consider that in the following light: what sorts of worldwide or regionwide "communities" would have a reasonably strong potential interest in what any given international radio service would have to say to them, in terms of what's going on in that broadcaster's region, what has gone on in the past, what might go on in the future, what viewpoints the broadcasting nation's

leaders - not just governmental - and people have. In some cases, those interests also might be served well through inclusion of material from other nations.

There are many such communities, and some broadcasters address one or more of them now. Among the most worldwide, I would include (in no necessary order of importance):

DXers
Teachers and students (of foreign language and culture in particular)
Popular music lovers
Sports enthusiasts (far more for some sports than for others)
Tourists
International businesspersons
Indigenous peoples (remember that was the year of indigenous peoples, and there turned out to be a lot of curiosity about them all over the world)
Diplomatic and foreign office personnel
Expatriates
Philatelists (a good example of a small but worldwide commu nity of individuals who are "internationally curious")
Medical personnel
Scientists, e.g. agronomists

There are many communities that may have greater interest in certain parts of the world than in others, or in certain nations more than others: various government officials, other than foreign office staff, who have international responsibilities; armed forces officers; religious authorities and adherents to certain religious faiths or denominations which enjoy broad international membership, to name a few. They will be good potential customers, but certainly not for every broadcaster.

The community of interest approach has characterized the periodical market for many years now. Many of the industrialized nations have a few to several magazines devoted to a single subject, whether skiing, cookery, philately, or foreign affairs. That approach obviously appeals to

people with common interests, and it is not surprising that a number of the magazines are edited in one country, but distributed regionally or internationally, sometimes with items of more specific local or regional interest added.

The concept of communities of listeners should prove attractive to international broadcasters in search of ways to avoid sounding too self-centered or even propagandistic. A program prepared with a specific community in mind is especially well-suited to worldwide distribution. It largely obviates the need for regional variations, so long as the approach taken maintains a focus on the elements shared by the community as truly mutual interests. For example, while there may be several different approaches to treatment of AIDS patients, there remains the overriding interest in treatment of the disease, and the desire to follow developments in its treatment.

The provision of "community" programming also helps to mitigate the criticism that international radio stations favor certain nations or regions over others. They often do, of course, but programs for worldwide communities can be a vivid symbol of a station's desire to reach out universally, to exhibit more than narrow interests of the sort often associated with the more pejorative dimensions of propaganda. That symbol will be all the more powerful if community programs reflect not only developments in the broadcasting nation, but also developments elsewhere, so that the program becomes something of a clearinghouse for information on the subject of the community's shared interest.

Why Would the Broadcasters and Their Paymasters Want Listeners to Hear the Material? A sense of purpose for international radio was easy enough to assume during times of major international conflict. World War II and the Cold War brought many international stations into existence, or resulted in their expansion. While wars continue, they have become much more localized or regionalized, and sometimes seem almost irrelevant to the interests of many nations. In such a climate, it is no wonder that some of the stations face pressures to "downsize," to consolidate, or even to cease operating. The paymasters of many of the stations - especially legislative bodies coping with slumping economies - have become so accustomed to thinking of international radio in terms of its role in major and prolonging conflict that that has become its only role.

International radio had other purposes long before World War II, and some of those purposes remain relevant. However, they may need a bit of refurbishing if they are to catch the attention and win the approval of those paymasters. Those purposes certainly can include such hardy perennials as communicating with any or all of the following:

1. **Expatriates** (These are a good bet for nations such as Lebanon, Mexico, or China, which have seen so many of their people leave over the decades.)

2. **Citizens temporarily residing abroad** (Nigeria, Iran, India, and several others have seen tens of thousands of students going abroad for further studies; the U.S.A., Japan, Germany, and other nations have many businesspeople overseas at any given time; tourists, military

personnel, workers for humanitarian agencies, and others constitute quite sizeable aggregations for some countries.)

3. **Customers for one's products** (Several international stations long have carried programs promoting the nation's goods and services, e.g. the BBC's "New Ideas." Some international stations carry advertising. International religious broadcasters can be said to "sell" Christianity or Islam to some listeners abroad, even if they may not find it attractive to think of their activities in that light.)

Still, some audiences which seem quite logical bets for international radio often seem to be neglected. A few examples:

1. **Citizens of other nations who have resided in the broadcasting nation** (Germany, Japan, Great Britain, France, Canada, the U.S.A., and others have attracted considerable numbers of temporary residents over time; many of those residents would seem likely to appreciate the opportunity to follow developments in their temporary homelands, but may have especially great interest in developments within those institutions - business and industry, education, or whatever else - that attracted them in the first place.)

2. **Tourists** (Great Britain, Australia, Japan, Brazil, Egypt [even if not at present], France, Spain, Italy, the Scandinavian nations, the North American nations, Russia, China, and others, have been tourist "magnets" for some time now, yet few of their international radio services do much to serve such audiences, which also are helpful for the national economies.)

3. **Students and teachers of a broadcasting nation's culture and language** (Most international stations broadcast language lessons, but few furnish programming that would be of specific help and interest to students and teachers in formal educational settings. Yet this is a group that almost certainly will be interested in keeping up with developments in the country which is a major focus of their attention, and in receiving help with the teaching and learning of a foreign language.)

Certain international stations do carry programming aimed at some of the audiences noted above. What seems to be more crucial now than ever before is to present paymasters with specific evidence of that activity, backed by the rationale which shows why it is in the interest of the nation or organization to continue to support or expand such activity, or to initiate it if it has not been undertaken already.

That rationale may prove somewhat elusive for stations which haven't thought very deeply about why they should wish to attract various categories of listeners. And many stations seem not to have done so, very often because they could tell themselves, "Where else would they get it, if not from us?" But that is precisely what is changing so rapidly in our world. There are increasingly numbers of alternative sources. Also, the attitude expressed in that question rests on the assumption that what stations have to offer is inherently interesting and valuable to listeners.

But there is little broadcast material of any sort that will be inherently interesting. Consider the long-standing programming practices of the many stations broadcasting to the Soviet Union during the Cold War. Orthodox church services, certain kinds of Western popular music, **samizdat** literature, all had their place, because they were largely unobtainable through any other channel.

Now, they would have very little attraction for most Russian listeners - and perhaps Western popular music least of all, because so many Russian private stations carry large amounts of it.

But certain communities of Russian listeners might appreciate programs about starting small businesses, visiting once-forbidden countries on modest budgets, or struggling for women's or ethnic minority rights.

Will paymasters support such programming shifts? After all, they, too, became accustomed to thinking of international radio programming in relatively narrow ways. Also, the importance of certain audiences will be difficult to illustrate, at least to the satisfaction of paymasters. But if they can be shown that the "new" audiences are made up of fair shares of opinion leaders, present and future, it should be possible to show why a revised program schedule makes good sense, and justifies the continuing investment in the station.

Where Else Could They Obtain Such Material? In this increasingly multimedia world, it will be more and more vital to become aware of alternative media sources available to one's target audiences. That isn't always easy, especially within closed societies, but there usually is some material on at least some aspects of media availability in most countries. Most industrialized nations have magazines which report on domestic business developments, and many of the larger Third World nations, e.g. India, Brazil, or Nigeria, have them, as well. It may be worthwhile to subscribe to such magazines, especially in parts of the world that are especially important target areas.

There are other sources, as well: international distributors of videocassettes, movies, television programs, records, audiotapes, magazines, and newspapers, often have a very good idea of media availability in various countries, particularly when their firm has major interests in one or more of them. Reporters and correspondents, including those working for international radio stations, often can make anecdotal observations about changes in media availability in countries from which they report, IF they're asked about it. (It isn't a subject that they're called upon to cover very often.)

Finally, there is a somewhat unlikely source: magazines which specialize in coverage of developments in electronic technologies, whether satellite, terrestrial, industrial, mass consumer, video, audio, or all of those. There are not many such magazines, and most are published in North America and Europe. But they are particularly useful for their provision of glimpses of what lies ahead, and thus an excellent way to keep one's long-term planning on track.

How Will Listeners Know What the Stations Offer, When, and Where? One very commonly-shared assumption of international radio broadcasting over the years has been the perception that listeners will take the time to listen to stations often enough so that the program schedule, and perhaps frequencies in use, become familiar. Of course there are stations that try valiantly to provide printed schedules, and even purchase space in local and national newspapers for displays of their frequencies and program times. But many of the smaller international broadcasters appear to rely heavily on the strong desire of audiences to seek them out.

That is likely to be less and less common as media channels multiply, particularly if the new services are more accessible than international radio often is. As a result, stations would do well to consider how to reach **potential** listeners more effectively. Purchasing space in newspapers will continue to have some effect, although newspaper reading appears to be in decline among younger population groups in most parts of the world. Careful on-air promotion of one's own programs is fine for "preaching to the converted" (those who already know where to find a given station), but of little help in reaching the new or lapsed listener.

Recalling my observations about communities of interest, it may be possible to think of discovering presently unused or little-used channels through which to convey specific material which is designed to persuade members of such communities, and others, to listen. Consider the possibility that sample audiotapes, which certainly can be produced at low cost, could be a way of reaching certain communities of listeners, if they are sufficiently important. (Audiotape even may end up being a far better vehicle for delivering a program series to a certain community of listeners than is broadcasting itself, if that community is small and scattered, but sufficiently important to be worth the extra effort. Fortunately, there is a single worldwide standard for audiotape.)

Imagine, for example, an international broadcaster about to initiate a major and long term series aimed particularly at teachers of the broadcasting nation's language. It would be possible to mass-produce a sample audio tape of the series, include a brief description of the series with the tape, along with an indication of frequencies and times of broadcast, and arrange to distribute it through one's embassies or other representing organizations abroad. Most of them work quite closely with educators, who often have national associations through which such material can be distributed.

Other approaches might include placing specific information about programs likely to be of interest to given communities in certain of the specialized magazines catering to such communities. Also, as subscriber lists are becoming increasingly available (for a price), direct mailings of scheduling and frequency information to subscribers may be effective. So may working through associations or clubs with specific interests, much as I have just suggested with respect to teachers' organizations.

Because such effort will be fragmented, it will demand time and money. But international radio stations will have to realize that finding new and more precise ways to reach potential listeners is absolutely essential if they are to remain effective in a multi-channel world. It should be worth the effort to convince paymasters that program publicity is of increasing importance. Unfortunately, most international stations have accorded low or even no priority to publicity, so they may have to reallocate their own budgets to provide for it at first, and then, with demonstrations of its effectiveness, approach the pay-masters.

How Will Broadcasters Know That Listeners Are Receiving What the Broadcasters Want Them To Receive?

If we assume for the moment that physical reception of international radio will improve within the next several years, then attention can be focussed more squarely on the attractiveness of the material for given communities of listeners, and on the degree to which those listeners actually comprehend the messages contained in the programs.

Those relatively few international radio stations which conduct their own audience research, and the larger number which purchase results of research done by someone else, have paid considerable attention to the numbers and demographic characteristics of listeners, but far less attention to the attractiveness of messages, and virtually no attention to the issue of comprehension: of the language itself, of the images it seeks to evoke, of the overtones of bias (both positive and negative) that it is almost certain to contain.

Perhaps the most constant in its devotion to audience research of several types has been the BBC World Service, which has managed an impressive record of quantitative studies over the decades, but which also has taken what is easily the most rigorous approach to the most widely used of all forms of contact with the audience: listener mail. Whereas most international broadcasters use that source to gain some impression of the overall size and composition of their audiences - a futile task, since there's no way to accurately extrapolate reliable figures from such a source - the BBC has used them as a base from which it draws a sample of known BBC listeners. Members of that sample then are contacted and asked whether they would agree to become part of a listener panel; although they are not required to listen to any programs in particular, they are asked a number of questions touching upon their reactions to such things as the speaker's pace of delivery, clarity of pronunciation, ability to put across the meaning of a given program, etc.; there are questions along similar lines regarding the scripts themselves.

While no one would argue that such reactions constitute the full range of audience opinion, this method of audience analysis does rest upon one very important element: the respondents are known listeners who have volunteered to share their thoughts. If they have difficulty understanding speaker or text, it seems quite likely that other listeners will fare no better, and quite possibly, not as well.

The method also has the virtue of being relatively inexpensive, although any station using it - as a few, e.g. Radio Nederland, now do - should be prepared to make a fair amount of staff time available for processing the data, which will come in all of the shapes and forms of human handwriting and expression of thought.

There also is the live listener panel approach taken by BBC, VOA, and a few others, in which individuals are brought together to discuss specific programs, which they may already have heard on tapes provided for them in advance, or which they may hear collectively. That approach, too, can yield data on comprehension and relative enjoyment, as well as believability, but it is time-consuming and quite expensive.

Time consuming and expensive or not, international radio broadcasters will have to increase their use of such methods as those just outlined if they are to compete successfully for listeners in a multimedia environment. The concept of communities of listeners noted earlier would require those approaches to audience research: successful communication with communities demands a more detailed knowledge of their likes and dislikes, levels of comprehension, and ideal listening times, since programs directed to them would of necessity be more narrowly focused.

There is yet another reason for increasing the amount and sophistication of qualitative research. As our world becomes increasingly multi-channeled, the possibility of misunderstanding and confusion well may increase. Listeners confronted with three, four, or more channels of information on a given subject could feel not just overwhelmed with information, but also at a loss to recall who said what, who supported which position, etc. That is where pre- and post-program research can help tremendously in determining whether a given international broadcaster's programming is likely to accomplish, or has accomplished, its purposes. (Without a sense of purpose, of course, research efforts are largely wasted.)

It also seems to me that research on comprehension will become increasingly vital for yet another reason: changing standards of usage for the world's leading languages: English, Chinese, Spanish, Arabic, French, Russian, and others. Actually, the word "standards" is a misnomer, since few languages are "governed" by one single set of all-inclusive rules. The multiplication of media channels is almost certain to expose more and more individuals to a wider range of usages of those languages. Long-held assumptions regarding the universality of primary meaning, pronunciation, and other facets of language use will have to be tested and retested. That is likely to be especially true for second language listeners, where absence of the ultimate security that characterizes most primary language users will lead to an even greater possibility of misunderstanding and confusion.

Conclusion.

When writing **Common Sense** over 200 years ago, American patriot and propagandist Thomas Paine spoke of the American Revolution as "the times that try men's souls." As a propagandist, he probably welcomed the challenges presented by such a time of trial. However, the challenges of wartime often are much more obvious than those of peacetime, however uneasy that peace may be. Yet another (probably unwilling) propagandist, George Orwell, seemed quite disillusioned by his World War II experience of preparing material for the BBC's broadcasts to Burma. He doubted that his supervisors, or <u>their</u> supervisors, were able to look beyond the war to the peace that would follow, and the implications of that peace for Great Britain's Burma policy.

Neither Orwell nor Paine had to consider the implications of a multi-channel world of the sort now emerging, although both certainly had to consider how to get people to listen to (or read, or see) and understand their messages. Both seemed to possess the flexibility of mind that would lead them to question the efficacy of yesterday's approaches in light of today's realities and tomorrow's prospects. That flexibility is more necessary than ever as international radio moves toward the 21st century, and should be an essential element in the approach of any international radio station that hopes to be a vital part of the next millennium.

HOWARD ASTER
PROFESSOR
DEPARTMENT OF POLITICAL SCIENCE
MCMASTER UNIVERSITY
HAMILTON, ONTARIO - CANADA

Integration of the Media
Axioms and Quandaries.

How ought we to think about the integration of the media? Is there a model, or some past examples, which can guide us in thinking our way through the present into the future?

The answer is a cautious yes.

What we are now witnessing - and the pace is remarkably quick - is the crossing of lines or the blurring of distinctions between different media and industries. Not ten years ago, for example, the world of telecommunications appeared to be quite distinct from the realm of television and broadcasting and the world of computers appeared to be quite different from the other two worlds.

Now, however, we have moved quickly into a period of the collapse of demarcating lines and industries and corporations which previously operated in one domain are moving quickly into the domains of other corporations and other industries.

In this new era of cross-over and integration, there is also the process of globalization. Newly integrated corporations operate globally and they practice the "high art" of vertical integration nationally and horizontal consolidation both nationally and trans-nationally. As early as the end of the last decade, the *Wall Street Journal* of March 7, 1989 proclaimed boldly, "The leading media companies see the world dominated by a few giant concerns by the end of the century, each company controlling a vast empire of media andentertainment properties that amount to a global distribution system for advertising and promotion dollars."[1]

In his study, *Split Screen: Home Entertainment and the New Technologies*, David Ellis (Friends of Canadian Broadcasting, Toronto, ON, 1992), the author, argues that this "merging traffic" is characterized by three fundamental trends and factors. First, "consumers are spending more and more entertainment dollars in the home, in many cases because of a lack of disposable time and money to go out. Rights holders and distributors of movies, sports events and other program material are using new video technologies to move the box office into the living room - accelerating the changeover from free TV to pay-TV."[2]

The second factor is "Technology has undermined the existing rationales for regulating broadcasting and will make such regulation more difficult to apply in the future....Technology will help initiate a re-evaluation of the ground rules for TV at a time when these ground rules have become inadequate or outmoded for other reasons anyway."[3]

The third factor which is characteristic of Canada but is also a factor shared by many other countries is "The domestic market in Canada has always been too small to provide adequate economic support to any of the cultural industries, including film and television.

A few years ago, it was largely up to our TV broadcasters to aggregate sufficient financial resources within Canada to get indigenous drama and entertainment programs produced. The constraints of our domestic market have obliged Canadian producers to rely on the international marketplace for financing partners - with the sanction and encouragement of the federal government."[4]

Much has changed, indeed, in the past few years. Let us simply identify a few of these major trends and, for purposes of dramatization, let us treat them, for a very short time, as 'axioms' or self-evident truths which follow an ineluctable, necessary, global logic.

I. The dawn of a new age: The promise of integration.

The pattern seems clear - the integration of telephone/telecommunications, television and computers to create a new form of communication. This is commonly called now the "information highway" or as *TIME* called it, the "Electronic superhighway". No less a 'guru' of modernity than John Naisbitt states:

"The long anticipated fusion of personal computer, television and telephone is a reality....Whether they are merely important new business tools or are ushering inconvenient ways to communicate, these amazing technologies will dramatically change the way we live and work during the latter half of the Nineties."[5]

Naisbitt has elaborated upon these ideas in his book *Global Paradox*: The Bigger the World Economy, the More Powerful its Smallest Players[6]. He argues that this integration of technologies "..is simultaneously creating the huge global economy and making its parts smaller and more powerful."[7] This era is characterized by four tendencies. First, we are witnessing the blending of technologies which are creating the new telecommunications industry. Second, we are experiencing more and more strategic alliances between established industries and entrepreneurial upstarts who are all looking to gain a toehold in the consumer-driven information age. Third, we are seeing the creation of a global network which is allowing anybody to communicate with anybody through the digital global web of networks. Finally, we are witnessing the spread of personal telecomputers and we will reach the stage where telecomputing will be totally decentralized and individualized.

Quandaries:

> *   We may think that the process of integration is taking place quickly, but the reality is that the pace of integration and the spread of integration of the media is limited to a small part of the world and involves a relatively small part of the world's productive and entrepreneurial capacity.
> *   The new 'information-age' is being played out before a very, very small part of the world's population and those who are literate in these new integrated technologies are still relatively very few.

II. In Big Games only Big Players can Play.

Clearly, one of the major elements which is driving interest and concern in this new, integrated technology, is the desire to be a 'player' in a larger and larger global system of information and entertainment.

The assumption is that only big players can play in this new era. Hence, mergers are rampant. Rogers and McLean Hunter in Canada. In the US, Bell Atlantic Corp. and America's largest cable TV provider, Tele-Communications Inc. announced a $30 billion mega-merger. That merger was then put on hold.

On March 22, 1994, *Reuters* and *New York Times* carried the following story.

"A startup company backed by billionaire executives William Gates and Craig McCaw has unveiled an ambitious $9-billion (U.S.) plan to build a satellite communications network to link the farthest reaches of the globe.

The venture by the chairmen of the world's largest computer software and cellular telephone companies would launch a network of 840 small satellites by the year 2001, creating an electronic web for voice and data communications.

The network would transport information, ranging from telephone calls to high-resolution computerized medical images and two-way video conferences, to and from almost any spot on the planet."[8]

The following day [9], there was a story reported by Jim Erickson of the *Seattle-Intelligencer*. "It's a bold and ambitious dream, but the proposed $9-billion (U.S.) satellite network backed by high-tech billionaires William Gates and Craig McCaw faces huge technical and financial obstacles before it can bring advanced telecommunications services to remote corners of the globe.

In a filing Monday with the U.S. Federal Communications Commission, Teledesic Corp. requested radio frequencies needed to build a system likened to a cellular telephone network in space.

The company said it would use the U.S. Defence Department 'Star Wars" technology to build a network that could transmit digital data at speeds competitive with the advanced fibre-optic networks that form the backbone of the planned information superhighway."

Quandaries:

> *   Mega companies are bound neither by concerns about national sovereignty nor by national laws. They operate trans-nationally and they redefine the national regulatory framework of any nation.
> *   Mega companies tend to build empires in big countries and then enter smaller markets which they treat as 'dumping' grounds for existing product.
> *   While we may think there is place for innovation, innovat ors, entrepreneurs, the reality is that in the unfolding of the integrated technologies, only the very, very large will play a role and only the big players will determine the future.

III. In Big Games, the Stakes are Very, Very High!

The stakes are thought to be enormous - monstrous! It is estimated by Jocelyn Cote-O'Hara, head of Stentor Telecom Policy Inc., that "this new kind of communications network - combining the power of telephones, televisions and computers - is expected to generate $1.3 trillion worth of global business by the turn of the century..."

The costs of building the fundamental infra-structure for this information highway in Canada alone, according to the same person, namely the 'feeder roads, on-ramps and driveways' is expected to be some $30 billion.[10]

However, the numbers are imprecise, 'guesstimates', at best. Another person, Fred Bacher, states:

"In Canada, the estimate runs as high as $100 billion over a period of 30 years; in Japan, $500 billion; in the United States, $1 trillion."[11]

There are, however, some known facts which make the stakes real and potential staggering. For example, at the present time, there are

$4 billion spent every year, in the United States alone on video games. In the US alone, video rentals are a $12 billion a year business. Residential phones are a $65 billion a year business . Catalogue shopping is a $70 billion a year business.

WHERE ENTERTAINMENT DOLLARS GO

Consumer spending on recreation and entertainment, 1993
(U.S. Commerce Dept.)

	Billions of Dollars
Toys & Sporting Equipment	$ 65
VCRs, TVs, Consumer Electronics	58
Books, Magazines, and Newspapers	47
Gambling	28
Cable TV	19
Amusement Parks and Other Commercial Participant Amusements	14
Movie Admissions and Video Rentals	14
Home Computers For Personal Use	8
Personal Boats and Aircraft	7
Live Entertainment Except Sports	6
Spectator Sports	6
Other Recreation & Entertainment	70
TOTAL	**$ 341**

Add on other entertainment and service functions, integrate them into a few megacommunications corporations, and you begin to see the enormity of the market.

However, to integrate these communications functions you must invest enormous amounts of money.

FUN POWERS SPENDING...
Increases in consumer spending, 1991-93*
(U.S. Commerce Dept.)

Billions of 1987 dollars

Entertainment & Recreation**	$ 20
Motor Vehicles	19
Medical Care	13
Apparels & Shoes	13
Personal Business	12
Housing & Utilities	10
All Else	26

* Growth in real spending above that accounted for by population growth.
** Except home computers.

...AND EMPLOYMENT GROWTH

Thousands of workers	Employment growth 1992-93	Employment 1993
ENTERTAINMENT & RECREATION. All producers and distributors of entertainment and recreation products and services.	204	4,482
HEALTHCARE. Makers of pharmaceuticals and medical equipment; drugstores; hospitals; doctors' office; and related industries.	187	11,793
AUTO INDUSTRY. Makers of motor vehicles and parts; auto dealers; gas stations and auto repair shops; and related industries.	33	4,272

289

Quandaries:

> * How and who funds this enormous investment? Is this another 'star wars' episode?
> * If the investment costs are so high, then very few countries or mega-corporations can become players.
> * Is the integration of the media a 'business' solely for first world countries?

IV. Information is a Public Good and is Central to Education.

It is a truism that in a democratic society, the free flow of information is a vital sign of social and political life, just as the flow of blood is a sign of physical well-being. Moreover, in this day and age, information is a critical - some would say 'the' critical - ingredient in education. No society can exist without the ever increasing productions and free-flow of information and a huge investment in continuing educational processes.

In western societies, education has always been thought of not just as a private need for personal growth and gain, but also as a public good. The good of society in general is enhanced through the ever-increasing levels of public education. Hence, there must be public investment in public education.

Quandaries:

> * Does the integration of the media signal an end to infor mation and education as a public utility and a public good?
> * If mega-corporations are the purveyors of and gate-keep ers to information, does this mean that public education will either be impoverished or priced out of sight?
> * The coincidence of education and information appears obvious today. Yet it is not obvious at all. The increase in information which is implied in the integration of the media will not necessarily lead to better education. It may lead to fewer people having more information, but that has quite little to do with education as a public good.

Some further Questions.

What does the integration of the media mean in terms of the communications environment we now live in?

* First, it means that the regulatory framework must change. Cross ownership will become the norm. Indeed, it now appears to be a corporate rule. Regulation appears to be impossible. But if there are no rules and no possibility of having national or international regulation, does that mean there the public good is 'lost'?

* Second, huge investments assumes that there must be huge profits. So, who makes it? Who provides the investments, who takes out the profits? Does it mean that governments provide the 'risk' capital but corporations 'reap' the profits?

* Equally important is who uses or who has access to the 'information highway'? Is it a public utility, as we have thought of broadcasting in the past, or is it a user-pay principle?.

* Does it mean that those who own and control delivery systems occupy the strategic place in the evolution of the 'information highway'? Are they to be the roadkeepers and, also, the toll-takers?

Some further Concerns.

Antonia Zerbisias, reflecting a fine scepticism, states that: "The superhighway hasn't yet been paved but already we've had overblown hype and mega media mergers in the U.S.

What we haven't had is a serious public debate about what it all means for our society, culture, economy, even our democracy."[12]

The issues surrounding the debate about the 'information highway' are only now beginning to emerge. Who will pay for it? Who will own it? Who sets the rules? Who designs it nationally and internationally? Who takes the profits?

It is widely accepted now that given the user-pay view, cable fees in the US are expected to rise from $30 to $75/month. Who will be able to afford it? We will have a society of entertainment and information 'haves' and entertainment and information 'have nots?'

Let us pose the problem is slightly different terms. Who gets best served by a 500 channel universe? The fact is that the median age group 18-34 in North American society are also functionally illiterate.

We are now on the threshold of a most peculiar phenomenon where the increase of information and entertainment choice is creating a larger and larger illiterate 'lumpen-proletariate' in our advanced societies.

Michael Clark sagely admonishes us: "To say that the aim is to make this new-age autobahn accessible to all is utter nonsense; those who do not seek knowledge now are not likely to develop a sudden interest simply because information is on-line."[13]

The advent of new technologies does not necessarily serve the public good. Nor does technology mean, necessarily democratization. If present reality is an indication of the future, we will see diminishing levels of information dissemination in spite of the fact that we have greater potentials.

This issue was captured in a wonderful headline:

A controlled-access highway. Corporate mergers are taking the 'mass' right out of 'massmedia'.[14]

The fundamental issues.

The Senate Committee on the Mass Media in Canada some 20 years ago was concerned with three issues:

1/ **Quality**. It's not just how much but what is carried in the mass media that counts. Quality or content is of primary concern. A 500 channel universe which broadcasts fundamentally the same programs does not mean anything.

2/ **Corporate ownership, competition and concentration.** Monopolies in the field of media, or information or entertainment, are fundamentally antithetical to democratic values. Scale itself does not serve the public interest. Diversity and choice are the hallmarks of freedom.

3/ **The issue of Canadian content.** Information is not abstract. It has a cultural base. It is the duty of government to ensure that citizens in a state have access to their own cultural production.

To those issues we can add a few more.

4/ **Nationality is important for cultural production.** Internationalism may well be a simple camouflage for monopolistic practices where the 'big' try to exclude the 'small' or the 'national' from the screens of the world - and themselves.

5/ Size and scale have little to do with quality or content. What counts for cultural survival are quality and content. Imagination and ingenuity have little, if any, relationship to size and scale.

6/ The issue in the media and in culture is always content, programs, not hardware.

As we enter more deeply into the era of the 'electronic superhighway' it would be wise to remember and pay close attention to the admonitions of the Senate Committee some two decades ago.[15] While the hardware, the terminologies and buzz words may change, the issues confronting public policy makers and societies have hardly changed. Understanding and foresight is one thing. Making decisions which enhance the public good of particular societies is another! It is imperative that we not succumb to arguments of historical inevitability and that we make decisions which preserve and nurture the public interest.(16)

Endnotes:

[1]. March 7, 1989

[2]. Friends of Canadian Broadcasting, Toronto, ON, 1992 p. 189.

[3]. Ibid p. 189-190.

[4]. Ibid p. 190.

[5].John Naisbitt's Trend Letter, reported in the April/May 1993/Volume 7/ Number 2 *INSIDE GUIDE* p. 4.

[6]. William Morrow and Company Inc., New York, N.Y., 1994.

[7]. Ibid p. 53.

[8]. Reported in the *Globe & Mail,* March 22, 1994, p.B1.

[9]. The *Globe and Mail,* March 23, 1994, p. B4.

[10]. Reported in *The Toronto Star,* Thursday, October 28, 1993, p. D10.

[11]. *The Toronto Star* of January 28th, 1994, p. A25.

[12]. *The Toronto Star* of January 29, 1994 p. B1.

[13]. *The Toronto Star* of February 14, 1994, p. A15.

[14]. *The Toronto Star* of January 28th, p. A25.

[15]. "That he will call the attention to the Senate to the state of the media in Canada, today, as compared to its state at the time of the *Report of the Special Committee of the Senate on Mass Media,* tabled in the Senate 20 years ago."

Senator Davey stated that he "wanted to find out if we did have the media we deserved or the media we needed. Two years later we would conclude that we did not have the media we needed, but rather, thanks to the Canadian public, we simply had the media we deserved." (*Senate Debates*, May 9, 1990, pp. 1588-1589.)

After a very prolonged analysis, Senator Davey asked: "Finally, honourable senators, the media we need or the media we deserve? Twenty years later, regrettably, it is still the media we deserve. Then, as now, we do not have the media we need; we still have the media we deserve." (*Senate Debates*, May 9, 1990, p. 1595.)

The issue have not changed very much, over those 20 years. The problems remain as identified, but the solutions have not emerged to provide Canadians with the media they need.

It is not incidental that there is a growing awareness among some academics who concern themselves with international political economy that communications and the globalization of communications is a major field of study. See for example Edward A. Comor, Editor, *The Global Political Economy of Communication: Hegemony, Telecommunication and the Information Economy*, New York, St. Martin's Press, 1994.

16. There is a contemporary fashion which would like us to assume that political pluralism, liberal economics and the free market define the new "end of history" and that a new universalism, propelled by technology, will wire the globe and create a new global culture. The best representative of this view is Francis Fukuyama, *The End of History and The Last Man*, The Free Press, New York, N.Y., 1992. Given the emerging chaos of much of the world one has strong grounds to dispute Fukuyama views. More significantly, there are strong grounds to dispute the view that nations must cede their national sovereignty to the Gates and McCaws of this world.

GERALD DUDA PRESIDENT
JOHN LUIK SENIOR ASSOCIATE
THE NIAGARA INSTITUTE
NIAGARA-ON-THE-LAKE, ONTARIO - CANADA

Fluidity, change and chaos at 20,000 feet above sea level.

As we enter the 21st century the perplexing changes are as daunting as they are reassuring.

The rapidity and the fundamental nature of the change we are experiencing can be unsettling, exhausting a times and seemingly endless. It feels like attempting to navigate through heavy traffic with all the noise, confusion, unpredictable movement and without any clear end. On the other hand, we could literally rise above it all, view this traffic from 20,000 feet above sea level. From this prespective what was at ground level confusion has now symmetry and order. Below, the roads are set out in grids and the cars travel in patterns governed by traffic lights set in neatly congruent geometric units and the natural surroundings frame these patterns with a sense of calm and order.

The Niagara Institute has studied the dimensions of change as we enter the 21st century. The following is a synopsis of fundamentally changing patterns and the requisite capacities required in this age of discontinuity.

We hope this short piece value adds to international broadcasters' perspectives on their changing role. We also hope it can levitate your vantage point to 20,000 feet above sea level.

Charles Handy, the distinguished British management writer, has described the 21st century as the age of discontinuity. What he means by that phrase in not the usual truism-that the 21st Century will be a time of significant change, but something more unsettling -that it will be a time of discontinuous change. Every century, to a certain degree is a time of change. What makes the 21st century unique in a problematic sort of way is that its changes will be without context-that is they will not be incremental changes that build gradually over time. Instead, they will be dis-continuous in the sense of being radical and seemingly unrealated. What discontinous change does is to rob us of our ability to place changes in an understood context by de-linking the familiar past from the present and emerging future.

If the first characteristic of the 21st century then is discontinous change, the second characteristic-or actually group of characteristics derives from discontinous change-namely ambiguity, complexity, unintended consequences, uncertainty and the unexpected. What links these features together is the thread of difficulty, surprise and the absence of the straight forward. Indeed what binds them together as well is a profound aversion on the parts of humans, either individually or collectively to live in an environment described by these characteristics. Yet if the 21st century is an age of discontinuity, then its political, social, economic and cultural features will all be somewhat disconnected from what proceeded them.

The third feature of the 21st Century will be its radically different economic organization. For the most part those nations and trading groups-not to say individuals who will dominate the creation of wealth in the 21st century will be those who understand the nature of the post-industrial global economy-those who are producers of knowledge and solvers of problems. In a word, those who have developed the abilities to discern patterns and be analytical and creative. The 21st century will not be the century where wealth is produced, as it has been for much of this century by economies engaged in low skilled mass production. The raw materials for wealth creation-land, raw materials, even technology can all be purchased and while important for the creation of wealth they are not as crucial. What is crucial is creative intelligence, the ability to perceive patterns not through mechanical causality but a capacity which is deeper built on intuition and a systemic view of the universe.

The fourth characteristic of the next century is the importance of technology, particularly what is called information and communication technology. The importance of technology is that the scope of technological change will be much greater than it has been in this century. Technology in the next century will quite literally redefine the way we work, live and to a large degree, think both about ourselves as persons and about the natural world. The 20th centry has been an age of technological change as well, but the change has neither been as universal or comprehensive in its influences nor as rapid as it will be in the next century.

The fifth characteristic of the 21st century is the widening and determining role that our deepening environmental problems will play. I suspect that in many respects our current environmental policy of gradualism will no longer be an option in many areas and that even the current fashionable talk of sustainable development will be supplanted by something much more radical, borne of necessity rather than choice. Deep ecology will not be popular but the continuing development of the South coupled with the traditional pattern of consumption, pollution and resource management of the North will necessitate a radical reappraisal of how we think about nature and how we manage our relationship with the natural world as well as how we handle crossnational relationships in that context.

The sixth characteristic of the 21st century is what might be called its significant demographic imbalance. This is two things. First, in the countries of the North there will be a growing scarcity of the young, relative to the old with all of the implications that such an imbalance has for societal conflict. Second, in the countries of the South there will be an excess of the young. Much of the wealth of the world will thus still be controlled-though some of the economies of the South, particularly of Asia, will be increasingly dominant-by countries dominated by the relatively old.

The last feature of the next century is what might be called its increasingly skeptical character. The century, of course, is not itself skeptical. It is rather those who will live within it. And what will thet be skeptical about? For the most part, a good many many of the values and institutions that in our 20th century have been more or less taken for granted. One can already see a substantial degree of distrust and indeed, cynicism about many of the core values that have defined, at least in the Western world, the way things are. For instance, there is a growing disenchantment with power and authority, with conventional political processes, with work and commitment and even with success. By referring to the next century as the age of skepticism this is not to suggest that skepticism is necessarily wrong. It is to argue that some of the assumptions that in quite crucial ways have defined this century might in the next century no longer have their compelling force for large numbers of people. In many respects, we should perceive this skepticism as a necessary stage as we move through various developmental stages of denial, desperation and anger towards more positive and aspiring perspectives.

An aspiring vision of the future suggests there are a minimum seven core competencies we must, especially in the West, develop and cultivate. These competencies or capacities require a culture shift in our thought, emotion and behaviour. These are not lightly suggested nor easily incorporated into our everyday life. They represent our significant departure from our culture-bound attitudes towards ourselves, each other, our work, our institutions and our political processes.

The first of these is the capacity to decode and understand our implicit personal and organizational assumptions. This is often called the process of mental-mapping and is perhaps the most difficult and sometimes painful process of change. Part of this difficulty stems from the fact that implied assumptions are many times difficult to articulate. This decoding process also present personal challenges as we explore the sub terrain often never expressed personal deeply held beliefs about how we understand and order our universe. This first attribute giving expression to the unexpressed and suspending those beliefs for examination in times of radical change can spark emotion and conflict. For this reason, unfortunately, they are left most times in their unexamined state.

The second attribute is based upon the first, it is the ability to tolerate the conflicting assumptions. It is the ability to accept ambiguity and complexity - to hold a variety of perspectives in tension without forcing a neat resolution. You might describe this skill as the ability to resist the neat, analytical solutions, strategy and allow the dynamic of the ambiguous to dominate at least for the minute. For many, if not most, the usual quest for certainty, predictability and control can make this a difficult undertaking.

The third attribute is again based on its predecessor, for it is the capacity of taking the complexity and ambiguity and re-ordering, re-defining, in a word creating something new, whether in terms of organizational structure, product, knowledge, strategy. It is the ability to create, to innovate, to change the existing structures to the way things are done and understood and to take the seemingly contradictory and make something different and compelling. This capacity also implies we do not freeze and unfreeze to create a new solid structure but see the need to create as dynamic, continuing and unfolding.

The fourth competency is the capacity for collaboration, for not simply engaging others but working with them in situations of considerable difference and diversity. This is more than the 20th century's dreadful rhetoric of empowerment. It is more than de-layering. It is the capacity to structure organizations and the process of problem solving and crafting new knowledge to be maximally participative and minimally hierarchical. The ambiguous state of being yourself and belonging to an organization, nation state or community will need to be re-defined. We need to hold in creative tension a re-defined role of the individual and the communal context. This is a revised sense of "both" rather than our usual "either/or" perspective. Advances will only be possible if we re-construct this basic paradigm and seeing new energy and direction emerge from the combined community's self re-definition.

The fifth competency is the capacity for reflection, for the discipline of putting aside the immediate and the pressing and allowing oneself the opportunity to take the longer and deeper perspective. It is the capacity for asking the difficult questions about purpose, commitment, means and yes, about ends, questions that too often are brushed aside or ignored as not central. Implicit in this ability to reflect is, of course, the ability to discern the trivial from the compelling, the right from the wrong, the good from the bad.

What emerges then from this set of core competencies are people who can create an organization that in the face of the unexpected, the complex, the ambiguous, the uncertain and the difficult can nonetheless understand themselves, re-invent itself, engage in both analysis and creation, overcome the problems of difference and diversity and do all of this in the context of values that affirm rather then degrade everyone whose life it touches.

CATHERINE MURRAY
PROFESSOR
SCHOOL OF COMMUNICATION
SIMON FRASER UNIVERSITY
VANCOUVER, BRITISH COLUMBIA - CANADA

The Infobahn.

I think that one of the rules that we can all probably agree to, is that interpreting whatever will be the "Infobahn" or the "information superhighway" of the future and its opportunities, is going to be rife with cultural differences and economic differences which stem, I think, from a fundamental problem that we have in economic theory in capitalism and in our understanding of communication theory. And that fundamental problem goes to the heart of what information is and whether it constitutes a public good or a private good. And where in the transition to the so-called information economy which is now underway in all parts of the world in the global marketplaces, where the two apparently opposite goods collide and where they complement each other?

I think one of the most exciting areas of contribution in theory currently is in the radical law of intellectual property where we begin to look at early emergence of innovations in multimedia production, as we heard today from Mark Starowicz. Whether it's in information software or new forms of radio broadcasting to new channels with new products, it seems to me that the common factor is that early innovation that is happening in communications. Whether it's on the Internet highway, whether it is in the development of new handheld portable video devices that will be able to simultaneously send and transceive, what Mr. Starowicz fails to realize is that the $ 100,000 desktop video production that he was talking about - that unit - is probably already coming down in cost and probably already portable now, in certain of our imaging developments and other sectors of the economy.

The rate of change is astronomical, the rate of precompetitive innovation is accelerating. The difficulties in our legal system and understanding intellectual property regimes and how things are organized are enormous.

But I think that it's Professor Browne who has identified the core problem. And that is why we are undertaking many of these developments anyway. Is there any social consensus or any market demand out there for many of these new services?

I think, Professor Aster, anyway, shares with me some profound reservations about the degree to which we have proven that there is public demand for these new services.

International broadcasters like computer software manufacturers today, share in common one thing. And that is that you have been marketing and providing your services to a very narrow elite, an elite of decision makers, policy makers and global knowledge workers. What is at issue here is the degree to which, in order to support the new investments required for the information highway, for the development of programming involved, for new audiences, the degree to which that elite market can hold and support the changes that we are looking at for the next ten to twenty years. And I think that we are very much having to move to new audiences, new constituencies of interest, and move in the process of the diffusion of innovation, if you like, beyond the 2.5 percent of our respective populations we perhaps have been serving, to the next wave of early innovators, to early adopters.

I am finding as I work in the field more and more, I am devolving back to some of the early theory on the part of Everett Rodgers and others, in understanding that the future of innovation is in information and video markets.

I would simply like to conclude with one major question. That is, I think, the fifth question that was raised by Professor Browne. To what degree as international broadcasters can we make sure that what we are providing is being understood, and our product is being valued by our target markets?

What I would like to ask is the following. I am not sure that institutional models for international broadcasting which were based very much on assumptions of bureaucratic control and a set of well-founded ideological assumptions about how certain foreign policy communication ought to be happening and so on, originating out of the pre-cold-war and cold-war regimes, -I am not sure how well these models are really adapting to the new realities of the broadcasting universe.

I am struck by how Radio Romania could very profitably export many of its programs here to Canada and to our local markets, in the city of Vancouver for example, and, in fact, share with us the process of discovery of the values of democracy and the role of democratic communication in our societies.

The irony is that in Canada, with our highly developed infrastructure, high degree of investment in content production and so on, we are despairing at the level of political culture, of political disintegration and cultural disintegration of the national product. We are worried about political immobilization, apathy, and we are worried about the emergence of new parties and interest groups fragmenting what we have seen as being a civic democratic consensus. I think, in many cases Canada shares the interests in democratic communication and political communication of other regimes, and in fact, we may be looking at importing this sort of focus on political communication to advanced industrial democracies.

I guess, my last comment is simply this - that we have assumed that much of what will drive the unfolding of the information highway is in fact going to be the commercial kind of demand for programs that we have seen in the last generation of development, whether it's demand for movies, or home shopping, or the kinds of things that Prof. Aster has talked about this morning.

It's not at all clear to me that this sort of demand will hold. And, in fact, what the more interesting work on the part of the telephone companies now in the United States, and, in fact, on the part of McCaw Cellular, is finding is that consumers and citizens are much more interested now in information products rather than entertainment products. But their expectation of information is being more and more grounded by what we call "information that makes sense", helps them make sense of their everyday worlds. And, certainly, they are becoming much more critical of the information designers and providers, and I think we are going to be seeing an increased call for accountability not only on the part of software designers, but also those who are involved in the carriage of the content itself.

It's an extraordinarily exciting time, it's extraordinarily promising, if you like, for those who, like Mark Starowicz, hold great aspirations for the implication this revolution may have for democratic communication. A lot remains, however, on the part of the researchers, to understand at core, how economic theory must change, and how our understanding of cultural theory and cultural formation must change.

CHAPTER NINE

SUMMARY AND RECOMMENDATIONS

Editors' Note:

At the end of all previous conferences, the organizers have attempted to provide a "summing up" so that the agenda of the past may be assessed and the possibilities for future agenda may be established.

TERRY HARGREAVES
EXECUTIVE DIRECTOR
RADIO CANADA INTERNATIONAL
MONTREAL, QUEBEC - CANADA

We've had, I think, a very heavy, tough and productive three days and I praise you all for your diligence and concentration. We've gone over a huge amount of material and subject areas. One of the themes was broadcasting to and from Asia and I think we've had some very valuable contributions in that regard. In audience research, stalwarts like Kim Elliott and Graham Mytton, Nicole Beaulac, and the head of research from Radio Moscow, have all made major contributions.

The subject of transition in the post-communist world which we addressed at the beginning is in a sense, a particularism. At the same time, it's transition in post-everything world. There have been great upheavals, political and technological, changes in the variety and methods of delivery.

As Howard Aster was saying this morning, information is not abstract, it allows you access to a culture. One of the issues for international broadcasters and for communicators in general is as the sophistication of our respective audiences, both at home and abroad, increases inevitably with the increased access that they have to all kinds of information, there is also a certain disenchantment with the representative democracy and a desire for more direct democracy. People want to have their own input on certain issues. The information flow for many years was a kind of command, of a dirigiste method, of transmitting information, and people were to accept it and learn in effect, as if we were primarily educators and leaders. And do we still lead? And do they still want us to lead? Or, do we still have a responsibility to lead? So, do we just follow and serve and just listen and react?

I think, however, there is still a responsibility to lead because somebody has to be at the head of the parade, somebody has to stimulate the ideas, somebody has to put forth the propositions. The rush and the anxiety to have participation from the grassroots is very valuable and useful, it should happen, does happen, it will increase. But that doesn't allow us to abdicate the responsibility we have in our field to try and put forward the propositions. While the milkman is busy delivering milk and the brain surgeon's busy saving lives, they can't devote the amount of intellectual time to worry about all of the things that we spend our full time worrying about. We, in the society, rely on the brain surgeon to do his job, we don't try to take over his job, we don't try to take over the milkman's job. We expect that they'll be responsive to our needs, particularly the brain surgeon. But we have a responsibility to be responsive to their needs, and to bring thoughts and attitudes they can consider. They'll bring them too but the fact of having a more direct democracy, with some areas of information becomes a setback. If they want triple murders and they want to have the courtroom trial and the explosion but they don't really seem all that interested in hearing about something that's a little deeper - that responsibility still lies with us.

HOWARD ASTER
PROFESSOR
MCMASTER UNIVERSITY
HAMILTON, ONTARIO - CANADA

I wanted to address just three or four themes, mainly because it seems to me, there is endless, unfinished business that these conferences raise. And it's always important to begin to set an agenda for the next one and I presume there will be a next one. I would just like to throw out three or four ideas as a basis for the thematic character of the next conference. Obviously, they are a function of my own particular interest but perhaps, I am sure, that there will be views, ideas coming from the floor in relation to the themes and the core of the next conference.

One of the things that always emerges in a discussion where you have such divergent views and varied presentations is the need for collaboration of some form or other. One of things I thought that came across very, very clearly is the need for some sort of collaboration in terms of research. It came through the audience research session but I think that might be one focus, but it might very well be that there are other ways of developing collaboration on research. I would suggest that that's a very, very important area which might be a valuable theme for the next conference.

Another, second theme which I think comes through often, and again it's a matter of the unfinished business of this audience, is the tension between the role of the public broadcaster and the demands of commercialism and commercialization. We've dealt with the theme of "The Evolution of the Role of the Public Broadcaster" but it seems to me it is clearly not only a matter of unfinished business but it may very well become much more urgent in the next few years than it has in the past.

Certainly, if I reflect upon the experience in Canada, the way in which the government tends to reduce public funding, but also there is an increasing abdication of the precise role which the public broadcaster plays in an increasingly commercialized and commercially driven broadcasting environment. I think much more thought has to be given to that. And I had the pleasure of listening to a discussion between Father Borgomeo and Pierre Juneau, and that theme seems to me a very, very important one which cuts across East and West, North and South, as well.

A third theme which, I think, is always there, and perhaps it's worthwhile taking up, perhaps in a slightly different language, is the question of intercultural understanding as a basis for international broadcasting. It tends to be an academic subject in many, many ways, and I think from my own personal academic point of view, it's an interesting subject. But there might be another way where we can address roles, definitions and objectives for the international broadcasting community, as it evolves over the next number of years.

There is always the issue which is the fourth issue, of the "haves" and the "have-nots", the rich and the poor, the North and the South. It seems to me, in this conference we have had some discussion about this. My own concern with the so-called information highway is that it'll be a highway for those people who can afford it. And it'll be a slum for those people who can't afford it. And I think the question of North-South, have and have not, the two worlds in relation to international broadcasting is an important theme which should be revisited.

The final one, of course, is always there. And it's a matter of speculation. I think we had one really helpful go at the question in fairly precise terms: the ideal receiver for the next generation, which obviously raises the larger issue of technological change, and the impact on the character and definition of international broadcasting. That, too, it seems to me, is a theme of endless fascination and absolutely unfinished business.

DANIEL OLLIVIER
DIRECTEUR DU DEVELOPPEMENT
RADIO FRANCE INTERNAITONALE
PARIS - FRANCE

Nous avons entendu beaucoup de choses pendant ces trois jours. Les défis vus par différentes personnes en fonction des positions différentes que nous occupons les radios d'Europe de l'Est n'étant pas dans la même situation évidemment - ou d'Europe centrale - que d'autres radios comme Radio France Internationale. Cependant sur certains des défis, j'ai retenu moi, trois phrases, trois défis qui ont été dits et que je vous re-citerai. On a entendu dire que le monde est entré dans un univers de l'amusement et il est évident que nous autres, les radiodiffuseurs internationaux, nous ne sommes pas véritablement des amuseurs publics. Donc, quel est notre rôle dans ce monde de l'amusement, est-ce qu'on en a encore un? C'était le premier défi.

On en a entendu un deuxième, à savoir, lorsqu'on parlait de l'Asie, qu'il y a de moins en moins de demande pour les radios internationales parce que les médias locaux s'améliorent et donc, il suffit d'écouter ce que vous avez localement. Pourquoi aller chercher plus loin ce que vous apporte votre radio locale. Et puis, le dernier défi et qui n'est pas des moindres : on nous a dit que la plupart des radios internationales n'ont pas d'auditeurs donc, pourquoi existent-elles?

Alors ces trois défis, qui sont les vraies questions, m'ont fait penser à une chose. Je me suis dit : "mais Terry est en train de faire du sabotage! Il nous a invités pour nous tuer, pour nous montrer qu'on ne servait à rien et donc on rentre chez nous et on arrête tout, on coupe les fils!" Bon. Ceci dit, ce n'est pas si idiot parce que vous savez que, parmi les radios internationales, beaucoup ont eu des problèmes ces dernières années parce que précisément, ces points de vue ont été retenus par des gouvernements qui en ont profité pour couper les crédits. Cependant, connaissant Terry, je ne pense pas qu'il nous ait amenés ici pour nous démoraliser mais justement pour rebondir sur autre chose. C'est le thème que j'ai retenu et qu'on a entendu plusieurs fois : le repositionnement. Or, ce repositionnement repose finalement sur les thèmes qui viennent d'être abordés et qui pourraient justement être les thèmes de la prochaine conférence, pour voir comment on a évolué sur une période de deux ans.

Premièrement, le monde de l'amusement. Alors, est-ce qu'il faut qu'on devienne tous aussi des amuseurs comme les radios commerciales qui, évidemment, n'ont pas comme intérêts premiers ceux enfin que nous, nous définissons - au moins à Radio France Internationale et je pense que l'on partage avec vous - qui sont d'informer, d'éduquer et quand même de distraire un petit peu. Bon, ces trois objectifs, il faut certainement les garder mais peut-être faut-il modifier leur répartition à l'intérieur de notre grille de programme. Il faut certainement distraire un peu plus; il faut qu'on évolue dans ce sens-là. Il faut qu'on change quelque chose pour justement, pouvoir entrer dans la compétition, sinon il est vrai qu'on risque de disparaître.

Le deuxième point de vue, donc, cette demande qui diminue pour les radios internationales parce que les programmes locaux s'améliorent et c'est très vrai, eh bien, c'est la concurrence. La concurrence, elle est très bonne et il faut savoir l'utiliser. Pendant très longtemps, c'est vrai, dans de nombreuses régions du monde, il n'y avait pas de concurrence, donc nous étions la source d'information. C'est une position très confortable; maintenant, ça, c'est fini. Mais depuis la chute du communisme il y a trois, quatre ans, il faut absolument s'adapter à un monde nouveau. Et là, je citerai une phrase qui a été dite aussi, c'est que cette nouvelle identité, elle doit être plurielle : c'est-à-dire que nous avons été, pendant très longtemps, des radiodiffuseurs qui diffusions de loin mais qui étions une voix qui apportait quelque chose qui était soit-disant la vérité, tout au moins l'objectivité, et maintenant, grâce aux techniques nouvelles, aux satellites, nous devenons à la fois une radio distante - parce que nous restons des radios distantes - mais nous devenons également une radio de proximité. Et c'est là que l'on retrouve justement ce thème qui a été abordé hier, celui de la globalisation et de la fragmentation, à savoir, nous devons être à la fois cette radio globalisante qui prend donc une vision générale et qui va apporter un autre point de vue - qui est, je pense, ce que nous devons faire - mais nous devons aussi fragmenter, nous devons aussi apporter quelque chose qui est proche des auditeurs que nous avons. Sinon, nous allons les perdre parce qu'ils auront quelque chose d'autre tout près. Et ça, ces nouvelles technologies, il faut les utiliser pour pouvoir multiplier des programmes et donc être à la fois globalisant mais aussi à la fois localisant si je peux utiliser un euphémisme pour montrer la dualité qui nous attend et à laquelle nous allons devoir faire face.

Une autre question importante a été posée : Faut-il continuer à diffuser? C'est la Radio Suisse qui s'interrogeait et puis les Anglais ont fait la même chose et les Français. Nous apportons tous quelque chose de spécifique. Mais est-ce qu'il y a un besoin pour tout ça? Alors, une des possibilités, peut-être une des pistes de réflexion pour l'avenir, est peut-être l'unité, s'unifier. Est-ce qu'il y a besoin d'autant de choses différentes. Alors, il y a un projet qui est en cours, en Europe, entre Radio Netherland, la BBC, Deutsche Welle et Radio France Internationale. En Europe où il n'y a sans doute pas besoin de cette diversité de points de vue et où nous devons avoir des points communs quelque part, il y a donc ce projet de créer une radio internationale qui serait nouvelle, qui offrirait un autre point de vue, une sorte d'unité et qui serait peut-être une solution à cette multiplicité qui, peut-être, se justifie un peu moins maintenant.

Un texte vous a été distribué hier par le président de RFI, André Larquié - et il n'a pas été commenté - un texte qui s'appelait "Charte des radios internationales". C'est un projet, un brouillon, une première version qui a besoin d'être certainement très améliorée, très discutée, qui a déjà été vue donc, par Radio Canada International, par Radio Netherland, par RFI et peut-être par d'autres. Je vous invite, peut-être, à le regarder et si vous avez des commentaires, faites-les à Terry Hargreaves qui est ici, faites-les au Président de Radio France, à Radio Netherland car je sais que ces trois radios-là ont été particulièrement concernées. Faites part de vos commentaires; ça peut être aussi quelque chose qui peut nous permettre à nous, radios internationales, de trouver une unité, de trouver une raison d'être et de nous définir face, et ça, c'est un autre problème qui a été abordé aussi, face aux radios nationales parce que des radios nationales accessibles également via satellite, font de l'international.

Une dernière question : les responsabilités des radios internationales. Nous avons parlé, je crois, des "have" et "have not". Nous arrivons avec notre pouvoir, notre puissance, notre professionnalisme sur les satellites dans des zones du monde où il n'y a pas la même chose qui est offerte. Et là, deux attitudes sont possibles : ou bien, nous avons le pouvoir, je pense, de tuer l'information qui existe sur place et de la faire disparaître ou de coopérer pour la maintenir, la développer. Je rappelle d'ailleurs ce que disait François Demers : "il faut garder les langues locales parce que sinon, dans quelque temps, le monde entier sera anglophone". Donc, il faut continuer à maintenir ces cultures locales. Et ça, c'est une responsabilité des radios internationales lorsque nous arrivons dans des zones où le monde audiovisuel est moins développé : est-ce que nous

décidons d'étouffer ce qui existe, ou bien de coopérer. Ces avenues de l'information qui n'existent que d'un côté, pourront servir ou bien à creuser le fossé et à tuer une partie de la culture qui doit exister ou bien, au contraire, à coopérer et à tirer vers le haut quelque chose qui est en voie de développement. Je crois que la radio internationale est à un moment de son histoire qui est particulièrement intéressant parce que la situation est changée. Nous ne sommes plus les instruments des ministères des Affaires étrangères de chacun de nos pays, nous ne sommes plus des instruments politiques. Nous devenons des radios comme les autres et je crois, que nous sommes à un moment où il faut créer quelque chose de nouveau, où il faut se créer une nouvelle identité, une nouvelle mission avec des moyens techniques nouveaux. Nous pourrons voir dans deux ans, si nous avons évolué par rapport à la situation antérieure.

TATYANA ANDREYEVA
DEPUTY DIRECTOR
RUSSIAN FEDERAL STATE RADIO AND TELEVSION
KANAL 5
ST. PETERSBERG - RUSSIA

I will try to speak English because I want to communicate with you on some very serious topics. I am learning English only one year but I will try, because my desire to discuss the questions are great. If I speak terrible, very bad, tell me, "Tatyana, speak Russian, OK?"

Summary and Recommendations

I want to tell about my impression of this conference. It is very interesting to me, it's great. In Russia we have a lot of the same problems. We discuss problems of international radio: why we need so many international radio companies if in Russia I can freely talk now, there is a lot of radio companies, there is a lot of journalists in Russia, why do I need to listen to BBC? I know one person in the Radio building, Lev, he works in the Radio building in St. Petersburg for 36 years. He listens to BBC, he knows everybody in BBC - young boy, good journalist, old person. And he says he keeps his mind because he listened to BBC. In Russia not many people listened to BBC and a lot of foreign radio stations, during all the communist times. But he is a person of culture. Now is another time. A lot of people listen to new radio stations. Of course, when we discuss a lot of questions, how better to speak with Russian people - it is better to use radio stations in Russia, private, government radio stations - now it is possible to buy time, and we have this experience in Russia. But I want to give you another example.

Last October I stayed in our Radio building because Khasbulatov and Rutskoi said, "Bye-bye, Yeltsin, we want to have power". And at that moment people with guns and a red flag went to Ostankino (radio and TV premises in Moscow), and we could not listen to anything. I work with Radio Russia, and we must broadcast news every evening. We called Radio Russia and I heard that an engineer was killed. I cannot broadcast my news, I cannot understand what is the matter in Moscow. At this moment our private radio station Baltika transmitted Radio Liberty. I listened and decided that I needed to use Radio Liberty broadcasts via Radio Baltika on my cable radio, because for me it is very important to explain the situation to the people, to know the news.

I called the Ministry of Communication. It's not easy in Russia to get in touch with the Ministry of Communication fast, it takes time. I sent a fax saying, please, organize the contact with Baltika, I need to know the news. At this moment one chief of my company called me and said, "Don't use these news. You are not a patriot, you are not Russian. How is it possible to listen to news from a foreign company?" It's a crazy situation in Russia now. It is possible to be together against the communists, but at the same time to have completely opposite ideas when we think about future.

My idea is that I want to have broadcasts from foreign countries, I want to listen to the news. And now, with this unstable situation in Russia it is very important to save international broadcasts, to have shortwave. It is very important, because it is very easy to ruin Baltika,

Radio Petersburg, any channel. Now is the time to save international radio. Please explain this to your government. We have an interesting person in Russia, Zhirinovsky. Zhirinovsky wants to be friends with every fascist party in the world. Post-communist countries do not have an easy situation now. Every fascist wants to be friends. Maybe tomorrow they will organize a great international company. We will present his ideas to people. Our people are very poor. We have a very difficult life. We cannot imagine our future. There is no structure, there isn't any idea about the future. It's so easy for a lot of people to believe fascist communists. And it's very important to have international broadcasts with the normal ideas, the democratic ideas. And I am thinking about the possibilities of working together.

Of course, there are too many foreign radio stations. You have the same problem we have in Russia. We have 3 government channels: Ostankino, Radio Russia, Mayak. Radio Petersburg - it's a great company where you must spend a lot of money. I want to save cultural broadcasts, I want to help children to listen to special broadcasts for children but it is expensive, and we must think that maybe tomorrow my company will go completely broke. What can I do? I must organize an advertising agency. I am not afraid to have a lot of commercial stations in Russia. We never had a possibility to listen to normal music. We listened only to the communist propaganda. In America I was surprised. There are 50 radio stations! If I like jazz - listen to jazz, if I like heavy metal (I don't like it, it's terrible, but I can understand that it's democracy) - welcome, if I want to listen to classical music - great, people can decide themselves. In London one of the best commercial stations is Classical Fan, competitor of BBC Classic. It's amazing but people like this radio station. I am confident that if people want to, people will find the good things. You must rely on the people's judgement. Very often, when I was working nearly all my life for the government radio station I thought, "Oh, I know what people should listen to. I graduated from the university and maybe other people are less "educated". This is a wrong approach. People understand what is true, what is right and what is wrong. We must think what the people desire to listen to. But, of course, we need to save a lot of our literature and cultural broadcasts. Maybe we should use the government money to save the system, and we must think how it is possible to organize an advertising agency. In Russia we have extensive experience, both terrible and good. We discuss this question a lot and it is very important for me to hear your opinions.

I can give you an example. In Ostankino any journalist could organize an interview taking the money under the table. One journalist organized a special sales and advertizing agency for a special program. It's very easy to make money but it is impossible to manage a company. But if the government cannot pay, what can she do, she cannot manage the company. It's bad experience but it can be worse still. The worst is if every journalist will sell himself - Zhirinovsky may pay one journalist, another party will pay another journalist - it's a very big problem in Russia.

I think it's better to organize an advertising agency to separate these things. I think that if we do not have money for Radio Petersburg, why don't we set up commercial radio stations - in fact, we could easily handle even five of them - it will be normal civilized practice. Maybe my company will have 80% of the shares, and I will have the money to organize broadcasts for children. It's very interesting, we need to think about it seriously. And we can discuss it with you, I'd love that.

And I want to tell you why I need to listen now to your broadcasts. Please save this possibility, please think, maybe we do not need 100 foreign international radio stations, maybe only 10, and your experience to organize work in a civilized manner to work together shared with us will help Russia. We must think about this too.

It was also very interesting to me to hear about the Christian broadcasts. We have this experience in Russia too. An American preacher, owner of a very big radio and TV company in Texas, came to St. Petersburg and told me, "Can you use my broadcasts? I understand you have difficulty. Only the Orthodox church wants to have power in Russia but the Orthodox church, everybody knows, worked with the KGB a long time." And I think that if I have government radio station I should do something about it. It is very important to help people to have Christian feelings, Christian thinking, to have a chance to listen. We were deprived of this in the past.

There are different ways to organize a Christian radio station, and we have one in St. Petersburg. It is possible to have cable radio, prepare broadcasts, and now it is time to buy the time. Sergei Korzoun from Ekho Moskvy talked about our very interesting problem. The engineers from our Ministry of Communication think that they can decide what kind of broadcasts people can have, because they will be selling our cable system, our transmitters. It's terrible because tomorrow only the fascists will be able to buy it, or Saddam Hussein pays for it - it is impossible to do this. If we need to listen, how is it possible to organize this system in a more civilized manner, how government can manage our TV and radio?

Situation in Russia, I think, is crazy, because people elected the president - I like some of his ideas - people elected the parliament, and now the deputies oppose the president. Who is governing Russia, the president or the deputies? And my company is all the time between the two fires. I must listen, I must make decisions, I need to do something. No, I prefer the system like BBC has. People will pay the money to the journalist, to the company. We need to learn about systems in foreign countries, how to organize it better. Maybe we can set up shareholding companies where the government owns 51%, we must think about this, and maybe it is possible to discuss this question if we can consider international broadcasts.

But now, I believe, we need to listen to the shortwave. My opinion is, please go to Russia, research different possibilities, work with different radio stations, help us change.

And what kind of broadcasts may now be most attractive in Russia? I think we can talk about politics, save BBC, maybe, the best international radio station. But it is so important to understand another style of life, of the cultural life. I would have a program about Switzerland, about France, with music, a few comments, some news, it will be very good. Our people like foreign people. Why not - it's only a political play - I am a patriot, I am not a patriot. People want to know, to understand another people's culture, and maybe it's not bad to think about this.

We have special questions we cannot find answers to in Russia, like how, what should be the status of our company? Your broadcasts can help us discuss, make decisions, it is very important to know. What is more important now to Russia (I talk about Russia, because I come from Russia)?

For me it was very interesting to listen about the future technical equipment. Of course, I don't understand everything but I realize that I must send my engineers to foreign countries. We must think about a new technological system, because our system is very old, maybe 50 years old - it's terrible, equipment that we use. Maybe it is better to ask for assistance, to ask to send us old equipment - maybe it is better to use a completely new technological system, to get the money somehow but to be like a modern country.

It is interesting, it is an experience, this possibility to talk, to learn different structures at different companies, it is great for me. I want to thank you - thank you very much, Radio Canada International, and thank you for the possibility to communicate, to discuss, to get acquainted. And please excuse my English. I was trying to communicate with you.

LI DAN
DEPUTY DIRECTOR
CHINA RADIO INTERNATIONAL
BEIJING - PEOPLE'S REPUBLIC OF CHINA

Last year CRI got a little bit over half a million letters from 173 countries but the major part of those letters came from Asia. I got a figure here: we got letters from Asia, as many as 479,481. So out of half a million over 479,000 letters came from Asia. That shows the importance of this area to China, to CRI. Also, as I said, CRI is broadcasting in 38 foreign languages and 5 Chinese dialects. And out of the 38 foreign language broadcasts the majority are Asian countries' languages. For instance, we even broadcast in two languages to India: we use Hindi and Tamil. So CRI stresses very much this part of the world.

Another factor that attracts our attention to this area is the new developments, I mean the rapid development of TV in this area. Mr. Mytton just said: "We might have the biggest audience group in Bangladesh." I tend to agree with him. Because in South Asia TV is not very much developed. In Africa TV is not very much developed. Last year I visited Tanzania. They were just talking about setting up, organizing TV broadcasts. But things are changing. Tanzania is talking about TV, and China has seen rapid development of TV in the past ten years or so, especially in the past two years. I would say 90 percent of the people, of former radio listeners, now turn to TV. On the average, a city would have around 10 channels. And last year Beijing started to have 24-hour TV broadcast.

I think that situation would create a new environment that our international broadcasters, our colleagues from the West should think about. Because we have difficulties to reach our audience in the West, or our potential audience in the West, because the difficulties are that most people in the West watch TV instead of listening to radio, even less to international radio broadcasts.

Number two, a point I'd like to touch upon is intercultural understanding. I talked to some of my friends yesterday that maybe we should narrow the topic, for instance, how to keep a normal relationship, first of all, between international broadcasters, especially how to solve problems between international broadcasters. We are sort of messengers, as the textbook says, messengers should be objective, fair, whatever you say, but very often we find ourselves entangled in confrontations, differences. We don't know where we are sometimes, although some people say, we know, we know very clearly where we are. My point is, unless our messengers know where we are, our messengers know how to solve problems, our messengers know how to take the role of a bridge, we cannot get a proper message across in a fair way, in an objective way. Now Chinese reporters like to say often, at least we don't, we shouldn't make troubles or act troubles. We, Chinese journalists, nowadays discuss such topics a lot. So when we talk about intercultural understanding, communication, I think, first of all, we might do a little bit self-education or orientation.

What is the third point? Suggestions. I, myself, attend this kind of meeting for the first time. I heard a lot about this meeting, I discussed this meeting with Mr. Familiant, I showed great interest in this meeting, and I hope this meeting can be enlarged, can be held regularly. And I have confidence in this. I even told Mr. Familiant whether at a certain point China can host this kind of meeting, so that everybody here can go to Beijing and spend a few days with your Chinese counterparts. Well, information is so important that more and more people get involved in this business in China. So, I think, at a certain point my suggestion can be materialized, at least on the part of China, on the part of CRI. Of course with the support of all my friends present here today.

COMMENTS:

Père Pasquale Borgomeo
Radio Vaticana:

Pendant ces jours que j'ai trouvés très intéressants, très riches en façons de voir nouvelles aussi, je me suis toujours demandé quel est le caractère propre à notre réunion qui devient désormais périodique. Je souhaite d'ailleurs qu'on continue avec cette cadence, grâce à Radio Canada International et aussi aux universités qui participent. J'ai comparé cette rencontre avec les autres réunions professionnelles que nous avons au niveau plutôt de continents, UER et autres et je crois qu'il faut garder ce caractère de réflexion assez libre, pas trop dirigée, dans lequel il y a le côté interdisciplinaire : des professionnels qui sont préoccupés par des problèmes concrets et quotidiens et des personnes qui peuvent entrer avec l'apport de leur réflexion. Mais je suis d'accord qu'il faudrait, pour que cette assise soit un peu plus universelle, il faudrait que soient présentes l'Afrique et l'Amérique latine. Je me réjouis d'autre part, je l'ai déjà dit, de la présence massive de l'Europe centrale et orientale. Je suggérerais pour la prochaine édition, toujours au nom de ce repositionnement dont on parle, que nous puissions faire le point sur ce qui se sera passé pendant ces deux ans au niveau technologique, compte tenu de notre problème de rivalité/collaboration avec les services nationaux domestiques et quant à la politisation des fréquences sur satellites.

L'autre point que je trouve très important, à mon avis, vital, c'est de repositionner la radiodiffusion internationale dans le cadre social et politique en évolution. Compte tenu du problème actuel de la légitimité de moins en moins reconnue de ce qu'on appelle le service public, il importe de considérer la radiodiffusion internationale comme une forme de service public, qu'on ne peut pas ramener à la logique, à la philosophie de la loi du marché. Mais alors, si nous ne sommes plus, comme il a été dit, la voix de nos pouvoirs publics, nous devrions être, ça me paraît plus normal, la voix de nos pays ou de nos régions culturelles - j'appuie sur "culturelles", plutôt que politiques. Cela postule un certain consensus aussi parmi les contribuables. Et donc, il faudrait de plus en plus être transparents vis-à-vis des pays ou des cultures - je préfère dire les cultures - dont nous sommes les représentants. Il faut donc aussi faire non pas de la promotion mais je dirais simplement, faire des efforts pour mieux faire connaître les régions du monde que nous sommes sensés représenter à ce dialogue interculturel.

Et enfin, il serait vital d'aborder la question de la programmation, si on veut se repositionner. Par exemple, quelle est la conséquence sur la production des programmes, lorsque l'on fait de la retransmission, est-ce qu'on tombe dans la programmation d'autres radios qui retransmettent nos programmes sans aucune attention au contexte culturel dans lequel ces radios sont sensées apporter leur message. Mais il y a plus encore. L'arrivée de la télédiffusion internationale va nous amener à repositionner notre programmation, de la même façon que l'avènement de la télévision a bouleversé la radio nationale. Et alors, pour cela, je suggérerais qu'on invite expressément des représentants de la télévision internationale de manière à voir si on peut être complémentaire à leur activité. Pour le moment, nous sommes à la traîne, heureusement à l'ombre, pour ce qui est de la diffusion par satellite de l'activité des télévisions en général. Est-ce que cette synergie technique qui s'impose d'elle-même ne pourrait pas devenir une collaboration complémentaire pour ce qui concerne les programmes?

Graham Mytton:

Tatyana Andreyeva was talking about the continuing need in Russia for information. This graph plots the need for information. By the way, I did not produce this, this comes from one of the consultants in the BBC at the moment, using data from my department. I don't entirely agree with it, but I thought it might be helpful. I wasn't intending to show it, but when Tatyana said what she did in such a moving way about the growing need for information in a situation like the one in Russia, the continuing need for information, I thought this illustrated it quite well.

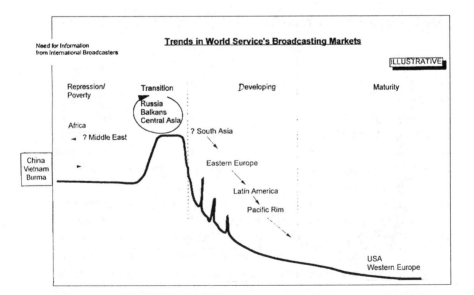

It's not a quantitative graph, the height of the graph doesn't represent any number, this is time - across here, and this is information need. And you have countries in this area which experienced government monopoly, government control of the media, or they experience poverty, there is a poverty of information.

There are many countries in Africa where the government doesn't control media too much. There is just lack of media. In countries like Botswana, for example, there is only one radio station. It's a very liberal radio station but it's one radio station, so there is no information if people want to hear alternatives. So you have both, either repression or you have poverty or the mixture of the two. And there is a fairly high level of information need and the theory of this consultant who produced this chart has that this information need grows during the period of transition that Russia, or Balkan states, Central Asian states are going through. And then, as things begin to liberalize, begin to develop, and you can have crises when information need rises again, and gradually falls off until you reach a point where the information need is at a very, very much lower level. That in, a lower level of need for alternative sources like foreign radio.

I've got another chart here. Those of you who were in Quebec will remember this second chart. This chart I did produce myself.

BBC Audience by Number of Domestic Radio Channels

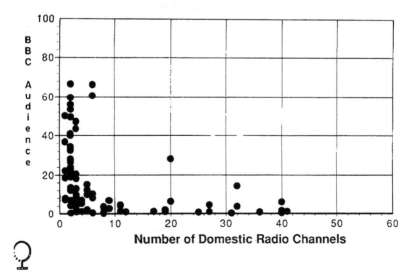

It's a different one, and it's more quantitative, where what I did was to plot a number of audience measures. Remember, I said yesterday we have measurements for about a hundred different countries (they are not all plotted here).

What I've done is to look at the BBC's audience by country here as a percentage weekly reach of speakers of the relevant language in various countries. Along the bottom I've plotted how many domestic radio stations have people to choose from. Here in Vancouver you've got about 19 or 20, correct me if I am wrong, in New York you've got about 60, in Botswana you've got 1, in Zambia you've got 3. Audiences for the BBC and other international radio stations, get bigger audiences only when people have limited local choice. As soon as local choice rises, audiences fall. So if you like, this is the graph showing how information need falls off as the number of local stations increases. So these two charts in different ways confirm some of the things that Tatyana was saying.

DR. ABDUL W. KHAN
COMMONWEALTH OF LEARNING
VANCOUVER, BRITISH COLUMBIA - CANADA

I'd like to make these two points taking cue from distinguished members of the panel, from Radio France Internationale and the distinguished delegate from China. The question is the repositioning of international broadcasting. Distinguished delegate from China has just reiterated the point that I made earlier, that in the wake of technological changes we, international broadcasters, the same as domestic broadcasters have to redefine their role, have to reposition their role. With due respect to the learned head of the research audience, you know, the penetration of television is bound to affect radio listening as it has done in case of the domestic, it has got to make a difference, we can't deny that.

I think it will be foolhardy on our part to say that it will make no difference. The point is that in the wake of technological changes what it is that radio can do best? What it is that we believe radio can deliver in the wake of technological changes? In my view, perhaps, one of the roles that radio can play more effectively, and I have found that it can do, and that is education.

Comment from the floor:

International broadcasting can be a rich learning resource, the broadcast aspect itself. But apart from the broadcasting, I think, lots of distance education organizations are starving to use material in audiocassette form. They don't have, it may be difficult for majority of the students to use broadcasts on shortwave, but they can always play the audio cassettes and so on and so forth. Would this convention consider the possibility of at least some way that resources that are available with the various international broadcasting organizations, could be made available to distance educational organizations in some form or another? The Commonwealth of Learning has just initiated a project of educational media, resources project, and we have just gathered some 7000 audio and video programs on various aspects of education in Asia alone. And there is a lot more available and it can be utilized for educational purposes.

Wayne Petrozzi:

I guess, one of the things that's struck me the most, is that it seems to be assumed, that there is a congruence between societal boundaries and state boundaries. And on the basis of that congruence there's an assumption that these are integrated societies that we broadcast to.

There's been some references made to broadcasting in the Hausa language which is one of many languages spoken in Nigeria. It is also spoken in various other countries in Western Africa.

The Secretary of State received last year a briefing book on Nigeria, claiming that the likelihood of Nigeria's surviving as a nation-state for the next 10 years is close to zero.

I wonder if we think through the consequences of whether we decide to broadcast in Hausa language if there is already occurring within Nigeria a notion that wants to redefine a political unit around Hausa and Hausa alone. Broadcasting in Hausa you might be facilitating a process of disintegration in Nigeria and in Ghana and in other countries in that region where Hausa speakers live in significant numbers.

We might think of this as a problem that is only rare, that occurs only in a few places, but I would suggest that if you look at the globe the potential for that kind of fragmentation is significant. You might be looking at the number of nation states increasing by one-third over the present number. Old states in Europe have this potential, whether it's the Lombards in Italy, or whether it's Basques in Spain. And again, I understand the need to want to identify one's audiences and speak to them in their language. I am not sure whether it might be fruitful to spend some time thinking about just what might be the implications of that, what kind of programming we choose to provide in what language.

Ousseynou Diop:

Je voudrais faire deux propositions rapides. D'abord, j'ai appris beaucoup - évidemment, on apprend beaucoup dans ces rencontres, que ce soit à la rencontre à Hamilton, à Québec et aujourd'hui, à Vancouver. On a suivi une certaine ligne qui me permet maintenant, après réflexion, de devenir un peu provocant, disons. On est en train, peut-être, de suivre le même sujet, le problème des anciennes démocraties dépendantes de l'Union Soviétique; on parle de l'Asie, et à mon sens on arrive à une espèce de consensus où tout le monde s'entend entre radiodiffuseurs internationaux. J'aurais aimé peut-être que l'invitation ici, soit étendue aux jeunes génération. On a parlé - quant on parlait de repositionnement des radiodiffuseurs internationaux - on a parlé du manque de relève, du manque de sang neuf. Peut-être qu'on pourrait dans les prochaines éditions - maintenant qu'entre professionnels du même âge, de la même génération, on s'entend sur ce qu'on veut faire - rencontrer les plus jeunes afin qu'il y ait un choc d'idées pour qu'on puisse arriver avec des idées neuves dans cette autoroute et qu'on ne vienne pas avec une vieille Chevy de 1959 alors que eux, ils vont commencer à rouler avec des Jaguars. Alors je pense qu'on a besoin des jeunes pour nous rencontrer et pour qu'on sorte un peu du consensus. Sur trois conférences, on a eu un consensus, peut-être qu'on devrait devenir un peu plus provocant et chercher des idées nouvelles.

Deuxième proposition que j'aimerais faire à la conférence : l'Afrique, l'Amérique latine, l'Asie - l'Asie est représentée, alors je vais parler pour l'Afrique et l'Amérique latine - sont peut-être les lieux les plus couverts par nos ondes. Ils sont certainement très bien desservis, mais c'est dommage qu'ils ne soient pas là, parce que même s'ils n'ont pas les moyens d'être des radiodiffuseurs internationaux comme la BBC, Radio France Internationale, Radio Canada International, etc. ils ont à faire face exactement à la même problématique de diffusion et ils utilisent les ondes courtes. Moi j'ai commencé ma carrière au Sénégal et je travaillais sur la chaîne internationale - il y avait la chaîne nationale et la chaîne internationale - mais la chaîne internationale utilisait les ondes courtes, non seulement pour pouvoir rejoindre le Sénégal en long et en large parce qu'il n'y avait pas de relais mais aussi pour rejoindre les pays autour. Donc, on se posait en situation de radiodiffuseurs internationaux. Mais dans des pays grands comme le Nigeria par exemple où on a affaire à plusieurs ethnies, à plusieurs langues et à plusieurs cultures, la radiodiffusion internationale est utilisée à l'intérieur d'un pays. Il serait, je pense, extrêmement enrichissant pour tout le monde que dans les prochaines éditions des DÉFIS, on puisse entendre ces radiodiffuseurs donner leur point de vue sur le service que nous leur donnons, sur notre manière de diffuser - et en cela j'appuie le professeur Aster et Monsieur Ollivier. Nous décidons en ce moment de ce que nous allons faire dans les autres pays mais il serait bon de savoir quel est leur point de vue. Et peut-être qu'on apprendrait à parler comme eux parlent parce que ça, c'est aussi une plaque à côté de laquelle nous passons souvent.

Elzbieta Olechowska:

I would like to make a comment and an appeal on behalf of the organizing committee. Some of you are aware to how many people and how many countries we sent invitations but for those who are not I would like to say that we have invited 15 radio stations in Africa, we have invited 15 radio stations in the Arab world and we have invited around 30 radio stations in Latin America. We have even offered to fund two people from Latin America and they almost came but, as you see, they are not here. As far as the African and Arab representatives, we have requested from UNESCO a special contribution to cover part of the costs of their trips and stay in Canada which was unfortunately refused, because all these organizations have their own money problems. This is the comment.

The appeal is that we would like very much to have from all of you suggestions as to whom we should invite from these regions that are under-represented at this conference. If you have contacts, if you have possibilities to help us for the conference in St. John's or wherever it will be, if you have any possibility to help us - either materially or in any other way - through giving us names, through explaining ways of doing it best, and so on - we would be most happy, because there is nobody in this room that deplores more this situation than the organizing committee.

Graham Mytton:

It's a bit unfair to come to the mike twice but there were some more, some further comments made that I thought were worth responding to. And before doing so let us just think back the last two days. We've talked a lot about public service, we've talked a lot about international radio as something which provides a service for the public that in different countries is a source of information, entertainment and education. And I am sure that most of the broadcasting organizations here, if not all of them, would agree that it is a part, if not all, of their mission.

Therefore there is something lacking in this conference, and that is being able to identify the results of these discussions, what areas there are for development, what areas there are for future initiatives.

You remember, yesterday afternoon after M. Larquié spoke, I talked about the opportunities. I just used one example of West Africa, of the opportunities of some larger languages which are not presently being broadcast in, and I mentioned Bambara. And Prof. Petrozzi raised this question about the choice of language having political implications.

This is a difficult question. It's not one which I am going to dismiss now. It would take far too long to debate this morning. But the choice of language for international broadcasting must have to do, or ought to have to do, with two things. One is information need, and the other is efficiency.

Most international broadcasters choose those languages or tend to choose those languages which are spoken by large numbers, sufficiently large numbers of people to make the international broadcasting activity worthwhile. Thus, in Africa most of the major international broadcasters broadcast in Swahili and Hausa.

There are no other international broadcasters now broadcasting in other African languages with the exception of Radio South Africa which broadcasts in Lozi and Cewa for Central Africa. As I explained yesterday, Radio Moscow used to broadcast in some other African languages but dropped them. But I used the example of Africa because it is an area where there is information need and where broadcasting in some of the larger languages would meet a genuine information need.

I can't quite understand this argument that somehow or other this might be the cause of some national breakup. How providing a service for listeners can lead to national breakup or national breakdown is beyond my understanding, but perhaps Prof. Petrozzi has some mysterious argument there which we could talk about during the break.

Ousseynou Diop also refers to the importance of shortwave and the importance of broadcasting in the West African region. He was involved in that himself and he knows how powerful and how important it continues to be. There is nobody broadcasting in his mother tongue Wolof - apart from the Senegalese broadcasters themselves. There is Mandinka, there is Bambara which I mentioned before, there is Yoruba, there is Lingalla, there is Kicongo. There are many languages spoken in Africa which could be broadcast and provide genuine services to people who have information need and who are presently inadequately served.

I think, the record of many international public service, public broadcasters in this field has been remarkable. I can point to the BBC's activity at the moment in Somali language and providing a lifeline for the Somali refugees and making links for them and their families, putting them in touch with their families in different parts of the world. This is something which the BBC does, but there are many examples of other broadcasters doing similar kinds of things.

I refer, for example, to the international broadcasting activities of Saudi Arabia who provide special services, especially during the period of the pilgrimage which is a very important public service.

I could give other examples. I entirely agree with Dr. Abdul Khan that there is a need for more use of international radio in education. And the BBC now has an initiative: we have a full-time educational organizer who is now making and encouraging the production of educational programs for transmission.

During the war in Afghanistan we've had a series of programs on health and on how to recognize mines in the field. Many of you know that much of Afghanistan is littered with mines which blow people's legs off and hands off or even kill them. We have a program on the air which actually explains, helps people to understand how to spot a mine, what to do with it and so on.

There are a lot of areas like that. Health, education, infant nutrition, and so on, which many international broadcasters are involved in. And we've heard from Bob Fortner and Walter Scragg about the contribution of the Christian broadcasters in that field. I think there are many things there that may be developed and I entirely agree with Dr. Khan about that. I think that's really all I wanted to contribute in response to what has been said.

Just to come back to what I said about the Somalis, the Somali language. There are many other examples like that of international broadcasters providing services which are of particular need during times of great difficulty, and great hardship, and war, and stress. The situation in Somalia is one at the moment. During the great drought in the 1970s in West Africa, some international services, most particularly Radio France Internationale, Voice of America and the BBC played an important part in informing people during that period.

Donald Browne:

As you probably guessed from my interest in the languages such as Maori and aboriginal Australian and so on, the point comes up quite often about whether language is divisive. In my own research, quite the contrary. It tends to be something that is taken by the people who speak that language as its wider acceptance which helps actually to integrate them into the national and international communities. One of the greater dangers in international broadcasting does not come from such languages as that but a sudden introduction of a language service for a nation at a time of crisis when there is an attempt to actually divide within the country or get it to fight against some kind of suppression.

CHAPTER 10

LIST OF PARTICIPANTS AND ORGANIZATIONS

Derek White
General Manager
ABC Radio Australia
699 Highbury Road
Glen Waverley 3150
GPO Box 428 C
Melbourne
Victoria 3001 Australia
Tel: 61 3 881 22 66
Fax: 61 3 881 23 46

Walter Scragg
 Director
Adventist World Radio
 Radio Mundial Adventista
12501 Old Columbia Pike,
Silver Spring, MD 20904 USA
Tel: 301 680 6304
Fax: 301 680 631

Graham Mytton
Head, Audience Research
& Correspondence
BBC World Service
3rd Floor North West Wing
Bush House, PO Box 76, Strand
London WC2B 4PH, U.K.
Tel: 44 071 257 8139
Fax: 44 071 257 8254

Aleksey S. Vlasienko
Program Director
Belorussian Radio
vul. Makayonka 9
220807 Miensk, Belarus
Tel: +7 0172 338870
Fax: +7 0172 366643

John Kennedy
Regional Director
CBC-British Columbia
Tel: 604 662 6330
Fax: 604 662 6712

Alexander Picha
Director, Radiozurnal
Cesky Rozhlas
Vinohradska 12
12099 Praha 2
Czech Republic
Tel: 42 2 24222195
Fax: 42 2 24218237

Li Dan
Deputy Director
China Radio International
2 Fuxingmenwai
Beijing 100 866
People's Republic of China
Tel: 861 6092171
Fax: 861 851 3174

Lynn E. Gutstadt
Vice President
CNN Audience Research
1 CNN Center
P.O. Box 105366
Atlanta, Georgia 30348-5366
USA
Tel: 404 827 1436
Fax: 404 827 3169

Dr. Abdul W. Khan
Senior Program Officer
Peter Kenyan-Jui
Commonwealth of Learning
Suite 1700
777 Dunsmuir Street
Vancouver, BC V7Y 1K4
Tel: 604 775 7906
Fax: 604 660 7472

Arno Selders
Head, The Technical Director's Office
Deutsche Welle
Raderberggürtel 50
D-5000 Köln 51, Germany
Tel: 49 221 389 3104/4
Fax: 49 221 389 3100

Sergei Korzoun
Program Director
Ekho Moskvy
11, Novy Arbat
12803 Moscow, Russia
Tel: +7 095 202 9229
Fax: +7 095 291 4643

Robert S. Fortner
Director
InterSearch
4588 Haywood Drive SE
Grand Rapids, MI 49512-5340
USA
Tel: 616 698 5096
Fax: 616 698 2672

Vasili Georgikia
Deputy Head
The President's Press Office
Tbilisi, Georgia
Tel: +7 8832 99 04 88
        99 08 79

Al Corenblum
Government of Canada
Department of Communications
Vancouver, B.C.

Lisa Lavoie
Department of Foreign Affairs
Head, Foreign Policy Communication
Government of Canada
125 Sussex Drive
Ottawa, Ontario K1A 0G2
Tel: 613 992 9280
Fax: 613 995 0667

Dr. Jinling Lee
800 South Arlington Mill Drive
#302
Arlington, Virginia 22204
USA
Tel: 703 998 7316

Kazimiera Mazgeliene
Program Director
Lithuanian Radio
Konarskio 49
Vilnius, Lithuania
Tel: +370 2 66 13 33
Fax: +370 2 26 32 82

Ian MacFarland
6 Coolbreeze Ave.
Pointe Claire, QC H9S 5G4
Tel: 514 697 4969
Fax: 514 697 2615

List Of Participants and Organizations

Howard Aster
Professor, Political Science
McMaster University
1280 Main Street West
Hamilton, Ontario
Tel: 905 525 9140 ext. 23705
Tel. & Fax: 905 844 0963

Alexandru Dorogan
Director
Moldovan National Radio & TV
Maison de la Radio
Miorita str. 1
277028 Chisinau-Kishiniev
Moldova
Tel: +3732 72336
Fax: +3732 723329

Gerald Duda, President
John Luik, Senior Associate
The Niagara Institute
Box 1041, 176 John Str. East
Niagara-on-the-Lake, Ont.
L0S 1J0
Tel: 905 468 4271
Fax: 905 468 5671

Frank Lloyd
Ontario DX Association
920 Davie Street
Vancouver, B.C.
V6Z 1B8
Tel: (604) 684-5981
Fax: (604) 684-7520

Dr. Walter Salmaniw
Ontario DX Association
1736 St. Ann Street
Victoria, B.C.
V9R 5V8
Tel: (604) 383-6031
Fax: (604) 383-3042

Sen. Raymond Perrault
The Senate of Canada
Ottawa, Ontario

Roman Czejarek
Vice-President
Polskie Radio S.A.
Al. Niepodleglosci
00 950 Warsaw, Poland
Tel. 48 22 45 91 03
Fax: 48 22 44 38 11

Levon Ananikian
Director General
Radio Agency ARAKS
Ul. Aleka Manukiana 5
Dom Radio
375025 Yerevan
Armenia
Tel: +7 8852 552650
Fax: +7 8852 551513

Babek Huseynoglu-Mamedov
Radio Azerbaijan
Mehdi Huseyin Av. No. 1
Baku, Azerbaijan
Tel: 92-38-07
Fax : 39-85-85

Anguel Nedialkov
Director
Radio Bulgaria
4 Dragan Tzankov str.
1040 Sofia, Bulgaria
Tel: +359 2 66 20 30
Fax: +359 2 65 05 60

Radio Canada International
Montreal, Quebec H2L 4S5
1055, East, René-Lévesque
Tel: 514 597 7500
Fax: 514 597 7953
Terry Hargreaves, Executive Director
Allan Familiant, Program Director
Sandra Basile, Manager, Americas
Ginette Bourely, Manager, News Services
Ousseynou Diop, Manager, English and
French Programming
Elzbieta Olechowska, Manager, Europe
Roger Tétrault, Manager, Asia
& Middle East

Jean-François Bolduc,
Announcer-Producer,
Edmonton
LornCurry,Announcer-
Producer,Vancouver
Mikhail Brodsky, Announcer-Producer
Andrey Loginov, Announcer-Producer
Mark Ryjik, Announcer Producer
Maya Wegrowicz, Announcer-Producer
May Abou-Saab, Announcer-Producer
Zhang Xiao-Ling, Announcer-Producer
Marie-Josée Metivier, Journaliste
Gordon MacDougall, Journalist
Frauke Vollert, Departmental Assistant
Steeve Côté, Radio Technician
Denis Aubin, Radio Technician

James Latham, Station Manager
Melanie Debo
Albert Hillsmith
Radio For Peace International
P.O. Box 88
Santa Ana, Costa Rica
Tel: 506 49 1821
Fax: 506 49 1095

André Larquié
Président-Directeur général
Daniel Ollivier
Radio France Internationale
116 avenue du Président Kennedy,
75786 Paris Cedex 16, France
Tel: 33 1 42 30 29 91 or
33 1 42 30 29 78
Fax: 33 1 40 50 39 96
Telex: RFIDG 615 229F

Masaomi Sato
Director General
Katsumi Komeiji
Radio Japan NHK
Jinnan, Shibuya-ku,
Tokyo 150-01 Japan
Tel: 81 3 5478 5100
Fax: 81 3 3481-1413

Arnolds Klotins
Director General
Radio Latvia
Doma Laukums 8
LV-1505 Riga, Latvia
Tel: +371 2 206722
Fax: +371 8820216

Valentina Zlobina
Head of Audience Research
Marianna Postremova
Consulting Editor
Radio Moscow International
Piatnitskaya Ulitsa 25
113326 Moscow, Russia
Fax: +7 095 230 28 28

Bert Steinkamp
Director, Planning & Development
Diana Janssen
Researcher
Radio Nederland
P.O. Box 222,
1200 JG Hilversum, The Netherlands
Tel: 31 35 72 4211
Fax: 31 35 72 4207

Dr. Natalka Berezhna
Director
Radio ROKS
2, Ukrainian House, office 104
Kreshchatik
252001 Kiev, Ukraine
Tel: +7 044 229 7652
Fax: +7 044 229 8764

Marian Bistriceanu
Deputy Editor-in-Chief
Radio Romania
General Berthelot str. 60-62
70749 Bucuresti, Romania
Tel: +40 1 3121053
Fax: +40 1 3121057

List Of Participants and Organizations

Father Pasquale Borgomeo
Director General
Radio Vaticana
00120 Vatican City
Rome, Italy.
Tel: 39 6 6988 3945
Fax: 39 6 6988 3237

Richard McClear
Raven Radio
Alaska, USA

Eugene Parta
Director,
Media and Opinion Research Department
RFE/RL
Oettingenstr. 67 am Englischen Garten,
W-8000 Munich 22, Germany
Fax: 49 89 21023835

Tatyana N. Andreyeva
Deputy Director
Federal Teleradio Service ROSSII
191011 Sankt Peterburg, Russia
27 Italyanskaya
Tel: +7 812 219 96 71
Fax: +7 812 312 94 71

Kevin Wang
President
SANGEAN America Inc.
2651 Troy Avenue
South El Monte, CA
U.S.A.
Tel: 818 579 1600
Fax: 818 579 6806

Faouad A. Taher
Assistant Deputy Minister
English Affairs
Ministry of Information
Kingdom of Saudi Arabia
P. O. Box 3949
Riyadh, Saudi Arabia 11481

Chen Wen-Bing, President
Jin Xian
Luo Jia Ling
Shanghai Radio
2 Beijing Road
Shanghai 200002, P.R. of China
Tel: 8621 321 8177
Fax: 8621 329 0087

Vladimir Stefko
Slovensky Rozhlas
Mytna 1
81290 Bratislava
Slovakia
Tel: +42 7 494462
Fax: +42 7 498923

Nicole Beaulac
Service des recherches
Société Radio-Canada
Montréal, Québec H3C 3A8

Jocelyne Limoges
Coordonnatrice des relations
internationales
Société Radio-Canada
1500 Bronson Avenue,
P.O. Box 8478,
Ottawa, Ontario K1G 3J5
Tel: 613 738 6862
Fax: 613 738 6749

Hélène Robillard-Frayne
Directrice de la programmation
et diffusion de la radio française
et des échanges radiophoniques
Société Radio-Canada
C.P. 6000 Montréal, Québec H3C 3A8
Tel: 514 597 4785
Fax: 514 597 4794

James Spears
2820 W 12th Ave
Vancouver, B.C.
V6K 2P9
Tel: (604) 688-9337
Fax: (604) 688-5590

Nicolas D. Lombard
Deputy Director General and Program
Director
Swiss Radio International
Giacomettistrasse 1
CH-3000 Berne 15,
Switzerland
Tel: 41 31 43 92 22
Fax: 41 31 43 92 56
Telex: 911 538

Boris V. Maksimenko
Director General
Tikhyi Okean
Primorskaya Teleradiokompania
Ul. Uborevicha d.20A
690670 Vladivostok, Russia
Tel: +7 4232 26 55 94
Fax: +7 4232 22 65 69

Viktor I. Nabrusko
Director, Radio Ukraina World Service
Vice-Chairman, Ukrainian State Radio
& TV Company
26 Kreschatik
Kiev, Ukraine
Tel & Fax: +7 044 229 8545

Douglas A. Boyd
Dean, College of Communications
University of Kentucky
106 Grehan Building,
Lexington, KY 40506-0042 USA
Tel: 606 257 3874
Fax: 606 257 7818

François Demers
Doyen, Faculté des arts,
Université Laval
Pavillon Louis-Jacques-Casault,
Ste-Foy, Québec, Canada G1K 7P4
Tel: 418 656 2833
Fax: 418 656 7807

Donald Browne
Professor
University of Minnesota
Dept. of Speech-Communication
460 Folwell Hall, 9 Pleasant Street S.E.,
Minneapolis, MN 55455 USA
Tel: 612 624 5800
Fax: 612 624 6369

Pierre Juneau
Professeur
Université de Montréal
165, chemin de la côte Ste-Catherine
PH 1
Montréal, Qué. H2V 2A7
Tel. & Fax: 514 495 8457

Gaetan Tremblay
Professeur
Département des communications
Université du Québec à Montréal
C.P. 8888, Succ. A
Montréal, Québec H3C 3P8
Tel: 514 987 8591
Fax: 514 987 4164

Milan Vitek
80 Montclair Avenue #104
Toronto, Ontario M5P 1P7
Tel & Fax: 416 481 3293

Kim Andrew Elliott
Voice of America
Audience Research
330 Independence Avenue S.W.,
Washington, D.C. 20547 USA
Tel: 202 619 3047
Fax: 202 619 1241

Alan L. Heil Jr.
Deputy Director of Programs
Voice of America
330 Independence Avenue S.W.,
Washington, D.C. 20547 USA
Tel: 202 619-2538
Fax: 202 619-1241

List Of Participants and Organizations

Karl Miosga & Jeffrey Cohen
World Radio Network
408 The Strand
London WC2R ONE, U.K.
Tel: 44 71 304 4343
Fax: 44 71 304 4347

Semion Afanasievich Protodiakonov
Chairman
Yakutian National Tele-Radio Company
Ul. Ordzonikidze 48
Yakutsk, Yakutia
Tel: +7 411 22 53 951
Fax: +7 095 230 29 19

Arthur Siegel
Professor, Social Science and
Mass Communications Studies
York University
4700 Keele St.
North York, Ontario, M3J 1P3
Tel: 416 736 5054

Juhani Niinisto
Head, External Broadcasting,
YLE Radio Finland
Box 95,
Helsinki 00251, Finland.
Tel: 3580 148014316
Fax: 3580 1481169

**ACCREDITED MEDIA
(OTHER THAN RCI)**

Scott Sutherland
Broadcast News/ Canadian Press

Greg Joyce
Canadian Press

Steve Mertl
Canadian Press
Cal Koat
CJVB

Kathy Danford
CFUN - QM FM News
Guy Buchholtzer
Société Radio-Canada

Marc Beliveau
Société Radio-Canada

Claudine Viallon
Société Radio-Canada

Denis Pronovost
Journaliste à la pige

Index

Index

ACHEVÉ D'IMPRIMER EN AVRIL 1995
SUR LES PRESSES DE
L'IMPRIMERIE D'ÉDITION MARQUIS
MONTMAGNY (QUÉBEC)